CHOSEN NATION

THEOPOLITICAL VISIONS

SERIES EDITORS:

Thomas Heilke
D. Stephen Long
and C. C. Pecknold

Theopolitical Visions seeks to open up new vistas on public life, hosting fresh conversations between theology and political theory. This series assembles writers who wish to revive theopolitical imagination for the sake of our common good.

Theopolitical Visions hopes to re-source modern imaginations with those ancient traditions in which political theorists were often also theologians. Whether it was Jeremiah's prophetic vision of exiles "seeking the peace of the city," Plato's illuminations on piety and the civic virtues in the Republic, St. Paul's call to "a common life worthy of the Gospel," St. Augustine's beatific vision of the City of God, or the gothic heights of medieval political theology, much of Western thought has found it necessary to think theologically about politics, and to think politically about theology. This series is founded in the hope that the renewal of such mutual illumination might make a genuine contribution to the peace of our cities.

FORTHCOMING VOLUMES:

Peter J. Leithart
Empire

Artur Mrówczynski-Van Allen
Between the Icon and the Idol: Man and State in Russian Thought and Literature: Chaadayev, Soloviev, Grossman

Chosen
NATION

Scripture,

Theopolitics, and the

Project of National Identity

BRADEN P. ANDERSON

CASCADE *Books* • Eugene, Oregon

CHOSEN NATION
Scripture, Theopolitics, and the Project of National Identity

Theopolitical Visions 13

Copyright © 2012 Braden P. Anderson. All rights reserved. Except for brief quotations in critical publications or reviews, no part of this book may be reproduced in any manner without prior written permission from the publisher. Write: Permissions, Wipf and Stock Publishers, 199 W. 8th Ave., Suite 3, Eugene, OR 97401.

The Scripture quotations found herein are taken from the New Revised Standard Version Bible, copyright 1989, Division of Christian Education of the National Council of the Churches of Christ in the United States of America. Used by permission. All rights reserved.

Cascade Books
An Imprint of Wipf and Stock Publishers
199 W. 8th Ave., Suite 3
Eugene, OR 97401

www.wipfandstock.com

ISBN 13: 978-1-61097-392-2

Cataloging-in-Publication data:

Anderson, Braden P.

　Chosen nation : scripture, theopolitics, and the project of national identity / Braden P. Anderson

　　xviii + 280 p. ; cm. —Includes bibliographical references and index(es).

　Theopolitical Visions 13

　　ISBN 13: 978-1-61097-392-2

　1. Christianity and politics — United States. 2. Nationalism — Religious aspects — Christianity. I. Title. II. Series.

BR517 .A545 2012

Manufactured in the U.S.A.

Contents

Preface vii

Introduction xi

1. Theopolitics and Nationalism 1
2. Nationalism and Christian Theology 36
3. Scripture in Theopolitical Scholarship 63
4. Old Testament Theopolitics 81
5. New Testament Messianic Theopolitics 127
6. Nationalism in the American Christian Right 150
7. Nationalism in American Political Theology 198

Conclusion 249

Bibliography 255

Index 267

Preface

This is a work operating at the conjunction of several different concerns and several different disciplines. First and foremost, it is a theological work, attempting to come to grips with the phenomenon of nationalism, a particular challenge to Christian identity and mission both historical and contemporary. Nationalism is a challenge that rewrites the Christian salvation narrative, reconstructs Christian politics, and reorients disciples of Christ away from solidarity with each other and with those suffering around them. It is a theopolitical challenge, I believe, that we do not fully understand. Secondly, this is a work informed by the social sciences, and particularly by a field of study—nationalism scholarship—that is itself interdisciplinary, consisting of social-scientific and historical work in both theory and empirical study. As I began taking note of the more detailed concerns of nationalism studies, I began to realize that our theological scholarship had only begun to take account of the nuances involved in the process of formulating and propagating national identity, a process that is ongoing within our churches even today.

This study therefore takes into account several types of discourse. The first is the theopolitical scholarship that has both informed my understanding and that requires supplementation if it is to fully address the challenge of nationalism. Then there is the discourse of nationalism scholarship, which provides, I believe, some helpful theoretical and empirical frameworks from which to understand the internal processes of nationalism and national identity development. The third and most significant discourse for this study is the biblical text, which provides a narrative standard of correction over against selective and distortive nationalist appropriation of the same. The fourth type of discourse is that of American Christian nationalists, who, in both popular writings and in more academic political theologies, interweave the narratives of the Christian theological tradition with those of American history and myth to formulate a particular national identity that, when examined, is found to be in great tension with the Christian salvation narrative.

Of course, I had always envisioned myself as undertaking interdisciplinary work, just not quite in this fashion. I was once, in fact, a Christian nationalist myself. I entered graduate school in political science in order to go into national security policy development, with the hope of both teaching and of serving in a national security policy role in the future. I did this as a committed Christian, having justified in my own mind (and even in personal writing) that God had uniquely blessed America, and that it was biblically justified to contribute to America's engineering of international forces toward the furtherance of its own interests. Yet in that first graduate experience, I fell unsuspecting into the clutches of a reading group belonging to our graduate-faculty chapter of InterVarsity Christian Fellowship. There, partly under the guidance of one of my mentors, political philosophy professor Thomas Heilke, I read works by authors like John Howard Yoder and Stanley Hauerwas, works that forced me (nonviolently, of course) to reevaluate my understanding of what "Jesus is Lord" really means. These works, among others, eventually prompted me to change in significant ways: theologically, politically, and professionally. I realized I could no longer study political science on the discipline's own terms, since its methodological presuppositions were too narrow for what I had come to understand as reality, and that entering into formal theological study was my best course of action. It was during this process that the attacks and aftermath of 9/11 occurred, an experience that ironically served to reinforce my own reorientation.

Since then, I have undertaken most of my theological education at Marquette University, where I wrote the dissertation that has, through some significant reconfiguration, become this book. There, I benefited tremendously under the direction of D. Stephen Long, who read my work and taught me to be generous to my interlocutors, fair to my sources, and true to a robust notion of theological study while engaging in interdisciplinary conversation. He provided throughout both wise and intelligent guidance on how to understand and articulate matters that are at the very heart of my theological passions, and he has continually pointed me toward further study and deeper understanding. I also thank Thomas Hughson for his gracious support and careful reading (and challenging) of my arguments, Deirdre Dempsey for her careful review of my biblical engagement, and Lowell Barrington for both introducing me to nationalism studies and for helping direct my engagement with that literature. As an evangelical with Anabaptist sympathies studying in an ecumenical, Catholic context, I am very thankful to the Marquette University Department of Theology for nurturing and sustaining me throughout this process, both in my studies and in my teaching. This community of teachers and colleagues has proved to be a substantive, ecumenical theological setting where genuine faith is considered to be part and parcel of the academic theological endeavor, and where collegiality and mutual support are practiced as essential to our work and to the service of our calling.

Within the process of revising the dissertation for publication, I especially wish to thank Douglas Harink for his review of the biblical discussion, William Cavanaugh for his patient interaction regarding the theopolitical literature (especially his!), and Chad Pecknold for generously giving his time to hone both my theopolitical understanding and the language of my argument. I thank Charlie Collier, Christian Amondson, and Jacob Martin at Wipf and Stock Publishers for all of their help along the way, and especially the editors of the Theopolitical Visions Series—Thomas Heilke, Steve Long, and Chad Pecknold—for endorsing this project. Any errors found herein are mine alone.

I also thank Meadowbrook Church of Wauwatosa, Wisconsin, who welcomed my family and me with open arms a month into our relocation to Milwaukee. Meadowbrook has been an ecclesial space of considerable love, hospitality, and support, both to me in my academic work and to my wife and children as we live in and through this rigorous and often surreal stage in our journey together. I thank the pastoral leadership, our New Life Community, and our cell group for caring deeply for my family, for providing me space to teach where other churches fear to tread, and for engaging with me in many conversations over who we are as a church and the implications of that for our life together and in all of our other communities.

Finally, I thank my family: my parents, Ken and Evelyn Anderson; my sister, Kerri Anderson; and my parents-in-law, Annette and Jim Singletary. They have been a constant source of encouragement even while deprived of their children/grandchildren/niece and nephew for many years. And to my wife, Elizabeth, and my children, Benjamin and Madelyn, I give my love and gratitude for all of these years of distance from family, for toleration of my often difficult schedule, and for living into a journey, uncertain both in length and destination. Wherever we go, may we all find our place in the people of God.

Introduction

The painting *One Nation Under God*, by artist John McNaughton, tells a story quite prevalent in certain Christian circles regarding the place of God in the life of the American nation, and conversely, the place of the nation in the divine project of global redemption.[1] When viewing it, the eye is immediately drawn to the central figure of Jesus Christ, who is portrayed as a Caucasian dressed in a white garment underneath an open golden robe. According to the captions on the web page (available in a convenient zoom window to the right of the painting), the golden robe, with the Greek letters alpha and omega stitched upon it, represents Christ's sovereignty over all creation. Upon the white garment underneath is the golden figure of the "Tree of Life," the fruit of which represents the twelve tribes of Israel.

Christ is adorned as well in a red sash around his waist symbolizing "the blood spilt by Americans for God and country" and displaying the Hebrew for Psalm 33:12: "Blessed is the nation whose God is the Lord." He holds up in his right hand a parchment copy of the US Constitution, which the artist describes as "inspired of God and created by God-fearing, patriotic Americans." Indicating those with an "important role in the preservation of our country," Christ's left hand points to the Constitution, as well as a "good" mother and her nearby son, whom she is "releasing to come forth and touch the Constitution." Indeed, in a moment reminiscent of the hemorrhaging woman who strains to simply touch Jesus' garment to be healed (Luke 8:43–48), the young boy is reaching out to gingerly touch the Constitution with his fingertip.

---

1. Available at http://www.mcnaughtonart.com/artwork/view_zoom/?artpiece_id =353# (accessed July 30, 2010).

Behind Christ stands an array of figures from American history, and behind them, the United States Capitol and Supreme Court buildings, as well as the US flag, occupying the highest point in the painting, save the Statue of Freedom atop the capitol dome. Historical figures include George Washington, Abraham Lincoln, and a number of other US presidents, soldiers from different eras of American warfare (including one named "King" who ironically doubles to represent the nonviolent civil rights leader Dr. Martin Luther King Jr.), and other heroes, from abolitionist Frederick Douglas to astronaut Christa McAuliffe to Nathan Hale, "martyr soldier of the American Revolution." Christ and the historical figures stand at the top of a stair, down the right and left sides of which sit figures from various contemporary American walks of life. The ones on the left (to Christ's right) represent "good Americans," and include a contemporary Marine, a family doctor, a college student, an immigrant, a schoolteacher, and a mother with a baby in her arm and a son nearby. On the right (to Christ's left) are "those who have weakened the country,"[2] and include a Hollywood director, a politician, a Supreme Court Justice, a "liberal news reporter," and a college professor. The devil himself lurks in the dark background of this group.

What is so telling about this painting is the way the images interweave the biblical narrative with the American national narrative. Christ and Israel are placed at the center of America's story, which is thereby made continuous with their own. America is of special concern to Christ and his reign, and Jesus is in turn directly involved in the preservation of the nation. Indeed, the painting, which the artist says he received in a vision,[3] is a powerful, albeit less than subtle, depiction of a particular understanding of the meaning of American identity. There

---

2. These descriptors are applied on another page where McNaughton explains the symbolism of the picture: http://www.mcnaughtonart.com/artwork/list_of_symbolism?artwork_title=One%20Nation%20Under%20God (accessed July 30, 2010).

3. See http://www.mcnaughtonart.com/artwork/interview_with_the_artist (accessed July 30, 2010). According to the artist, "I saw the painting in my mind as clear as if it were unveiled right in front of me, like standing before a stage when the curtains are slowly pulled back. I even had the name of the painting come to my mind. It hit me so hard that I knew I was supposed to paint it. I knew it would be one of the most difficult images I had ever endeavored to paint, but that it would be well worth it. Considering the time in which we live, I felt it definitely needed to be painted." The notion of providential responses to the exigencies of the day will play heavily in the discussion to follow, especially in the discussion of American Christian nationalism in the final two chapters.

is little doubt, between the picture and the artist's explanations, that the images contained therein are intended to have a claim on the understanding, particularly by Christian Americans, of America's true self, its authentic character. The nation is in crisis, divided between those who would direct America according to their own interests and aggrandizement and those who would sacrifice for its safeguarding as a special nation, ordained to greatness if only it is faithful to its providential founding. Those who acknowledge Christ as Lord are at the same time called to allegiance to America's traditions and ideals, and conversely, to be faithful to America is to be faithful to Christ.

As over the top as it may seem to many, McNaughton's painting presents vividly what is an all too common challenge to robust ecclesial identity and faithfulness today, namely, *nationalism*. Often understood erroneously as a fanatical form of patriotism—a disordered manifestation of an otherwise healthy and proper national identity—*nationalism is actually the process that leads to national identity in the first place.* Nationalism entails among other things the effort to authenticate and propagate an understanding of the "true self" of the nation, which is normative for the social identity of its members and thus integral to their politics. Politics is understood in this study as the processes by which members of a given community understand how their community is to be defined and how their communal life is to be ordered, as well as how they work out that understanding in practice. Insofar as nationalism entails the fusion of the political with the theological, it constitutes a *theopolitical* project of identity formation and communal construction.

Generally speaking, Christian scholarship on the theopolitical—by which I mean work associated with John Howard Yoder, Stanley Hauerwas, and certain of their students—engages politics not as an independent sphere of activity apart and autonomous from that of theology, but rather as a function of salvation history. Put differently, theopolitical scholarship assumes that every salvation narrative entails a politics, and every politics presumes a salvation narrative. As narrated in the Christian Scriptures, God's redemptive project entails at its heart a communal outworking in the form of Israel and the church. Christian salvation history therefore implies a sort of theopolitical ecclesiology, a theory of the church that entails particular understandings of identity and mission. Yet, theopolitics also understands that other salvation histories are operative in the world, complete with their own communal manifestations, their own political embodiments, which often vie with the church for a claim on human life and meaning. Part of the challenge for the church in this regard is to be able to identify and evaluate these narratives, their attendant political embodiments, and the degree to which the church itself perpetuates a competing gospel.

Theopolitical scholars provide unflinching examinations and trenchant critiques of the many ways in which Christian practice is co-opted by non-Christian politics, often concentrating on the theory and empirical behavior of the modern state and/or capitalism, which are understood to embody particular narratives of salvation. While such critiques are often helpful so far as they go, they address only incompletely or inconsistently how ecclesial identity and mission are compromised in such situations, namely how participants in one salvation history and its attendant politics can be brought over or persuaded of their own accord to participate in the politics of a competing salvation history. This is the purview of nationalism, a movement often distinct from the state and pursuing a particular communal embodiment of national identity. Nationalism is of crucial importance for theopolitics, for in many cases the nationalist narrative vies with the Christian gospel, resulting in a heavily syncretized and problematic theopolitical identity. More often than not, this takes the form of appropriating elements of the biblical narrative and/or Christian theology and fusing them with the national narrative, resulting in a syncretized understanding of identity and mission. Importantly, this appropriation emanates often from within the church itself, so attention to Christian responsibility for the problem is also necessary. Given that nationalism has been characterized in scholarship as "arguably the most powerful force in international politics in the twentieth century,"[4] and given its continued prevalence and proclivity for violence in the twenty-first, such a phenomenon requires explicit treatment. Given the attention paid to nationalism by ecumenical ecclesial documents in recent years,[5] its inadequate treatment in theopolitical literature is cause for concern.[6]

4. Barrington, "Nationalism & Independence," 3.

5. See, for example, the World Council of Churches' "Colombo Statement," published as "Ethnicity and Nationalism," and "Ethnic Identity, National Identity, and the Search for Unity"; see also the Leuenburg Church Fellowship's (now the Community of Protestant Churches in Europe) *Church-People-State-Nation*.

6. This absence is evident, of all places, in the *The Blackwell Companion to*

This study aims to supplement the literature in precisely this regard. In the first chapter, I review existing theopolitical scholarship in order to discern the state of the question and to set the stage for the subsequent theological analysis of nationalism. To be clear, the scholarship discussed in chapter 1 is not the main problem at the heart of this study; American Christian nationalism is. However, in examining the shortcomings of the literature in this regard—literature that, in light of its insightful nature and interests, one would expect to take up nationalism more explicitly—I am able to establish a framework in which to operate. To that end, I examine its treatments of the contemporary challenges to ecclesial identity, which either rightly note the importance of distorted identity emanating from within the church but leave their treatment of nationalism underdeveloped, or which locate those challenges primarily in the modern state, neglecting adequate treatment of how nationalism is formulated and propagated by non-state actors in non-state contexts. This examination necessitates engagement with nationalism scholarship as well, both because it helps delineate the nature of nationalism and its development, and because in the case of one major theologian, nationalism scholarship is engaged with the effect of overlooking key theological moves at work therein.

Chapter 2 then follows up that critique by providing the missing element, that is, the nature of the interplay between nationalism and theology, both in terms of their historical interaction galvanizing Christians behind certain national identities, and in terms of the theological elements of contemporary nationalism that produce what amounts to a competing salvation narrative to that of the gospel. Examining the work of several nationalism scholars, I show how theological Christian nationalism really is, in that it ultimately requires the deliberate task of interpreting the Christian Scriptures and intellectual tradition in such a way as to theologically underwrite a particular conception of national identity. This process interweaves the theological narratives with the national so as to present identification with the nation as part and parcel of Christian faithfulness. However, I also point out that the

---

Political Theology, coedited by William T. Cavanaugh and containing chapters by Stanley Hauerwas and a number of his students. The volume includes a section titled, "Structures and Movements," which contains chapters on "State and Civil Society," "Democracy," and "Globalization." Yet there is no chapter on nationalism, despite the phenomenon's prevalence in both social-scientific scholarship and ecumenical documents.

existing nationalism scholarship itself fails to take adequate regard for the theological moves involved in such a project.

Having established the parameters of the problem, I then discuss how any adequate response to Christian nationalism must include a robust treatment of biblical theopolitics, animated by explicit and thoroughgoing attention to the theopolitics of biblical Israel given form in the Torah as informative, and in some sense even normative, for the church. This, too, I find largely underdeveloped in theopolitical scholarship, which is the subject of chapter 3. I argue there that such works, if they discuss Israel much at all, tend to neglect Israel's election and covenant as prescribing and creating a particular identity within that nation. While these scholars rightly see Jesus as definitive and normative for both Israel and the church, it is unclear how he is normative since the covenant he claims to have fulfilled (Matt 5:17) is, with a notable exception, never discussed.

To attend to this problem, as well as to provide a theological criterion of evaluation for the empirical studies of recent American Christian nationalism in chapters 6 and 7, I offer in chapters 4 and 5 a constructive biblical theopolitics. Chapter 4 takes up the theopolitics of biblical Israel as related in the Old Testament. The promise of a people is made by God to Abraham near the beginning of the narrative, but the reader soon finds that people in bondage. This same God, Yahweh, delivers that people and then establishes it in election and covenant as a theopolitical community, alternative to both the empire from which it had been delivered as well as to the kingdoms surrounding its land of destination, to be before the world a visible sign of God's reign, resulting in human flourishing. However, the people fails to stay true to its divinely ordered life and chooses instead to conform to the ways of its neighbors. It is indicted by the prophets for its departure from covenant, and falls under judgment. However, exile becomes a new mission as well, aiming at Israel's restoration, which will be made real in the one person who will be Israel as Yahweh meant Israel to be.

That one person is Jesus Christ, as the New Testament presents him, who comes as both Israel and Yahweh to definitively fulfill covenant. He is the Messiah, and he inaugurates a new age wherein he establishes the church, as engrafted onto Israel, to be the communal embodiment of covenant fulfillment, as well as the form and manner—animated by the Holy Spirit—of the opening of Israel to the rest of the world. This is the subject of chapter 5, which examines the linkages between Israel and the church via Jesus Christ and determines that the character of the theopolitics of Israel is normative for the church, and is also singularly carried forth in the church throughout the messianic age. This is of central importance to the present study, for if Israel's theopolitics as perfected in Christ is to be embodied in the church, then the church is similarly accountable for faithfulness to Christ's covenant in the face of contending theopolitical communities. Christian nationalism in any form, then, directly challenges ecclesial identity.

Chapters 6 and 7 examine concrete instances of this very challenge. Chapter 6 takes on the nationalist discourse of the American Christian Right, which syncretizes elements from the biblical and American national narratives into a story of God's election of America as the New Israel. This fused narrative, which the movement then seeks to institutionalize in American politics for the sake of cultural renewal, fits well into the theoretical framework supplied by nationalism scholarship, which means that as Christian Right nationalists seek to authenticate their vision of American national identity as *the* national identity, they simultaneously distort the Christian biblical and theological traditions on which they rely for narrative content as well as for popular support. In the end, their nationalist narrative supplants the church with America, redefining for millions of Christians their primary community of theopolitical identity.

Chapter 7 takes on the ideas of two American political theologians who undertake more sophisticated projects of interweaving the Christian biblical and theological traditions with the American national narrative. In both cases, though by different routes, these scholars present an account of American exceptionalism that entails the distortion of biblical theopolitics in order to portray the nation as uniquely endowed and called by God to prefigure the kingdom of God on earth. I therefore examine their accounts and critique them both for their internal inconsistencies as well as their aberration from the biblical theopolitics presented in chapters 4 and 5.

This study is interdisciplinary, as demonstrated by its engagement with social-scientific and historical scholarship on nationalism. I appropriate such scholarship where it helpfully reminds theology of matters requiring theology's attention, as well as where it identifies nuances in the phenomenon of nationalism of which theology should be mindful.

However, this project is primarily a theological endeavor: I engage what I perceive as a prominent challenge to the faithfulness of the church in our contemporary context, and I aim to address that challenge via a theological appropriation of the Christian Scriptures, an appropriation I hope is faithful both to the biblical narrative and to the church that claims—and is claimed by—that narrative. With much appreciation, I leave it to the reader to discern to what extent this endeavor has been successful.

CHAPTER 1

Theopolitics and Nationalism

Introduction

Theopolitical scholarship is well known for its trenchant analysis of contemporary Western politics and economics and their widespread theological rationales. While specific approaches vary, this scholarship typically attempts to examine the roots of these phenomena, identifying soteriologies at work within them that contend with, and ultimately amount to simulacra of, the Christian salvation narrative. In response, the scholarship proposes a reorientation of Christian allegiances via a renewal of ecclesial identity, usually in the form of a recovery of traditional Christian beliefs and practices that would resist and ultimately subvert contemporary politics and economics by embodying an alternative, ecclesial community as defined and shaped by the gospel.

In view of their work, it would seem that nationalism would be at the forefront of their concerns, a distinct subject of robust theological analysis and evaluation. Yet all too often, nationalism is discussed only indirectly and imprecisely, or else it is simply subsumed under the activity of the state with little accounting for it as a distinct phenomenon, many of its manifestations independent of state agendas and activities or even contrary to state interests. When this happens, a key manifestation of the problem is obscured, namely, nationalist discourse and practice emanating from *within* the church itself. Such "Christian nationalism" is noticed in their work, to be sure, but it is inadequately examined and understood. This is in great part because no theological approach can adequately address such challenges to ecclesial identity without accounting for the *interweaving of narratives*, in this case theological and national. Yet such interweaving receives only limited attention in the work of these scholars, necessitating a more extensive and in-depth examination of the processes involved.

This chapter examines the work of prominent thinkers in theopolitical scholarship to take stock of their understanding of contemporary challenges to ecclesial identity, with special attention to whether and how nationalism figures into their schemas. While I am in agreement with much of their thought, I will show that they fail to give the processes of nationalism proper attention—particularly those involving specific theological moves in formulating national identity—and that this failure renders their approaches inadequate when it comes to diagnosing the habits of thought and practice that give way to altered ecclesial identity today. I attend here to the work of John Howard Yoder and Stanley Hauerwas, arguably the pioneers to the theopolitical approach in contemporary theological scholarship, as well as to one of Hauerwas's best known students of theopolitics, William T. Cavanaugh, who is a leader among his generation in influencing the direction of the scholarship. In my examination of their work, I raise questions having to do with their understanding of the challenge of nationalism, as well as engage pertinent nationalism scholarship that helps elucidate why it is important to pay attention to nationalism as a problem often distinct from the modern state and involving theological moves by and within the church itself. I see my project, therefore, as supplementing current theopolitical scholarship by fleshing out more precisely the nature of the church's role in the development of nationalism, historically to an extent, but with special emphasis on contemporary forms.

John Howard Yoder: The Challenge of Constantinianism

It is debatable whether John Howard Yoder considered "Constantinianism" to be the most central problem for the church today, but the concept is certainly central to Yoder's theopolitics. The term refers in part to a series of historical developments centering on the reign of the Emperor Constantine in the fourth century, but more importantly, it designates an ongoing theological problem encompassing the practices of the church and the effects upon both church and world of having the ecclesia aligned with the powers, those norms and institutions that were intended to serve the redemptive order by restraining sin short of the coming of the kingdom of God, but that absolutized themselves in rebellion to that order, attempting to exercise sovereignty over humanity.[1] It is therefore more a problem found within the church than one in which the church is victimized by some exterior entity. Indeed, for Yoder, "Constantinianism always begins before there is some Constantinian settlement proper . . . some other problems always arise before some emperor presents his tempting offer."[2] Constantinianism is best characterized as the church absolutizing itself—its own security and survival—and refusing to conform to its properly contingent role at any one place and time. This is most typically accomplished by acquiring a stake in the powers that be, by positioning itself as their indispensible support. Thus, the chief agent of the Constantinian challenge is the church itself, which, by seeking dominance, actually undermines its own distinctive identity, its own alternative political identity and ethic:

> Before Constantine, one knew as a fact of everyday experience that there was a believing Christian community but one had to "take it on faith" that God was governing history. After Constantine, one had to believe without seeing that there was a community of believers, within the larger nominally Christian mass, but one knew for a fact that God was in control of history. Ethics had to change because one must aim one's behavior at strengthening the regime, and because the ruler himself must have very soon some approbation and perhaps some guidance

---

1. Various historiographical characterizations of Constantine, Eusebius of Caesarea (Constantine's contemporary biographer and arguably the father of the theology of empire), and the Constantinian settlement can be found in Barnes, *Constantine and Eusebius*; Barnes, *From Eusebius to Constantine*, chapter IX; and Cameron and Hall, "Introduction." In terms of the historical portrayal of the settlement, these sources tend to support Yoder's understanding. Again, Yoder sees Constantinianism primarily as a type of problem, symbolic of a particular theopolitical move. Arguments that emphasize the accuracy of Eusebius' accounts (panegyric notwithstanding) or the authenticity of Constantine's conversion over against Yoder's characterizations are misplaced. Yoder's understanding assumes these elements; his concern is how the Christian church and theology change as a result.

2. Schlabach, "Deuteronomic or Constantinian," 454.

as he does things the earlier church would have disapproved of.[3]

This statement is key to understanding Yoder's theopolitics. Confidence in Christ's lordship within a situation of marginalization and threat concretized the Christian community and prompted a certain ethical orientation that emphasized humble faithfulness without certainty of immediate outcome. With the Constantinian shift, however, God's control of history seemed to be realized in the empire, and a contingent ecclesial life centered on faith in Christ's lordship was no longer necessary—securing the empire was, and Christian theopolitical practices changed accordingly, aiming at the moral and structural integrity of the imperial power. Rather than examining how to respond to social questions, Christian ethics becomes the question of how people in power should use that power. The role of the church, then, is relegated to chaplaincy, "i.e., a part of the power structure itself. The *content* of ethical guidance is not the teaching of Jesus but the duties of 'station' or 'office' or 'vocation.'"[4]

Undergirding the power structure takes on added meaning with the development of modern national identity acting as the primary form of social identity and historical significance. Globally, and even where governments oppose Christianity, "Christians remain patriotic." Not only does catholicity suffer as the church is divided among national loyalties, but so does the church's ability to be critical, either of itself or of the country in which a part of the church might reside. In the American instance, it has meant a "moral identification of church with nation," which has historically included a "Christian," and often Protestant, tone to political discourse.[5] Hence the rise of a particular American "civil religion," whose first problem is its theological underpinning of coercive politics, given that its political community is involuntary and overseen by the state.[6] Other elements include the belief that the

---

3. Yoder, *Priestly Kingdom*, 137.

4. Ibid., 138. For a literal example of this today, see the website of the US Army Chaplain Corps: http://www.goarmy.com/chaplain/. Earlier iterations of the site explicitly recruited chaplains to perform "religious support duties" to help "young men and women become effective Soldiers in body, mind and spirit."

5. Yoder, *Priestly Kingdom*, 144.

6. The problem here is at least the theological endorsement and support of the nation-state's politics, but consistent with Yoder's Anabaptist sensitivities, is likely also civil religion's implicit *theological* coercion. By "state," I refer to Yoder's description of

identity and interests of this civil community are of special concern not only to the citizenry but to the deity upon whom they call. By its very nature, this civil community has outsiders and enemies, defined in territorial, ethnic, or religious terms, and its special relation to God often necessitates violence against them. Therefore, no moral or theological commitments, such as "specific 'sectarian' matters of identity," should hinder the support religious resources provide to the establishment. For Yoder, those clergy or religious/humanist elites who do show such support are themselves part of the establishment in question: "They have access, as a group, taking turns, to subsidized chaplaincy services in public institutions. They reciprocate by assuring the powers that be of divine blessings in general and by reminding them occasionally of divine imperatives."[7] In this manner, the church gives up its ability and responsibility to embody an alternative to state politics.

Underlying Yoder's argument in this regard is a critique of the widespread notion that politics necessarily entails violence: "I have preferred to contest the meaning of the term [politics], insisting that nonviolence and nonnationalism are relevant to the *polis*, i.e., to the structuring of relationships among persons in groups, and therefore are political in their own proper way."[8] And it is not merely violence that is renounced by Christ and therefore his disciples, but "the compulsiveness of purpose that leads men to violate the dignity of others." The point, he stresses, is not that all of our legitimate ends are available without violence, but rather that "our readiness to renounce our legitimate ends whenever they cannot be attained by legitimate means itself constitutes our participation in the triumphant suffering of the Lamb."[9] For Yoder, the renunciation of coercive power and the taking up of active peacemaking thus constitute a fully fledged alternative, Christian politics.

I affirm Yoder's understanding of Constantinianism as an ongoing problem emanating primarily from within the church. I think he is right

---

a civil community in which "a function of coercively sanctioned organization claims jurisdiction over all the participants, normally within a territorial definition of physical frontiers and normally with a substantial degree of centralization of power" (Yoder, *Priestly Kingdom*, 173). The importance of the distinction between "state" and "nation" for this study will be explored below.

7. Yoder, *Priestly Kingdom*, 173ff.
8. Yoder, *Politics of Jesus*, 42n36.
9. Ibid., 243–44.

to perceive this as a central challenge to ecclesial identity, a challenge that too often has less to do with co-option from without than with idolatry from within. Calling attention to civil religion is quite helpful, especially in noting its "moral identification of church with nation" and its tying of political interest to a community's deity. Indeed, Yoder's discussion of chaplaincy can, with further development, be connected to discussions of "authentication" in nationalism literature, that process, discussed below, by which nationalists determine what constitutes the "true" nation.

Yet, while I find Yoder's analysis to head very much in the right trajectory, especially as it emphasizes the involvement of the church in the problem rather than merely being acted upon by forces outside it, his treatment of the problem of nationalism remains considerably underdeveloped. His discussion of political identity occurs firmly within the context of the state, without regard to the nation as a potentially distinct field of political claims and activities. Even where he mentions "nation" and "nationhood," or where he argues for the priority of "nonnationalism," the significance of these terms goes unexplored. What is nation? How is the national form of polity, or even of the state, significant for Constantinianism over against other forms? What is the nature of nationalism, particularly if its "compulsiveness of purpose" is formulated, justified, and propagated apart from the state apparatus, and why would its repudiation be important? Do we miss something by concentrating primarily or even solely on the civil order? Could it be that another potentially problematic framework of sociopolitical identity is being neglected, one that much more directly involves the deliberate involvement of the church?

This leads to other questions about Yoder's diagnosis. For instance, he writes that in America, civil religion has meant "the moral identification of church with nation," but how is such an identification accomplished? If Constantinianism in its various forms is at the root of the problem, that means the church itself is culpable in this identification, but Yoder does not explain how the church-nation link is made or how it is justified theologically by its propagators. So, too, for the claim that the identity and interests of the polity are believed to be of special interest to its deity. He is certainly not incorrect on this, but how is this kind of theopolitical rationale made for Christians in such a way as to galvanize them toward a corrupted and often violent politics? Might the answer to that question suggest possible solutions? Such an examination requires further precision, and a more precise evaluation would need to attend to how the claims of the nation are interwoven with those of Christianity in order to theologically justify a reorientation of Christian loyalties.

STANLEY HAUERWAS: THE CHALLENGE OF LIBERAL DEMOCRACY

Stanley Hauerwas shares Yoder's understanding that Christian theopolitics has been problematized by Constantinianism, which Hauerwas characterizes as the effort to make Christianity seem necessary to the powers that be in such a way that the church can feel at home in the world, thereby precluding witness and potential suffering.[10] Or, as he puts it starkly elsewhere, it is the project "to enable Christians to share power without being a problem for the powerful," such that the church would have a language intelligible to the powers in order to retain its cultural significance.[11] Like Yoder, Hauerwas sees this phenomenon manifested in relation to the modern liberal democratic state. In the United States, it is particularly present in those churches, both conservative and liberal (albeit in varying manifestations), which "assume wrongly that the American church's primary social task is to underwrite American democracy."[12] This has been reflected in academic theological ethics at least since Walter Rauschenbusch, insofar as the discipline's main agenda has been to demonstrate American democracy's "distinctive religious status," thereby making America itself the primary subject of Christian ethics.[13] In short, not only is liberalism an agent of modern Constantinianism, but it is abetted by those within the church who have conflated democracy with the Christian faith.

Yet "even a democratic state is not the kingdom."[14] Responding to the general claim that democracies have institutionalized the limited state, Hauerwas argues that any state, by definition, seeks to surpass its limits, democracy or not. Hauerwas is responding to an article by Richard John Neuhaus, wherein Neuhaus's theological justification of

---

10. Hauerwas, *With the Grain*, 221.
11. Hauerwas and Willimon, *Resident Aliens*, 21, 27.
12. Ibid., 32.
13. Hauerwas, *Christian Existence Today*, 177. Quoted in Rasmussen, *Church as Polis*, 224.
14. Hauerwas, *Against the Nations*, 122.

democracy and the limited state fails to provide the criteria for discerning when the democratic state actually exceeds its bounds. As Hauerwas writes, "There is no state we should fear more than the one that claims to be 'limited.'"[15] Arne Rasmussen notes that for Hauerwas, liberalism is associated institutionally with "an allegedly limited state in service to a social and economic order based on exchange relations." A central component of this project is to "emancipate people from the historical particularity of their traditions and communities," which essentially left the individual and the state as the two basic units in modern society.[16] For Hauerwas, no state is self-limiting, regardless of its constitution or philosophical undergirding, unless there exists "a body of people separated from the nation that is willing to say 'No' to the state's claims on their loyalties."[17]

The modern liberal state, although created to secure rights, is rooted in an irresoluble paradox: it claims merely to be a means toward an end, yet it must convince its citizenry that it can provide a meaningful identity since the state is the only means of achieving the common good.[18] This identity proves ultimate, since even democracies must ask their citizens to die on the state's behalf.[19] While confessional orthodoxy is kept private, general religion is advanced as functional in this context for both individual and society. This leads to the necessity of civil religion as a "transcendent principle of criticism which can sustain the democratic system and ethos."[20] Civil religion reconceives traditional faith as "the morality-bearing part of culture, and in that sense the heart

---

15. Ibid., 126. See Neuhaus, "Christianity and Democracy."

16. Rasmussen, *Church as Polis*, 250.

17. Hauerwas, *Against the Nations*, 123. Despite his rather strident tone in response to Neuhaus, Hauerwas has since become involved in conversations concerning "radical democracy," an approach to social life that emphasizes the importance of personal and local relationships, the "politics of small accomplishments" resulting from neighbors actually getting to know one another, i.e., a politics that ultimately subverts a modern liberalism that seeks to deny contingency. See Hauerwas and Coles, *Radical Ordinary*; see also Hauerwas, "Democratic Time."

18. Hauerwas and Willimon, *Resident Aliens*, 34–35.

19. Ibid., 35. Or, even more so, to kill on the state's behalf.

20. Rasmussen, *Church as Polis*, 299. See Hauerwas, *Peaceable Kingdom*, 12–13. Both the political left and right in the United States share a commitment to civil religion, which emphasizes "faith in the spiritual oneness of Christianity and democracy" (Hauerwas, "Christian Critique," 466). Quoted from Dawson, "Religion of Democracy," 47.

of culture,"[21] which requires Christians to make their religious speech accessible to the wider public and to continue to pursue a commitment to democracy as the appropriate social form for a Christian society. Furthermore, it posits that the lives of American Christians make sense only within the context of religious and political traditions that currently face the danger of erosion and that are our only hope "if we are ever to enter that new world that so far has been powerless to be born . . ."[22] In such a view, "Only the biblical religions can provide the energy and vision for a new turn in American history, perhaps a new understanding of covenant which may be necessary not only to save ourselves but to keep us from destroying the rest of the world."[23]

What bothers Hauerwas about such views, coming from both the right and left in American political discourse, is that they assume that "Christians should or do have social and political power so they can determine the ethos of society," taking upon themselves the responsibility to create "a nation structured according to the will of God."[24] This "habit of thought," asserts Hauerwas, must be surrendered, or Christians will continue to implicitly or explicitly assume that "insofar as America is a democracy she is Christian." When this happens, Christians have already lost the necessary skills to discern their own level of compromise, rooted in an assumption that their responsibility is to rule over American character and values. What is required, then, is a revitalization of a counter-politics, the theopolitics of the church in its liturgy and practice, to cultivate such skills of discernment, resistance, and alternative construction of community.

As with Yoder's, I find Hauerwas's take on Constantinianism compelling, and I concur with his reading of ecclesial accommodation to liberal democracy. I affirm his moves to at least partially locate the agency of this problem within the church, though I think he does so less centrally than Yoder, attributing the problem also to liberalism and the modern state. In particular, the centrality of politics to Christianity in Hauerwas's work and the socio-ethical role of the church *as the church*

---

21. Hauerwas, "Christian Critique," 469. Quoted from Neuhaus, *Naked Public Square*, 154.

22. Hauerwas, "Christian Critique," 472. Quoted from Bellah et al., *Habits of the Heart*, 282–83. It is difficult to miss the eschatological overtones of this statement.

23. Hauerwas, "Christian Critique," 472. Quoted from Bellah, "Revolution and Civil Religion," 73.

24. Hauerwas, "Christian Critique," 474–76.

have been central to my own theopolitical development. While, like Yoder, his work tends to stay within the confines of the state, he does at least mention the notion of societal or national ethos, which can be related to nation and nationalism with further elaboration.

However, I believe his response to the civil religion question to be illustrative of the shortcomings of his approach, which tends to overlook the fundamental problem of distorted theopolitical identity by concentrating too narrowly on the church's moral practices. Hauerwas is disturbed that Christian advocates of civil religion assume as appropriate the exercise of power by Christians to determine the ethos of society; in his view, such a move robs Christians of the ability to resist the temptation to rule, which contradicts Jesus' noncoercive ethic. While I believe he is correct on this point, it is arguably not the root problem, which is rather the misconstrual of theopolitical identity inherent in civil religion—the misappropriation of biblical theopolitics for one's given nation and/or state—that creates the possibility for such a contradictory ethic. Put differently, we can grant that such an ethic is problematic and contradictory to the gospel, but we must ask how or why such an ethic even exists.

Hauerwas mentions the "habit of thought" among Christians that the present nation should be structured according to God's will. This points to something deeper than a simple assumption of power over society, but it raises still more questions. What occurs theologically to allow such a habit of thought to develop? How is such a habit cultivated, and how does it exist—even thrive—within contemporary ecclesial communities? Moreover, is it just a question of "structure" at issue—that is, the political apparatus of the liberal democratic state—or are there deeper fusions being made between the identity and mission of the church and those of the nation, which Hauerwas seems to distinguish from the state? This distinction is indicated by his statement, "a body of people separated from the nation that is willing to say 'No' to the state's claims." Here, Hauerwas could be read to conceive of the "state" as that entity which rules over the "nation." Yet, what actually constitutes or coheres this distinct entity called "nation" remains unclear, obstructing identification of claims distinct or independent from those of the state, yet still constituting a challenge to ecclesial identity. For instance, it could be argued that the primary problem for ecclesial identity in the United States is not so much that America will be considered Christian because it is democratic, but rather because it is thought to be elect of God, the New Israel. Where America is considered a Christian nation, it is so primarily in terms of divine election by the Christian God to a particular mission, which is often interpreted to entail a certain state form. This alters Hauerwas's conception of civil-religious thinking, such that America is not Christian because it is democratic, but rather democratic because it is Christian. If America is considered Christian, it is not because modern liberalism has conceived of it as such, but because somehow Christianity and America are being fused. Certainly, Hauerwas would not deny this, yet he is unable to adequately explain it (and thus to resist it).

This places into question another claim by Hauerwas that part of the liberal project is to "emancipate people from the particularities of their traditions and communities." This is a key notion, and one that is developed much further by William Cavanaugh, as will be explained (and critiqued) below. This claim is partly justified; indeed, there are situations where the modern state does aim to dissolve more local identities and loyalties in favor of constructing a direct tie between the individual and the state. However, I do not believe this is an accurate portrayal of the overall theopolitical challenge posed to the church, even in modernity. Note Hauerwas's aforementioned claim that Christians in America have a habit of thought regarding America's sociopolitical conformity to God's will and the power necessary to accomplish that end, or his claims regarding the equivalence of Christianity and democracy in much of American political discourse. These phenomena have to do with quite particular theological claims being linked with national narratives of history and myth. As such, Hauerwas is pointing not to a people emancipated from the particularities of their traditions, but rather to *a people who have tied the particularities of their traditions to the nation-state, or to the nation and/or state.* Not only does this place into question generalizations about departicularization in modern politics, but it suggests that a fusion is occurring that can only be examined with careful attention to the theological and cultural particularities in question, attention that is as yet lacking in Hauerwas's corpus.

William T. Cavanaugh: The Challenge of Modernity

Perhaps of all the theologians of his scholarly generation, William Cavanaugh presents the most comprehensive account of contemporary Christian theopolitics. By his telling, modernity—particularly the modern state and its theoretical proponents—presents the greatest challenge to an orthodox ecclesial identity. It does so by conveying an alternative salvation history, of which the modern state is the definitive political embodiment. This salvation narrative contends against that proclaimed by the church, and the church ends up domesticated, reduced to the oversight of the interior dispositions of individual souls. Modernity, he argues, assumes the separation of theology and politics as proper, with politics residing in a different autonomous space from that of the church. The church must therefore approach politics indirectly and from a distance. Cavanaugh's alternative is to view politics as embedded in core Christian theological themes, reimagining the political as a direct response to God's activity in the world. Thus, "there is no separate history of politics apart from the history of salvation," and "the church is indispensable to the history of salvation." As he explains, salvation is not merely about "pulling a few individual survivors from the wreckage of creation after the Fall," but rather concerns the renewal of creation, central to which is the creation of a community of people who are to be a foretaste of that new creation, a community living radically differently from the world around it.[25]

I find much of Cavanaugh's overall argument to be profound and compelling, and my own theopolitical understanding is much indebted to him, as it is to Hauerwas and Yoder. That said, I am concerned that his emphasis on modernity and the state results in an incomplete understanding of how nationalism operates, especially when it emanates from within the church as grounded in a selective and distortive use of Christian Scriptures and theology. This section will attend to Cavanaugh's approach in some detail, with focused attention to his appropriation of nationalism scholarship, as he is the only major theopolitical scholar to date who has directly engaged with that scholarship. By examining his use of that literature, I will show that his approach is partially successful in identifying present theopolitical challenges to ecclesial faithfulness, but that it falters at crucial points in accurately

---

25. Cavanaugh, "Church," 394.

discerning the church's own direct and even primary agency in the problem of nationalism. This is not to say that Cavanaugh ignores or rejects church complicity, but rather that he provides an incomplete account of the nature of the relationship between theology and nationalism, and hence of the church's role. Such an examination will also provide a launching point for explaining how nationalism is understood throughout the rest of this study.

Modernity, "Religion," and Departicularization

Competing with Christian salvation history is the salvation narrative of the modern state and modern political theory, which presents religion as the source of violence from which the state saves us. Cavanaugh undertakes a thoroughgoing critique of this modern narrative throughout his work, most recently and comprehensively in his book *The Myth of Religious Violence*.[26] Here, he deconstructs the idea of "religion" itself. One of his central claims is that religion operates in both modern political theory and religious studies as an essentially *transhistorical* and *transcultural* phenomenon. His thesis is twofold: (1) there is no such thing as transhistorical and transcultural religion, inherently inward and private, and thus separated from politics; rather what qualifies as religion in a given context rests on how power is configured in that context; and (2) the attempt to assert such a transhistorical and transcultural "religion" separate from the "secular" is itself part of a particular configuration of power, that being the modern liberal nation-state.[27]

Examining the treatments of religious violence by a number of philosophers of religion and religious studies scholars, Cavanaugh concludes that not only is their understanding of religion unclear, but that their vague definition is applied far too specifically to things called Christianity, Buddhism, Islam, etc., when phenomena like nationalism or capitalism could likewise qualify as "religious."[28] By and large in their works, the categorical distinction between religious and secular is un-

26. This source provides the bulk of information for this discussion of Cavanaugh, given that it incorporates much of his previous work on the salvation narrative of modern liberalism. Previous writings by Cavanaugh on the same include "'A Fire Strong Enough'"; *Torture and Eucharist*; and "The City."

27. Cavanaugh, *Myth*, 9.

28. These scholars include John Hick, Charles Kimball, Martin Marty, Mark Juergensmeyer, and Scott Appleby.

critically presupposed. To demonstrate, he sorts contemporary scholarship into three groups according to their main characterizations of religious violence: absolutist, divisive, or insufficiently rational. In each case, he argues, the scholar in question has artificially and inconsistently attended to certain kinds of violence over against others, namely, "religious" over against "secular," and has subscribed to the prevailing understanding of the former as inherently more absolutist, divisive, and irrational than the latter. Such a distinction—firmly anchored in these authors' understanding of religion as timeless and universal—is neither explicitly examined nor justified, and ignores other prominent scholarship that recognizes that phenomena like "secular nationalism" can themselves be characterized as religious, thus negating such a distinction. He argues that for them then to attribute violence or a certain ferocity exclusively to "religion" is to miss the fact that not merely do nationalism, capitalism, etc., themselves underwrite extensive violence in the late medieval and modern eras, but that according to empirical investigation, there is no coherent method of separating religious and secular violence in such a way as to conclude that the latter is essentially more restrained than the former.[29]

In fact, Cavanaugh asserts, religion is a contestable term, its definition depending on the configurations of power and authority in a given context. Specifically, the understanding of religion operative in the studies he critiques is a product of the modern liberal state: "the religious-secular distinction accompanies the invention of private-public, religion-politics, and church-state dichotomies. The religious-secular distinction also accompanies the state's monopoly over internal violence and its colonial expansion." In particular, these distinctions perform "an ideological function in legitimating certain kinds of practices and delegitimating others." They make religion essentially interior and private, distinct from the secular, public sphere; thus, something like Christianity can coexist peacefully with patriotism since (private) loyalty to God is separated from (public) loyalty to the state.[30]

Historically, for Augustine, *religio* meant worship; true *religio* was worship of God as revealed in Jesus Christ, while false *religio* was directed to elements of creation. This *religio* is not contrasted with some sort of secular realm free from it; *religio* cannot be compartmentalized

29. Cavanaugh, *Myth*, 16, 56.
30. Ibid., 59.

from the rest of life, but rather, the rest of life put in proper order and relation to the Creator constitutes its true form. With Thomas Aquinas, *religio* is a virtue, a habit cultivated by repeated practice. Rather than being a "universal genus of which Christianity is a particular species," true *religio* reveres the Triune God.[31] *Religio* is a "virtue embedded in particular bodily disciplines,"[32] a habitual set of practices that brings the person to participate in the life of the Trinity, in both body and soul, in both private and public dimensions alike. This medieval conception is overtaken in early modernity by the invention of "religion," a universal category containing particular species demarcated by systems of propositions, an "essentially interior, private impulse," and existing as distinct from public, nonreligious endeavors like politics.[33] The process is catalyzed by the Reformation, in various strands of which religion comes to be associated with particular saving knowledge, "a body of objective truths to which the believer could assent or withhold assent."[34] Religion becomes essentially an intellectual exercise, a category of cognitive propositions. Subsequently, in both Protestant and Catholic understandings, distinct doctrines come to signify separate religions, an understanding that during the seventeenth century comes to include Christianity as juxtaposed with Judaism or Islam.

As religion becomes intellectualized, it becomes departicularized doctrinally. Cavanaugh describes this development under Lord Herbert of Cherbury, an early seventeenth-century religious theorist. With Herbert, "it became possible to speak of religion in general." Herbert attempts to boil the world's religions down to common essential beliefs that can then be internalized and privatized, detached from political embodiment. Consequently, particular doctrines or salvation narratives and liturgies come to be seen by Herbert as "a dilution of the original purity of the natural instinct . . . the particularities of the various religions are to be considered accretions and corruptions which distort the 'perfect sphere of the religion of God.'" Thus religion is departicularized, made "transhistorical and transcultural" for Herbert, a "timeless religion that is interior, universal, nonmaterial, and essentially distinct

---

31. Ibid., 63–65.
32. Ibid., 71.
33. Ibid., 69.
34. Ibid., 73.

from the political," one of many attempts that are "part of the creation of new configurations of power" inherent to the emerging state.[35]

Integrated into early modern political philosophy, religion is thus primarily a state of mind, something that cannot be enforced by civil authority or force. It is distinct and separate from the activities of the body. This is how, for example, John Locke can propagate a hard division between the public interests of the state and the private interests of the church, a line that neither must cross in order to secure civil harmony. Violence is the purview of the state rather than the church, which constitutes a voluntary society of persons rooted in their interior religious dispositions. Indeed, this is an underlying motif of early modern political philosophy. Discussing Thomas Hobbes, Jean Jacques Rousseau, Locke, and others, Cavanaugh explains how a transnational church becomes for them a threat to state unity. The church must therefore be "domesticated," a process that quite easily includes notions of religious liberty, though rooted in a notion of Christianity as a set of universal moral truths underlying all faiths, rather than "theological claims and practices which take a particular social form called the Church."[36] Here, departicularization becomes *depoliticization*: Christianity is privatized, while public, embodied loyalty transfers to the state. Thus "in Locke, we find a modern version of the spatial division of the world into religious and secular pursuits," as opposed to the medieval conception of the secular as "this world and age."[37] All this is to say that "religion" itself has a history, and therefore cannot be considered transhistorical and transcultural in essence. In the end, the modern notion of religion is not merely a *description* of a social phenomenon, but actually helps *create* and *reinforce* that phenomenon: in short, "religion is a normative concept."[38]

The normativeness of "religion" is nowhere more apparent than in the so-called Wars of Religion, whose commonly accepted interpretation Cavanaugh effectively debunks. He challenges the narratives put forward by contemporary political theorists such as Jeffrey Stout, Judith Shklar, and John Rawls, in which liberalism arises to save humanity from the ravages of religious strife. Rather, Cavanaugh finds that the

---

35. Ibid., 74–77.
36. Cavanaugh, "'A Fire Strong Enough,'" 404.
37. Cavanaugh, *Myth*, 78–80.
38. Ibid., 85.

historical record reveals that "the so-called wars of religion appear as wars fought by state-building elites for the purpose of consolidating their power over the church and other rivals."[39] Yet, rather than simply arguing that these wars were conflicts over political and economic interests rather than religious, Cavanaugh asserts that they were in fact part of the process of creating the distinction between those areas, a distinction that would serve to enflame the wars and support the rise of the modern state. In short, the myth of religious violence operates as part of Western folklore. Rather than merely relating history, it actually authorizes certain configurations of power. And it is quite theological, underwriting a distinct salvation narrative. The typical narrative of the Wars of Religion acts as the "creation myth for modernity," wherein the forces of order overcome some preexisting chaos. The myth is also the state's soteriology, its narrative of the salvation of humanity from religious division and violence: "It is a story of salvation from mortal peril by the creation of the secular nation-state. As such, it legitimates the direction of the citizen's ultimate loyalty to the nation-state and secures the nation-state's monopoly on legitimate violence."[40]

According to Cavanaugh, the state's soteriology fails on multiple counts. For one thing, it is rooted in a "'theological' anthropology which precludes any truly social process." Conceiving of human beings as essentially individual, relations can be had only by means of contractual arrangement, to which notions of participatory relationships with God and each other are threats. What follows is human unity in a "body of a perverse sort." Since individuals operate with no common ends, the best the state can do is prevent them from interfering with each other's rights. The modern liberal view is thus that of "a monstrosity of many separate limbs proceeding directly out of a gigantic head," the members of society adhering to the state, rather than to each other. This is particularly apparent as the state moves to replace other "local communities of formation and decision-making." Finally, and most blatantly, the state at the heart of its *mythos* has promised peace, but has brought violence instead. This is evidenced by the violence within a territory as a state tries to secure itself, but also "the establishment of territorial borders with a single authority within each assumes a 'state of nature' between

---

39. Ibid., 161–62. Cavanaugh's detailed analysis of modern depictions of the "wars of religion" can be found on 142–71.

40. Ibid., 226.

territorial states, heightening the possibility of war." Lacking shared ends, the modern state must be defined by its means, which is its supposed monopoly on the legitimate use of force. Thus war becomes "the primary mechanism for achieving social integration in a society with no shared ends." Violence is the state's "*religio*, its habitual discipline for binding us one to another."[41]

Cavanaugh's response to the theopolitics of modernity is a "Eucharistic counter-politics" rooted in the true story of the world, which by its very nature "is already to be engaged in a direct confrontation with the politics of the world."[42] In the Eucharist, a "stunning 'public' *leitourgia*," we are made members of Christ's Body and of each other. Such unity is a gift, thus subverting "the primacy of contract and exchange in modern social relations."[43] As opposed to the distorted state body, the Eucharist builds the Body of Christ by relating its members to one another, not through Christ the Head alone, "for Christ himself is found not only in the center but at the margins of the Body, radically identified with the 'least of my brothers and sisters.'" While state unity depends upon absorbing the local and particular into the universal, in "true catholicity," "the antithesis of local and universal is effaced." The Eucharist found in each local community makes the whole Christ present, so all are united in Christ. The Eucharist transforms political identity as well, as it "transgresses national boundaries and redefines who our fellow-citizens are."[44]

Cavanaugh presents a highly compelling portrayal of modernity's salvation history and its attendant politics. I find his narrative powerful and convincing at many points, particularly in terms of how he characterizes the motives and practices of the modern state, and I believe he successfully debunks certain significant liberal readings of history and politics since the Middle Ages. However, Cavanaugh's understanding of modernity and the modern state tends toward an overly narrow understanding of nationalism, conceived of as an exclusively mid-to-late modern phenomenon, and therefore a *primarily state-driven project*

---

41. Cavanaugh, "The City," 192–94.

42. Cavanaugh, *Torture and Eucharist*, 11–13.

43. Cavanaugh, "The City," 195. For an in-depth discussion of the Eucharist as solution to the state project of globalization, see Cavanaugh, *Theopolitical Imagination*, especially chapters 5 and 6.

44. Cavanaugh, "The City," 196.

rooted in a transhistorical and transcultural conception of religion. What I hope to show here is that such an approach can only account for some, not all, forms of nationalism, and less so for the forms that present the most direct challenge to ecclesial identity and mission today. In fact, those forms of nationalism are developed by non-state actors and rely not on the departicularized notion of religion with which Cavanaugh characterizes modern politics, but rather emanate from within the church itself and rely upon a syncretism of quite particular theological and national narratives. In order to move toward this understanding, we must next examine Cavanaugh's specific thought on nationalism, especially his engagement with contemporary nationalism scholarship.

Nationalism Theory and Cavanaugh's "Modernism"

Cavanaugh defines nation as "a unitary system of shared cultural attributes," consolidated by the state. Nations most commonly entail some sort of shared ethnicity, language, or history, but these are themselves constructed. National identity is "a matter of 'common feeling and an organized claim,'" but he argues, "this claim is first organized by the state." Only after the state's claims to sovereignty within a territory are established does nationalism arise to "unify culturally what had been gathered inside state borders." While nationalists construct myths of national origin stretching back into antiquity, nationalism itself only appears in the eighteenth century with the nation-state, which then comes to prominence in the nineteenth, as "the vertical relationship of state and individual is opened to include a horizontal relationship among individuals, an increasingly cohesive mass relationship."[45] This is a very strong argument for nationalism as a project primarily of the modern state, a process by which a given state creates national identity in order to socially cohere the diverse identities of its population under its auspices.

Cavanaugh relies for this understanding on a rather one-sided appropriation of nationalism scholarship, namely, the "modernist" approach, which argues that "nations are only possible once states have been invented, and that nations, even seemingly 'ancient' ones, are the product of the last two centuries."[46] Cavanaugh cites, among other

---

45. Cavanaugh, "Killing for the Telephone Company," 246, 250.
46. Ibid, 261.

scholars, Benedict Anderson, who argues that the conditions of possibility for nations and nationalism are inherently modern, primary among them the advent of "print-capitalism" and the proliferation of vernacular literatures.[47] As Anderson writes, "one of the earlier forms of capitalist enterprise, book-publishing felt all of capitalism's restless search for markets," which ultimately enabled increasing numbers of people to perceive themselves and relate to others in important new ways. Print-languages created a basis for national identity in three ways: (1) by creating "unified fields of exchange and communication" in between Latin and the spoken vernacular; (2) by imbuing a sort of "fixity" to language, thus attributing to it a semblance of longevity or even antiquity; and (3) by creating new "languages-of-power" that diverged from older administrative vernaculars.[48] Moreover, the spread of the use of vernacular languages was in many instances a spread in the use of *state* languages, which clearly implicates the state in the construction of these "imagined communities."[49]

Cavanaugh relies as well on the work of Eric Hobsbawm and his notion of "invented traditions" rooted in "exercises in social engineering which are often deliberate and always innovative, if only because historical novelty implies innovation."[50] For Hobsbawm, "invented tradition" refers to "a set of practices, normally governed by overtly or tacitly accepted rules and of a ritual or symbolic nature, which seek to inculcate certain values and norms of behavior by repetition, which automatically implies continuity with the past." Any purported continuity with the historic past is "largely fictitious"; rather, invented traditions are "responses to novel situations which take the form of reference to old situations, or which establish their own past by quasi-obligatory repetition."[51] The key agent in this construction is the state, which fuses the various invented elements of tradition—both through public education and public ceremonies—in a way ultimately decisive for the identity of its citizens.[52]

---

47. Anderson, "Imagined Communities," 89.
48. Ibid., 94.
49. Ibid., 90.
50. Hobsbawm and Ranger, eds., *Invention of Traditions*, 13.
51. Ibid., 1–2.
52. Hobsbawm, "Nation as Invented Tradition," 77–81.

The work of both Anderson and Hobsbawm is rooted in the thought of the so-called father of the modernist school, Ernest Gellner. In his landmark 1983 work, *Nations and Nationalism*, Gellner argues that "nationalism is primarily a political principle, which holds that the political and the national unity should be congruent." It is a "theory of political legitimacy," requiring ethnic boundaries not to violate political ones, nor to separate the elite from the masses within a given state,[53] and it is a phenomenon "inherent in a certain set of social conditions," namely, those of modernity.[54] Gellner does not provide a clear-cut definition of nation. However, he posits that persons can be considered of the same nation if "they share the same culture, where culture in turn means a system of ideas and signs and associations and ways of behaving and communicating"; yet they must *recognize each other* as belonging to the same nation, including mutually acknowledging rights and duties due each other by virtue of their shared nationhood.[55] It is this mutual recognition, and not merely the sharing of attributes, that is definitive.

Drawing on Max Weber, Gellner assumes the state as agent in a nationalism process driven and controlled by the interests of the state's elites. The state constitutes a particular manifestation of a social division of labor, namely that concentrating on "order maintenance,"[56] and over time, it is the state's consolidation and universalization of education—according to the interests of the modern economy—that is definitive for the rise of national identity.[57] Such education forms a "high culture" within a population, the imposition of which upon a lower culture (thereby dissolving social bodies at the local level) constitutes nationalism.[58] Nationalism, therefore, is not a reawakening of "an old, latent, dormant force," but rather a "new form of social organization, based on deeply internalized, education-dependent high cultures, each protected by its own state."[59] As political authority is concentrated in the central-

---

53. Gellner, *Nations and Nationalism*, 1. It should be noted here that "ethnic" need not be narrowly defined in terms of blood relations or biological attributes, but also includes elements commonly associated with culture. This broader sense of the term is operative for the present study.

54. Ibid., 125.

55. Ibid., 7.

56. Ibid., 4.

57. Ibid., 33–34.

58. Ibid, 57.

59. Ibid., 48.

ized state, each state oversees and is identified with "one kind of culture, one style of communication, which prevails within its borders and is dependent for its perpetuation on a centralized educational system supervised by and often actually run by the state in question," a rather "monolithic educational system" reflecting the economic interests of the modern state.[60] In this light, "it is nationalism which engenders nations, and not the other way around." Consequently, Gellner emphasizes the relatively arbitrary nature of any given national identity. Nationalist movements use "the pre-existing, historically inherited proliferation of cultures or cultural wealth, though it uses them very selectively, and it most often transforms them radically." He goes further: "the cultural shreds and patches used by nationalism are often *arbitrary historical inventions. Any old shred and patch would have served as well*."[61] The content of these inherited traditions is hardly binding in any way, but is rather a resource pool from which to draw for state-driven national identity fabrication.

The modernist school is to be credited with recognizing and deciphering the many ways in which nationalism has developed and has been influenced by various developments and structures in the modern era, as well as the ways in which states themselves can be agents of nationalism by engineering national identity through education and celebration. Anderson's notion of "imagined communities" is quite intriguing and in many ways accurate, and his argument attends to the very important element of language and its standardization as a factor in social identity. Hobsbawm's work is excellent for noting how the state uses education and ceremony—the latter of which clearly amounts to a type of liturgy—to reinforce or even inculcate elements of identity within a people, and rightly points to the way the state does indeed invent traditions to solidify its hold over a territory and populace. Gellner, for his part, rightly points to elements of political engineering and to the very important aspect of elite appropriation and reinterpretation of preexisting cultural elements. He also rightly points to the distortion of those elements that occurs in the nationalizing process, a key element to which we will return in the next chapter. It is clear how such schemas would be consonant with and reinforce Cavanaugh's own approach.

---

60. Ibid., 140.
61. Ibid., 55–56. Emphasis added.

However, the modernist school goes too far in suggesting that nation and national identity are peculiar to modern conditions, and especially that they are almost exclusively the products of state agency and can be largely fabricated according to the interests of the state elites involved. As to the issue of agency, certainly nationalism can be fostered by state elites in the pursuit of quite pragmatic political objectives; this is a common occurrence. But it is also true that many nationalist movements are born and catalyzed apart from the state, led by a different set of elites quite apart from state operations, and driven by independently derived goals that are sometimes even a threat to the state establishment. If nation and nationalism are primarily arbitrary creations of the state, then one would expect to find little if any nationalist resistance to the state. "Nationalist violence" would only ever be violence exercised *by states*, and state nationalism typically would be successful outside of local pockets of cultural-political nonconformity. Yet, as Josep Llobera writes, "An important characteristic of the modern development of nationalism is to realize that state nationalism is not always successful precisely because of the importance of *nationalisms against the state*."[62] In some contexts—one immediately thinks of anti- or post-colonial movements in Africa, as well as Yugoslavia, Chechnya, or former Soviet republics—often violent anti-state nationalisms command a loyalty and allegiance, even instilling an identity comparable or greater in power than the existing state itself; this suggests that nationalism should be treated as a significant phenomenon often distinct from state agency. And this is not to mention those movements for national renewal that revolve around contests over the very core of national identity and meaning, wherein the state is of relatively marginal concern, except insofar as it reinforces or subverts a particular identity primarily propagated in other quarters. It is often this last type of nationalism—featuring prominently in the United States—that most directly implicates the church in an artificial fusion of ecclesial and national narratives. Yet to the degree that Cavanaugh relies on this modernist conception of state-driven nationalism, his approach is unable to attend adequately or consistently to the processes of non-state-driven Christian nationalism, particularly its inherent theological moves.

Then there are the substantive critiques of the modernist position within the literature itself, overstatements and inconsistencies by

---

62. Llobera, *Foundations*, 48. Emphasis added.

the modernists that Cavanaugh seems to overlook. For example, while Anderson emphasizes the role of modern capitalism and publishing in solidifying written vernaculars, which then solidifies national identities, Adrian Hastings points out that Anderson completely neglects the centrality of the Bible in cultivating European nationalism from the late Middle Ages on; and indeed, it was not merely the biblical text itself, but clerical instruction in those texts that contributed.[63] This leads to a point by the constructivist Paul Brass that in some cases, communities can be mobilized politically apart from modern systems of mass communication, "especially through traditional networks of religious communication."[64] As such, not only is a central element of a specific faith tradition appropriated in nationalist development, but national identity is quite able to emerge without the mechanisms of the modern state.

There is also the tendency among modernists toward monolithic conceptions of popular allegiance, moving from programs of state nationalism to popular loyalty without really accounting for how that loyalty is in fact cultivated, or that multiple conceptions might be at play in a given context. However, Brass has convincingly argued that nationalism is almost always a significantly contested process. In his account, nationalism is the politicization of a preexisting ethnic community, wherein that very process of politicized identity formation revolves around cultivating the meanings of a variety of symbols in a given context, and attempting to achieve a measure of consensus on such meanings within a people.[65] Symbol selection involves competition among elites, as well as the uncertainty of transforming a given ethnic identity from its initial form. Importantly, Brass adds that such "striving for multisymbol congruence is pursued by ethnic group leaders as much as by state-builders."[66] Thus, nationalist elites need not be, and often are not, members of the state apparatus, nor is nationalism necessarily a monolithic, state-driven project. Yet, nationalism is by definition a political movement, and must be able to compete against other political groups as well as, where relevant, state efforts to suppress it. To the degree that the movement can identify with, rather than merely

63. Hastings, *Construction of Nationhood*, 12.
64. Brass, *Ethnicity and Nationalism*, 15.
65. Ibid., 20.
66. Ibid., 21.

represent, the community, it will be more effective against external political pressure.[67] No doubt, the degree of symbol competition varies on a case-by-case basis, but it is clear that in many instances, nationalism is a messy process made so by the agency of multiple actors, state and non-state alike. This insight goes considerably underappreciated in the nationalism scholarship of the modernist school. Cavanaugh's reliance upon that literature, as well as his emphasis on the totalizing and departicularizing modern state, therefore requires qualification.

Moreover, the modernist argument has been assailed in the past two decades for its lack of attention to preexisting culture and culture's constraints upon nationalist elites in determining what constitutes genuine national identity. Even granting that elements such as ethnicity (whether biological or cultural), language, and history are often constructed, can we claim that they only come about in the modern period, invented from scratch without so much as a premodern precedent? That would be a claim of utter discontinuity between premodern and modern periods, a claim Cavanaugh would not support. Yet if such elements are in some ways inherited, they inevitably affect the activities of nationalist elites, rendering nationalist construction of identity a process constrained by those elements in definitive ways. This means that, contra the modernist school, the process of nationalist construction of identity is often a significantly *constrained* process, requiring a closer examination of those elements and their selective reappropriation than Cavanaugh currently provides.

On this point, Anthony D. Smith has pointed out that Hobsbawm's notion of "invented traditions," like modernist scholarship generally, tends to overstate the ability of elites to be innovative, to craft the nationalist message from scratch. Hobsbawm states that the nationalist message must be on a wavelength that will resonate with the people hearing it, but as Smith points out, Hobsbawm fails to explain how such a wavelength arises if there are not key preexisting elements of national identity and culture—in short, *inherited* traditions—which have already formed the people and to which the nationalist can and must refer.[68] Indeed, according to both Smith and Brass, as well as Anthony Marx,[69] *nationalists themselves* are often preformed according to such cultural

---

67. Ibid., 48.
68. Smith, *Nationalism and Modernism*, 129.
69. Marx, *Faith in Nation*, 75.

and religious traditions, which then inform their understandings of what nationalist discourse would be both appropriate, that is, reflecting the "true" nation in their conceptions, and effective at galvanizing the populace. More importantly, not only do elite and popular formation point to the existence of prior elements of identity, they beg the question in Christian and other faith-associated nationalisms of what is going on *theologically* when various elements of faith traditions are appropriated and reinterpreted for national identity. If we do not assume that nationalist elites and peoples alike are initially blank slates, then a Christian nationalism, for instance, must replace some preexisting—perhaps more orthodox—theological understanding. Such an understanding must be there for Christian nationalism to have any traction, and there must be some sort of theological realignment going on in the process of its reception. Neither Cavanaugh nor his sources account for this.

The ethnosymbolism approach of Anthony D. Smith has demonstrated, contra modernist claims, that there are other drivers of nationalism besides the state, and that nationalists have limited options when it comes to crafting their message. They must, in fact, work within already existing parameters in order to effectively galvanize a populace behind a given conception of national identity. This suggests elements of national identity that in many cases precede or exist apart from the state. Cavanaugh dismisses ethnosymbolism, and Smith in particular, as having been criticized for overstating the "group consciousness" of premodern groups and for failing to attend to the lack of institutional undergirding there. Indeed, he reiterates that "most importantly, 'nationalism is not simply a claim of ethnic similarity, but a claim that certain similarities should count as *the* definition of political community.'"[70]

Unfortunately, Cavanaugh takes these critiques for granted and does not directly engage Smith's work. Had he done so, he might have seen that the heart of Smith's ethnosymbolic approach is the principle of *authentication*, the process by which nationalists determine from an assortment of available cultural, historical, and even theological elements what precisely defines their "true" nation as a political community. To be sure, Smith asserts the longstanding preexistence—indeed the perennial existence—of such cultural elements and ethnic identity, sometimes in rather sophisticated form. Smith leans on these elements

---

70. Cavanaugh, "Killing for the Telephone Company," 262. Quoted from Özkirimli, *Theories of Nationalism*, 185.

more heavily in understanding how national identities are formed than he does on the constructive work of nationalists because he wants to be clear on how those elements limit the range of action available to nationalists, both in terms of what might appeal to the people as well as how those very nationalists might already be formed in their thinking. This, Smith rightly recognizes, is part of what the modernist school overlooks about nationalism. However, I believe Smith overemphasizes the degree to which the preexistence of such elements constitutes the key determining factor in the shape of nationalism in every case, a disposition I believe is almost as problematic as the modernists' overemphasis on arbitrary state action.

I therefore diverge from Smith in area of emphasis, but I still take his work to be the best available explanation of the phenomenon in question. This is partly because I believe Smith to be more "constructivist" than he admits, given that his process of authentication requires the nationalists' own activities of selectively interpreting and reappropriating elements so as to galvanize the public. Such is, to greater or lesser degrees, depending on the case, a constructive process (though neither necessarily modern nor state-driven), and one, ironically, that Smith attends to in far more detail than do the modernists. This is why I think Cavanaugh would benefit from incorporating Smith's understanding into his own, at least in a somewhat qualified manner.

For Smith, authentication is what enables nationalists to present a convincing narrative of national identity to their compatriots and to outsiders. It entails selecting, interpreting, and reappropriating elements of a people's cultural heritage in such a way that the present community is galvanized toward the reembodiment of some ideal presented as the people's past and purified of foreign elements. This resonates to a degree with the claims by Gellner—Smith's former teacher—that nationalists selectively mine existing cultural resources and then reinterpret them. Yet Gellner, as a modernist, locates this activity squarely within the institutions of the state, and he overstates the degrees to which such a process is free and arbitrary and to which such preexisting elements are interchangeable. Thus, the notion of authentication, properly balanced between constraint and construction, both highlights the importance of received elements of identity that cannot simply be fabricated or appropriated at whim by nationalists, as well as the constructive process by which said nationalists then reinterpret those elements toward their vision of national identity. As such, it is key to an understanding of Christian nationalism as a process, not of *departicularizing* faith communities into an amorphous religious impulse, but rather of *reparticularizing* specific narratives of salvation history in new contexts for nationalist purposes.

Nationalism as Reparticularization

Cavanaugh's focus on modernity's "secular" nationalism necessitates that nationalism by definition relies on the modern notion of religion as transhistorical, transcultural, interior, and private. This is, after all, how the religious-secular distinction actually enables the rise of the state: private loyalty to God is separated from public loyalty to the state. Yet with regard to nationalism, this fails to acknowledge the fact that some nationalist movements do not consider religion to be transhistorical or private at all. In these movements, the identity, mission, and destiny of the nation are actually being syncretized with specific features of a given faith tradition, that is to say, with quite *particular* historical and theological narratives. Where this is the case, resisting the atomizing and departicularizing efforts of modernity and the modern state is not sufficient by itself to meet the current challenge of nationalism. Rather, we must understand nationalism to be often a process of reparticularization, wherein various nationalist elites, often quite apart from the state, seek to tie quite specific preexisting theological narratives to national narratives of history and myth in order to formulate, and galvanize people toward, a particular vision of national identity.

Cavanaugh himself mentions the "curious blend of Enlightenment and Christian themes and symbols" in American civil religion, for example, including the Puritan use of biblical images and the identification of their colony as a New Israel chosen by God; over time this New Israel becomes the United States (rather than the church), which acts as the world's savior via the propagation of democracy and capitalism. This notion of America as the New Israel, including Puritan biblical covenant imagery was combined with certain "Revolutionary ideals" into America as a "kind of metachurch."[71] The same idea is picked up by others in the eighteenth century—such as Herman Melville, who refers

---

71. Cavanaugh, "Messianic Nation," 262–64. Some of these themes are reiterated in his slightly later article "Empire of the Empty Shrine."

to America as the "political Messiah"—to the point where "we see a shift from a nation under God to a nation as God's incarnation on earth, the nation as Messiah." Here, explains Cavanaugh, "we see the blending of the biblical notion of election with American ideas of progress, expansion, and capitalism."[72] Note then that Cavanaugh finds quite specific theological elements to be tied to national ones here, a process ill at ease with his notion of modern nationalism requiring a transcultural and transhistorical understanding of religion.

Cavanaugh observes this "blended" narrative alongside another strand of American exceptionalism found in such Enlightenment ideals as political and economic freedom, where the "freedom of the human will" makes America the firstborn of universal nations. In this strand, "freedom is not a substantive good but a formal structure that maximizes the possibility of each person to realize his or her particular goods." This kind of exceptionalism uses a "kind of secularized version of providence" called "history." History calls America to be the "destiny of the rest of the world."[73] The main theological danger of this form of exceptionalism is a messianic nation "that does not simply seek to follow God's will, but acts as a kind of substitute God on the stage of history." The nation worships its freedom to worship, which is inherent to its identity, and thus it worships itself.[74]

Cavanaugh finds these two themes, biblical and Enlightenment exceptionalism, woven together in the work of American theologian Stephen H. Webb, who combines evangelism of the gospel with evangelism of American freedoms. This breeds a certain alarming evangelization-through-violence: regarding Muslims, for instance, Webb suggests that they can be forced militarily into democratic political arrangements so that they may subsequently choose freely to accept Christianity. Here, suggests Cavanaugh, "American-style democracy provides the empty form for evangelization, but the Christian gospel provides the content." Yet, there is great danger that this configuration would be inverted, such that the biblical narrative of God acting in history becomes the form, and American-style democracy and capitalism

---

72. Cavanaugh, "Messianic Nation," 264.
73. Ibid., 265–66.
74. Ibid., 268.

become the content, that is, "America itself becomes the criterion for locating God's activity in the world."[75]

Webb's arguments will be explored at length in chapter 7. What is important here is to note that what Cavanaugh critiques Webb for is actually a type of nationalist discourse. Cavanaugh does not identify it as such, perhaps because his understanding of nationalism as relying on transcultural, transhistorical religion would not really accommodate the interweaving of particular narratives. However, in examining the actual *content* of the discourse, what Webb is propagating is an authenticated vision of national identity. Webb's discourse is neither state-driven nor does it rely on a transhistorical, transcultural, private notion of religion. Rather, it is a message crafted from within Christian theology, deliberately tying the American national narrative to a preexisting theopolitical narrative, that of the Christian Scriptures. Cavanaugh's argument as stated cannot adequately account for this type of discourse, for here, loyalty to the nation (or state, or both) is not a public function alongside a separate and privatized faith, the situation produced for and by the rise of the modern state; rather, *loyalty to God and loyalty to nation or state are one and the same, and this syncretized loyalty is both particular and public.*[76] Therefore, these quite specific theological narratives must be disentangled from the national in order to rectify their nationalist distortions and thereby recover a genuinely Christian salvation narrative and its attendant politics.

---

75. Ibid., 270.

76. In personal correspondence on this point, Cavanaugh has said, "A lot depends, of course, by what we mean by 'Christianity.' When I say that Christianity becomes privatized, I mean that what I consider to be the true gospel does not have much effect on what Christians do with their money, their bodies during wartime, etc. When Christian themes are usurped for nationalist causes, I don't think of that as the deprivatizing of Christianity; I think of that as the 'migration of the holy' from the church to the state, the use of Christian language and practices for false purposes. So we both need to distinguish between empirical Christianity and—for lack of a better way of putting it—true Christianity, that is, what is normatively and theologically true. . . . So, in response to [the] statement that 'Christian faith is not privatized but rather redefined so as to be tied to loyalty to the nation,' I would want to affirm that this is the case empirically, but say that, insofar as it is so redefined, it ceases to be 'true Christianity' and becomes a species of idolatry" (Cavanaugh, e-mail message to author, April 22, 2011). This is an important statement on his part, but I maintain my argument above since I believe Cavnauagh's public argument on this score is ambiguous at key points and bears further qualification. The distinction between "empirical" and "true" Christianity, however, is the argument of the rest of this book.

Moving Forward: Nation, Nationalism, and the Process of Authentication

While I have touched on them in the preceding discussion, it is important here to be explicit about key concepts with which I will be working throughout this study, including nation, state, and nationalism. Anthony Smith defines *nation* as "a named and self-defined human community whose members cultivate shared myths, memories, symbols, values, and traditions, reside in and identify with a historic homeland, create and disseminate a distinctive public culture, and observe shared customs and common laws."[77] Lowell Barrington defines a nation as "a collective of people ... united by shared cultural features (myths, values, etc.) and the belief in the right to territorial self-determination."[78] Barrington is qualified by Ronald Suny, who refers to nations as "'collectives [who feel they are] united ... groups of people [who believe they are] linked by unifying cultural characteristics.'"[79] Indeed, as Walker Connor asserts, "nation is a self-defined rather than other-defined grouping"; self-perception is what matters, "not *what is* but *what people believe is*."[80] As Barrington's definition is contained within Smith's, I take those to be normative for this study, with the caveat by Suny and Connor that self-perception is key. Note that this definition need not preclude situations where the state itself creates said unity, but neither is "nation" limited to such situations.

What is particularly important for the nation, but is not often discussed explicitly, is its shared sense of purpose as a people, a common understanding of the nation's *raison d'être*. Barrington identifies such a sense of purpose as "controlling the territory that the members of the territory believe to be theirs." Yet, while this may be the foremost practical objective—and while it may constitute the ultimate objective for certain elites—within the various features of culture, such a sense of purpose typically entails something "higher," even spiritual, and often in relation to the divine. If self-perception is key, then how the members of a particular nation view its role in the world, often in relation to the

---

77. Smith, *Cultural Foundations*, 19.
78. Barrington, "'Nation' and 'Nationalism,'" 712–13.
79. Suny, "Nationalism," 279.
80. Connor, "Nation Is a Nation," 36–37.

divine and almost always over against other nations, can be critical to understanding the nation in question.

As the reader already will have noted, "nation" has been defined in contrast to "state." A state is the "principal political unity in the international political system corresponding to a territory, a relatively permanent population, and a set of ruling institutions."[81] The state, in other words, is the institutional apparatus over a given, politically demarcated territory. To reiterate, nationalist movements either undergird states (sometimes as state-driven projects, as the modernists and Cavanaugh conceive them, and sometimes even without state involvement), or they resist states, attempting to gain control over existing states or to achieve new states of their own; in any event, while the two are usually related, nations and states are distinct entities.[82]

As with nation, *nationalism* is a contested term. In addition to Gellner's aforementioned notion of a political principle, Smith defines it as "an ideological movement for the attainment and maintenance of autonomy, unity and identity of a population, some of whose members deem themselves to constitute an actual or potential 'nation.'"[83] Anthony Marx defines nationalism as "a collective sentiment or identity, bounding and binding together those individuals who share a sense of large-scale political solidarity aimed at creating, legitimating, or challenging states," or, in short, "a mass sentiment for or against state power."[84] In some contrast to Marx's heavily state-centered understanding, Barrington argues that nationalism is a *process* of "creation of the unifying features of the nation, or the actions that result from the beliefs of the group"; further, it constitutes "the pursuit—through argument or other activity—of a set of rights for the self-defined members of the nation."[85] Nationalism is necessarily ideological—it must be a movement rooted in ideas—but it is also a *movement*, that is, a dynamic process of development and pursuit of goals.

---

81. Barrington, "'Nation' and 'Nationalism,'" 713.

82. The term "nation-state," which technically refers to a correspondence between a people's national boundaries and their state's borders, is perhaps a situation where the distinction between state and nation is moot. Yet, to the degree that such correspondence is a less frequent occurrence anymore, the distinction between the terms is becoming increasingly salient.

83. Smith, "Culture, Community and Territory," 447.

84. Marx, *Faith in Nation*, 6–7.

85. Barrington, "'Nation' and 'Nationalism,'" 714.

In fact, Barrington's two comments here could be read to indicate that there are *multiple* processes involved. At the very least, there is a distinct process of discerning and defining identity, of cultivating and propagating it among the people, that is, cultivating popular loyalty and thereby creating and perpetuating the nation as such. This can be orchestrated either by state or non-state elites, depending on the context. There is also the process of the pursuit of political power, up to and including territorial autonomy, usually in the form of a state. In state-driven nationalisms, this might take the form of after-the-fact justification or reinforcement of the current regime; in non-state or anti-state nationalisms, this typically means taking over an existing state or assembling a new one. These two main processes are often concurrent and closely linked—even mutually influential—but they can be distinguished. Thus, nationalism is a multifaceted movement. It is also, to reiterate, a movement often in contention. This is true both for its internal cultivation of identity and for its external pursuit of political power. Moreover, because identity is relational—it defines and redefines "self" and "other"—that "nationalism does not simply 'express' a pre-existent identity: it 'constitutes' one."[86]

According to Barrington, any nationalist movement must address two questions concerning the boundaries of the nation, namely, territory and membership: "Who is the nation? And what territory does the nation have a right to control?"[87] To these I would add a third, namely, "What is the meaning or purpose of the nation?" What is it that sets one's own nation apart from others, not only in terms of people or geography, but in terms of its role in the world? It is quite conceivable that in certain situations—say, within an established and stable state—the question of the nation's *raison d'être* might be highly contested, while the questions of membership and territory are considered fairly settled. A nationalist movement concentrating on cultural renewal of some sort would be a prime example.

It is within the processes of nationalism that Anthony Smith locates his principle of authentication, a concept I find particularly helpful in addressing nationalism as a challenge to the church. This again is the process by which nationalists determine what constitutes the "true" nation, a vision they then propagate in movements to cohere a people

---

86. Ignatieff, "Nationalism and Narcissism," 92.
87. Barrington, "Nationalism & Independence," 10–11.

around a particular identity and/or achieve consonance between that vision and a state apparatus, either on the part of, or against (or even in the absence of) a given state. The past is especially decisive for present nationalism in light of the "tendency of later generations, especially of nationalists, to rediscover, authenticate and appropriate aspects of what they assume is 'their' ethnic past." This process, which Smith usually simply calls "authentication," constitutes an essential component of nationalism, enabling nationalists to provide a compelling account of their nation to both their fellow nationals and to outsiders.[88]

Here, argues Smith, the nationalist acts as archaeologist, actively intervening in national construction via a three-step process.[89] The nationalist first "rediscovers" the people's ethnic past ("ethno-history"), especially that of a golden age, which in reconstructed form becomes the standard of evaluation for the present community and the inspiration for its correction,[90] the "canon of authenticity and creativity for latter-day nationalists."[91] This then requires authentication of that past, a determination of what is both "distinctive" and "indigenous" regarding the community's origins and achievements. Finally, the past is reappropriated: "the people must be encouraged to take possession of their authentic vernacular heritage and their genuine ethno-history."[92] This process leads to the "purification of culture," characterized as "seeking to purge the communal culture of foreign elements . . . [and] cleansing the community itself of everything alien and extraneous."[93] Thus, authentication aims toward a purified national identity that then leads to a purified nation.

What happens, though, when there are *theological* elements appropriated and reinterpreted from a people's past? What happens when particular theological traditions are taken by nationalists and fused with certain narratives of national history and myth? How do we discern when and how this is being done? What is the significance to that nationalist movement? More importantly for this study, what is

88. Smith, *Myths and Memories*, 63–64.

89. Ibid., 177.

90. Smith, "Culture, Community and Territory," 450.

91. Smith, *Nation in History*, 67.

92. Smith, "Culture, Community and Territory," 451. "Genuine" refers here not so much to objective historicity as to what a given community can consider as truly "their own."

93. Smith, "Formation of National Identity," 149.

the significance of such moves to those theological traditions? What if those nationalists are engaged in authentication from *within* their theological traditions? What happens to the theological narratives at play as well as the people shaped by those narratives? These questions require a specific discussion of the interplay between nationalism and theology, and particularly for this study, the Christian theological tradition. The next chapter aims to provide just that, examining the work of several different nationalist scholars who have dealt with the interplay between nationalism and faith traditions. I will ask of them not only how the traditions are used, but what theological moves occur allowing those appropriations to be justified to the participants of the Christian tradition in question, as well as what the effect of such a nationalist appropriation might be.

CHAPTER 2

Nationalism and Christian Theology

Introduction

The first chapter ended with the question of what occurs theologically in nationalism when elements of faith traditions are appropriated by nationalists in their formulation of national identity. What happens when particular theological traditions are taken by nationalists and fused with certain narratives of national history and myth? How do we discern when and how this is being done? What is the significance to that nationalist movement? More importantly for this study, what is the significance of such moves to that theological tradition? And what if those authenticating nationalists are actually accomplishing their endeavors from *within* those traditions? What happens to the theological narratives at play as well as the people shaped by those narratives? These questions require a specific discussion of the interplay between nationalism and theology, and particularly for this study, the Christian theological tradition. This chapter aims to provide just that, examining the work of several different nationalist scholars who have dealt with the interplay between nationalism and faith traditions. I will ask of them not only how the traditions are used, but what theological moves occur allowing those appropriations to be justified to the participants of the Christian tradition in question, as well as what the effect of such a nationalist appropriation might be.

Within nationalism scholarship, the virtual neglect of religion or traditions of faith by modernists has constituted one of the more robust lines of critique against their conception of nations and nationalism, as it virtually ignores one of the most prominent sources of human identity. In many cases, religion is made central to the nation's sense of self, its *raison d'être*, particularly when that self-understanding is animated by some sort of divine sanction or mandate. This move involves appropriating elements of preexisting *theological* traditions in order to galvanize the public into action. In the case of Christian nationalism, this is done not only by appropriating various Christian symbols but also and especially the narratives of the Christian Scriptures. For this reason, theopolitical scholarship—especially as it engages with nationalism studies—must recognize where and how the biblical narrative is being used by nationalists to redefine the identities of Christians according to an altered theopolitical narrative, one that fuses an incomplete and therefore distorted version of the Christian salvation history with a national narrative of history and myth.

In this chapter I look at several different approaches to the study of theology and nationalism, all of which bring out vital issues for consideration by the scholarly communities of both nationalism and theology. As I present them, each successive scholar improves upon the work of the foregoing one in terms of delineating what is going on with the nationalist use of religious elements. Ultimately, it will be clear that central elements of the Christian salvation narrative are being redirected to define certain national identities in lieu of ecclesial identity. Nevertheless, I will also point out how the lack of adequate attention by these scholars to the theological nuances of the traditions they cite brings their explanations up short.

Anthony Marx: Selective Exclusion and the Consolidation of Loyalties

While sharing modernism's state-centered focus, Anthony Marx argues the modernist chronology falls short in failing to recognize considerably earlier attempts to consolidate public support either behind or against particular states. Moreover, it neglects the central element of religion—as opposed to economic factors, for instance—as a means by which elites and commoners alike could mobilize for or against a given regime. Marx argues that this is to miss the key element in the rise of nationalism, an element that actually locates that rise in early modern Europe, at least two hundred years before the French Revolution.

As early modern rulers attempted to consolidate centralized rule, establishing the loyalty of their subjects became a key concern, especially when the masses mobilized against such centralization. Both state and popular leaders attempted to garner public support by means of what Marx calls "selective domestic exclusion." State or anti-state elites would choose those who would be included and exhorted toward loyalty, and would "thereby identify and bind the core constituency of and as the nation, selecting, aggravating, and playing off established antagonisms against some other group thereby excluded." Marx argues that these political actors would give in to the prejudices of a particular constituency and aim exclusionary policies at that constituency's adversaries; by so doing, elites would win the former's support, often unifying it in the face of other divisive challenges. Thus, "by maintaining legal boundaries and excluding an internal 'other' as a common enemy, state and other leaders encourage the cohesion and support of those included, focusing tangible benefits and reinforced by symbolic manipulations. This allocation process is at the heart of politics."[1]

The convergence of political conflict resulting from state-building and emerging religious strife in the wake of the Reformation provided the context for selective exclusion during this period. Examining the cases of early modern Spain, France, and England, Marx notes that faith was the most prevalent form of identity among the people, and as such provided both a framework for popular engagement—which state and anti-state elites sought to duplicate in the secular arena—as well as the only feasible grounds for such engagement. In this manner, "faith became politicized and increasingly relevant to state- and nation-building," an effective course according to Marx, since "the passion unleashed by doctrinal conflict was precisely the sort of strong identity that states sought to bolster for their own ends."[2] Elites took advantage of such passions by implementing exclusionary laws in favor of their chosen constituency—particularly by branding the latter's adversaries as heretics—and thus binding together their supporters.

---

1. Marx, *Faith in Nation*, 22–23.
2. Ibid., 25–27.

Marx notes that this was not a purely rational-choice operation, where calculating elites selected allies and adversaries according to a simple and unfettered cost-benefit ratio. Rather, "historically informed ideology or prejudice, or the 'embeddedness' of identities, pose a constraint on viable coalitions." Contemporary circumstances influence the strategic perception of elites or common people about what is rational in a given situation. Stated differently, "culture produces preferences that are then acted upon via rational calculation, or identities make some outcomes more likely. Choice is conceived and interpreted according to past history." Nevertheless, asserts Marx, while elites both share and are limited by popular belief, "they simplify, distort, and select such beliefs to serve the purpose of unifying a core group." More specifically, "religious sentiments are inherited from the past but then may change or be used selectively, with both elites and masses combining cultural vehemence with strategic action."[3] As asserted in the first chapter, then, both construction and constraint characterize nationalist action.

In sum, Marx argues that state rulers sought a "passionate loyalty to their own authority" and identified religion as the most promising avenue to that end. As state leaders—and then their opponents—discovered, "while serving their own interests the surest way to enflame religious passion and redirect it was to attack heretics within as evident and present threats to religious homogeneity." While religious passion cohered cultural identities, political leaders on either side sought a more secular form of unity. These forces came together at the common point of identity, and "what began as religious fanaticism aggravated by elite conflicts was gradually transformed into more explicitly political identities reflecting the interconnection between issues of faith and power."[4] Hence, nationalism and national identity.

Marx presents a very interesting argument, one that effectively undermines the modernist timeline and rightly raises questions about the importance of religion in the rise of nationalism. I appreciate his attention to the constraints upon nationalist elites—both externally by what faith traditions might have most sway with the populace, and internally in the way those elites were themselves formed in faith—but also his delineation of instances and manners in which state or anti-state elites exploited religious belief for their own interests and objectives, as well

---

3. Ibid., 75–77.
4. Ibid., 93–94.

as the extent to which church leaders acquiesced. His description of the co-opting of churches corresponds in part to Cavanaugh's, though I believe Cavanaugh would undoubtedly and rightly resist the notion that such initial passion could be so commonly inflamed merely on the basis of doctrinal differences, without those differences being somehow framed in terms of political threat, usually to the very survival of the people as such. This begs the question of how and why such purposes were framed along those lines.

To address that question, I begin by noting a significant and unresolved tension in Marx that cuts to the heart of his theoretical commitments. On the one hand, political leaders deliberately select those groups whom they seek to unify and galvanize for the purposes of the leaders' own nationalist aims, either to undergird or undermine the current state. This is arguably the center of the action in Marx's model. On the other hand, preexisting identities and historical circumstances condition the "strategic" perspective of elites, their field of options and choices between them constrained, even defined, by "culture." This point begs several questions.

First, precisely how free are elites to select and maneuver vis-à-vis particular religious groups? Not only are the strategies of elites externally constrained, but Marx suggests the elites themselves have been in some ways formed by prior identity and culture. So to what extent and in what manner do these influences shape their strategic view, and if religion is particularly determinative in some cases, to what extent in those instances is the factor of elite selection even salient? Marx seems to want to acknowledge both aspects, but it is unclear why elite rational choice, however limited, should be so generalizable and central to his schema if its parameters could be so predefined. And if they are not significantly predefined, then how important is this qualification? Second, if both elites and masses are so profoundly formed religiously, why would they even seek "more secular forms of unity and support"? Why not simply pursue a religiously defined nation-state? Marx seems to overstate elite instrumentalism here.

More directly, framing doctrinal differences according to political allegiance and survival requires certain *theological* moves, which Marx does not really address. Let us be clear: the prevalence of "religion" in the cases Marx takes up means the prevalence of Christianity. This in turn means the prevalence of the church or churches, whose theological instruction of both elites and masses is implied at the heart of this matter. Yet Marx does not deal with this essential factor, neither in the matter of the framing of heresies and adversaries, nor even in the basic question of why "religious homogeneity" in a political, social, cultural, or territorial context would be of such importance to the faithful; its centrality is merely assumed. But what are the theological assumptions at work amongst the people that would end up making religion so indispensable to nationalist elites? How are those assumptions formulated and propagated, and are they so from within the churches or from without, or in combination? If from within, what theological rationale is developed to create such passion—often resulting in violence—and further, how is such passion theologically tied to the state, either in support or in resistance?

Conversely, if the elites are themselves formed by religion, then what accounts theologically for their undertaking a nationalist course of action? What prompts them theologically to consolidate power in the first place and to choose particular methods over others? Relatedly, if religion is merely a means to an end, then what accounts theologically for their instrumental use of it, given they are operating from within it? Of course, this begs the question of the reverse: What if in some circumstances consolidating power is rather a means toward achieving religious homogeneity for its own sake? Is the state so central in those cases, or is it instrumental? What might this do to Marx's overwhelming emphasis on "state governance, the central component of our definition of nationalism"?[5] In short, Marx neglects the theological content of "religious nationalism," and in so doing, he arguably leaves incomplete any explanation necessary to precisely address his research question. To begin addressing these questions regarding the role of theology in the development of nationalism, we turn to the work of Adrian Hastings.

Adrian Hastings: Nationalism in the Vernacular, and the Biblical Model of Israel

Hastings, a former priest and professor of religious studies, devotes a great deal of attention to the study of nationalism, focusing particularly on the biblical model of Israel as appropriated by nations beginning in the Middle Ages. He criticizes modernism, both for its timeline and for

---

5. Ibid., 193.

its neglect of "the impact of religion in general and of the Bible in particular." Among his primary theses is the priority of vernacular literature in fostering national self-consciousness. Particularly central is the Bible, which was for so long "Europe's primary textbook" and "provided, for the Christian world at least, the original model of the nation."[6]

Contra the modernist time line, writes Hastings, the word *nation* was already in use by the fourteenth century (at least referring to distinct language groups), derived in major part from biblical and Vulgate roots. Additionally, the Bible "presented in Israel itself a developed model of what it means to be a nation—a unity of people, language, religion, territory and government." As such, Israel acted as an obvious and available model of nationhood to readers of Scripture, "a mirror for national self-imagining."[7] Hastings concentrates on England, which he considers to be the prototypical Western nation, surveying English history from the time of Bede in the early 700s to early modernity to illustrate the myriad ways ideas of nation and national identity emerged, and particularly around the themes of divine favor and election.[8] He also cites English translations of the Bible and associated catechetical materials as integral in inculcating in the Bible's hearers and readers notions of nationhood and specifically English national self-awareness.[9] Later, as disillusioned English settlers reached America, they aimed to create a "true Israel of God," over against the deteriorating society at home. These New Englanders considered themselves "God's peculiar people,"[10] who were led into the wilderness, it becoming a matter of

---

6. Hastings, *Construction of Nationhood*, 12. Here, Hastings specifically challenges Benedict Anderson, whom he says makes no reference to the impact of the profusion of biblical texts nor to the Bible as "the prime lens through which the nation is imagined by biblically literate people."

7. Ibid., 18.

8. Ibid., chapter 2. Hastings refers to Bede's *Ecclesiastical History of the English People* (c. 730) as the earliest discussion of English unity and identity and, at least implicitly, the notion of a nation under God like Israel (38). Later writers expressed similar notions more explicitly. By the eleventh century, numerous allusions were made to biblical texts as applicable to England, such that England is "a nation to be defended as the Israel of the Old Testament was defended" (42). Later instances of "Christian nationalism" include John Foxe's *Book of Martyrs* (1563), which placed events "within a national Christian history, a sort of English Book of Maccabees" (58–59), and by 1719, Isaac Watts put forth a translation of the Psalms wherein "the word 'Israel' was regularly and ludicrously replaced by 'Great Britain'" (62).

9. Ibid., 24.

10. Ibid., 74.

providence that America's discovery had coincided with the Protestant Reformation and the expansion of "England, God's Israel."[11] In both cases, the written vernacular of the biblical text, and the model of nation interpreted from it, provided a remarkable and powerful force for national identity and cohesion.

Hastings considers both nation and nationalism to be "characteristically Christian" developments. To begin with, Christianity has helped shape and "canonize" national origins, either "canonizing" dynastic lines—wherein national identity formed in the "imaginative space" around kings, "precisely through the closeness of the church's identification with royal power"[12]—or via the context of religious conflict and contested frontiers, wherein political conflict takes on religious overtones (including crusade) when a people feels threatened by a group committed to another religion. Here, national and religious identity become fused. Integral to such conflict is the "mythologization of threats" to national identity, wherein "national salvation is, or seems to be, at stake." Hastings argues that it is not the events themselves that are so decisive, but rather that meaning has been read back onto them, "simplistically symbolized in public memory." The purpose of mythologization is to ensure that each generation is "socialized into a certain us/them view of the world, a view at once nationalist and religious." And it is the religious connotation that lends credibility to otherwise "quite secular events."[13]

There is also the social role of the lower clergy, who in their local residence and relationships mediated identity between the rulers and the populace. Living in parishes throughout Europe, clergy—poor but well educated, and therefore in touch with both peasantry and gentry—helped cultivate a sense of common identity across communities and provinces, as well as across socioeconomic divides. Hastings suggests that the proliferation of such clerical activity, "far more than anything specifically political," consolidated national identities as marked by their respective literatures.[14] This is another decisive influence of Christianity, namely, the encouragement of literature in the vernacular.

---

11. Ibid., 78.

12. Ibid., 189.

13. Ibid., 190–91.

14. Ibid., 191–93. Hastings cites the clergy in this capacity as a distinct class, which he argues effectively challenges binary class divisions like that of Eric Hobsbawm.

Christianity, Hastings maintains, is a "religion of translation" rooted in Pentecost, and never hesitating to appropriate the local vernacular for the propagation of its message, thereby lending itself to social cohesion at the linguistic level.[15]

The other highly significant factor, rooted in the diffusion of vernacular copies of the Bible, is what Hastings calls the biblical model of the Christian nation as found in Old Testament Israel. This is a model that arises despite a certain inherent tension:

> In central New Testament terms nations might be encouraged but there could be no place for a single chosen nation. It is the church itself which is the New Israel. Nevertheless the Old Testament provided a detailed picture of what a God-centered nation would look like and of the way God would treat it if it was faithless. Why would God behave differently now? Why should one's own, New Testament-sanctioned nation not be vouchsafed an Old Testament style providential role?[16]

Theologically, appropriating such a distinct status for a particular people might be considered suspect. However, "the more the Old Testament was translated into the vernacular and accessible to a theologically untrained laity, the greater the likelihood of claiming for one's own nation a divine election, so powerful was the Old Testament example working on the political imagination of a Christian people." Autocephalous state churches catalyzed this tendency; such ecclesiastical autonomy in a national church is a major factor encouraging nationalism in that it "vastly stimulates the urge to tie all that is strongest in God's Old Testament predilection for one nation and New Testament predilection for one church contemporaneously to one's own church and people."[17]

Perhaps the most pronounced influence of the model of Israel upon national formation is the notion of the election and special destiny of a given nation. The more these other factors are operative, the easier it is to go all the way and claim status as a chosen people with a

---

15. Ibid., 193–94. Hastings suggests that this view of Christianity places into question Benedict Anderson's argument that the rise of nations corresponds to a decline in "sacred languages." Christianity never really had one to begin with. Even the Vulgate, states Hastings, was an exception rather than the rule.

16. Ibid., 195.

17. Ibid., 195–96.

special divine mission to accomplish. And this is readily done, theology notwithstanding:

> The Bible is so easily indigenized. By its very nature and the church's retention of such lengthy Israelite histories it hints at a continuity of more than a theological kind between it and us. The whole concept of a "Holy People," divinely chosen but enduring all the ups and downs of a confusing history, seems very applicable to life nearer home. Of course for the early Christian and for the universal church's permanent theological vision that concept is realized in a universal community of faith and by no means in any one nation, but for ordinary Christians, lay and clerical, that can seem too remote, too unpolitical.[18]

Due to a "lack of evident political concern in the New Testament" or the early church, Christianity did not begin with any "clear political model."[19] Thus, two alternatives emerged: empire and nation-state. Empire corresponded both geographically and politically to the "religious society" Christians perceived themselves to be, and providence was seen to be at work in Rome. Even when that empire collapsed, the *idea* of empire did not, and would be revived again and again in European experience. However, fragmentation of the church eventually corresponded to that of empire, and ecclesiastical structures began to be tied to emerging national identities, particularly after the Reformation. Notions of election and destiny were transferred accordingly. In the West, Hastings describes Catholic Christianity as "both incarnationalist and universalist," both identifying closely with particular communities, cultures, and nations, and also insisting upon a transcendent community. "It oscillated," he writes, "between Old and New Testament sources of inspiration." Protestantism, on the other hand, generally tended to lend greater weight to the Old Testament, finding precedents therein (especially in the historical books) for its own contemporary political situations.

Such nationalism is not merely an early modern phenomenon. Hastings writes of several instances of twentieth-century nationalisms in various Christian contexts, including Afrikaner (Reformed), Ulster (Catholic), and Serbian Orthodox, as well as instances in post-colonial

---

18. Ibid., 197.
19. Ibid., 198.

Africa and Asia.[20] Many of these instances have direct ties to Christian missionary activity. However, Hastings identifies Christian nationalism in the United States as "the gravest nationalist threat to Christianity" of our times.[21] "The dual temptation of late-twentieth-century America," he writes, "basking in a prosperity and imperial power beyond anything hitherto known, has been to see itself in terms of God's preferred people and to see the American brand of universalism 'as simply universalism itself.'" And such is particularly true of the Christian Right.

Hastings does what Marx does not, namely delineate the outlines of the theological content of Christian nationalism. In this sense, he is able to go further than Marx in explaining why nationalist discourse took hold amongst the people, how it was that popular loyalties were reoriented, even theologically, behind nationalist agendas. With the proliferation of the Bible in local vernaculars, nationalists were able to find therein a model of nation to inspire and construct their own. Biblical narratives, particularly of Israel in the Old Testament, were interpreted and appropriated to formulate and reinforce nationalist discourse, and this, in league with the profusion of vernacular translations, contributed decisively to the solidification of national identities throughout Europe. Considering themselves extensions of Israel, these nations cultivated within their respective societal contexts—political, cultural, territorial—a commitment to religious homogeneity rooted in a theologically informed identity.

However, I believe Hastings's treatment of the nationalists' theological moves falls short with regard to the notion of Israel as the biblical model of the nation. I refer to two dichotomies Hastings assumes in his treatment, dichotomies that need not at all be taken for granted, and that contain and imply a number of problematic elements. The first is his dichotomy between Old and New Testament visions of the people of God. The Old Testament narratives about Israel present for him a model of the nation, which he interprets as a political community revolving around a centralized (monarchical) state apparatus. The New

---

20. Hastings, "Clash of Nationalism," 15–33.

21. Ibid., 32. Hastings alludes here to a conversation he overheard between American Catholic Archbishop Fulton Sheen and an African bishop: "Sheen represented American Catholic nationalism at its most earnestly international.... His commitment to the missionary cause was immense, but so was his belief in the American way of life as supreme expression of Christianity. The future he held out to the African bishop, a century or two ahead, to my shocked amusement, was that of becoming like America."

Testament seems to be for Hastings a decisive break from the Old in this regard, a wholly different discussion about the shape and function of the people of God. This dichotomy is problematic on several levels. To begin with, the Old Testament is not so monolithic as Hastings suggests. Rather, there are competing views of Israel as a political community in the Old Testament, and much of the narrative there is concerned—rather dramatically at points—with the conflict concerning whether national identity did in fact revolve around the monarchy or rather around an earlier covenantal conception rooted in core elements of Torah. Therefore, one must ask what prompted the later nationalist appropriation of one of these views over against the other. Moreover, it is questionable to what extent Old Testament Israel should even be abstracted as a model for other political communities, versus viewing it as a singular historical undertaking; Hastings seems to assume the former, with Israel as universal prototype rather than "peculiar people," but that is not at all necessitated by the biblical texts.[22]

Within this first dichotomy, there is the idea that the Old Testament is political while the New Testament is decidedly apolitical. Hence, for instance, his comment about a lack of political concern in the New Testament or about Catholic oscillation "between Old and New Testament sources of inspiration," or his assertion that empire corresponded *politically* to the early Christian *religious* society. Such an apolitical view of the New Testament (and particularly the gospels) is a myth John Howard Yoder and others have effectively debunked. However, Hastings assumes it at multiple points, which allows him to likewise assume the naturalness of "the church's identification with royal power" instead of questioning it,[23] and precludes him from inquiry into other points of theological incompatibility with nationalism, historical and contemporary alike.

This is related to Hastings's second problematic dichotomy, that of formal theology versus a more popular understanding of the Bible. He argues that the former, rooted primarily in an understanding of the

---

22. These points will be discussed at length in chapter 4.

23. As with the portrayal of Israel in the Old Testament, this is a question of monolithic description. The fact that there arose reactionary movements such as monasticism over against the theology of empire in the fourth century, or the Anabaptists beginning in the sixteenth over against ecclesiastical and nation-state hierarchies, indicates that such accommodation did not occur without critique, and therefore that alternative conceptions were indeed available, if not predominant.

New Testament, would naturally preclude notions of national chosenness: the church is the New Israel, there is no room for any other chosen nation. Yet, he indicates that this understanding is almost irrelevant to the experience of the common people, the "theologically untrained laity," for whom such an ecclesiology would have been "too remote, too unpolitical." But how is it then that the Old Testament conception he portrays became so dominant, for that conception is no less theological. Hastings seems to assume the people's understanding as a matter of happenstance or natural proclivity, but there must have been an active theology at work.

Leaving aside for the moment the question of New Testament politics, Hastings's assumption does not make sense if the clergy operated in the social role he described. As educators of the populace, he argues that the well-educated lower clergy acted as essential links for relations between rulers and ruled, aiding significantly in the solidification of national identity throughout Europe. In short, theological education was active across the board. Therefore, one must conclude that nationalism arose, not in the *absence* of theological teaching among the masses, but fully in the *presence*, and perhaps even in *consequence* of such teaching. Certain theological moves must have been at work in that teaching, but Hastings does not inquire into them. He does not, for instance, ask why the clergy did not instead contribute to a transnational ecclesial identity. Could it be that they shared in and propagated nationalist reinterpretations of the Old Testament, despite New Testament theology? If so, then it is not a question of the presence or lack of theology, but rather the content. These questions are crucial, for as Hastings reminds us, such religious nationalisms occur even in late- and post-modernity, and their formulations and propagations often occur along the same lines as early or even premodern nationalist discourses. To understand what is occurring theologically in these developments brings us closer to an adequate understanding of the roots and motivations of nationalism, and it also allows us to see how nation and nationalism are particularly important considerations for ecclesial identity.

Anthony D. Smith: Nationalism as "Political Religion"

Anthony Smith's work contributes to a fuller understanding of the theological moves being made within nationalist movements with regards to religion. For Smith, only religion could inspire the passionate commitments people make to their national identities, and nationalism, which he describes as the "religion of the people," has arisen as a fusion of national mythology with more traditional faiths. He therefore examines what he calls the "sacred foundations" of nation and nationalism. The objects of this sacredness are fourfold: (1) the community, particularly as the "chosen people"; (2) the holy land in which the people dwell; (3) the glorious past of the people, and particularly their "golden age" that preceded their current decline (prompting the nationalist reaction); and finally, (4) the people's sacrifice and sacred destiny. All of these revolve in some way around the "cult of authenticity" that lies at the heart of nationalism.

Modifying Rousseau, Smith conceives of such nationalism as a "political religion," wherein the nation is "the object of a secular mythology and religion, at whose center the cult of the sinless and seamless nation made any opposition to the regime a crime against the national state." In this model, the nationalist movement is itself a "church," its rites of celebration and commemoration taking the place of traditional religious ceremonies. Yet, nationalism is not simply an adjusted or secularized continuation of traditional religion. Many modern nationalisms appropriate elements and themes from traditional religion, but also reject many of their beliefs and practices, particularly any conception of salvation located in a "cosmic, other-worldly source."[24]

This "religion of the people" is not such because it has arisen *from* the masses, but because the people as a specific cultural community in its homeland constitute the object of this religion. It is not individuals who are sacred so much as the community as a whole, "or rather the image of an authentic (pure, pristine, natural, uncorrupted, and unique) nation in its own landscape." For Smith, the nation is envisioned as a form of community that coheres its members through ritualistic (liturgical?) practices, such that "[nationalism] is best seen as a form of culture and a type of belief-system whose object is the nation conceived as a sacred communion."[25] Nations synthesize certain elements of faith and ethnic communities in such a way that they are "invested with sacred qualities."[26] National identity thus becomes a matter of "the main-

---

24. Smith, *Chosen Peoples*, 17.
25. Ibid., 18.
26. Ibid., 23.

tenance and continual reinterpretation of the pattern of values, symbols, memories, myths, and traditions that form the distinctive heritage of the nation, and the identification of individuals with that heritage and its pattern."[27] Significantly, this religion of the people mimics and competes with particular theologies, as the "nationalist belief-system draws much of its content from *key elements of traditional religions, duly sifted and reinterpreted.*"[28] Not only is this last process a core feature of many nationalisms, if not *the* core feature, it has significant implications that I will explore later. Suffice it now to say, using our operative definition of theopolitics, that Smith understands nationalism to be a form of salvation narrative, which then entails a particular political outworking in the nation.

Nationalists build their national identity upon four "sacred foundations": community, territory, history, and destiny. The notion of community involves a fusion of ethnic (shared memories and common descent), cultic (unity as a single and holy moral community), and moral-legal (a moral community of equals with common rights and duties—"the people") conceptions of human community. Historically, this fusion has meant that "'the people' were not just the prime worshippers (and objects) of the popular nation; they constituted in themselves a holy congregation, for God spoke through the people and the popular will."[29] Such a conception is often the result of the self-appropriation of the biblical model of election and covenant. As we have noted, the nation here views itself as designated for a special purpose in service to the divine, thereby standing in special relationship to that deity. The nation is required to stand apart and follow a special course that is a function of divine promise, and to thereby play a singular role in "the moral economy of global salvation." The people accept this unique identity voluntarily, in Smith's understanding, and in so doing, "become God's elect, saved and privileged through their obedience to His will and their identification with His plan." As applied to historical communities of culture, this constitutes a "myth of ethnic election," where myth refers to a widely believed narrative justifying present nationalist concerns by

---

27. Ibid., 25.
28. Ibid., 42. Emphasis added.
29. Ibid., 32–34.

alluding to the nation authentically embodied at some point in the past, a golden age to which the people must return.[30]

Covenant entails notions of sacred law, collective sanctification, and a privileged status as witness to the acts of God. But covenant is not focused on the elect nation alone; rather, its fulfillment is integral to global salvation: "The chosen people act as a model or *exemplum* of what it means to be holy, and hence like God. And to be like God is to be free of sin and death, and thereby to be eternally saved." Since the ultimate end of the singular covenant is global salvation, "the doctrine of divine election harnesses universalism to particularism, and makes the salvation of all hinge on the conduct of a special few."[31] Such a covenant makes separation inherent to the nation's divine election and requires a stringent system of evaluation and judgment. This understanding of holiness is what marks out the covenant people, from Sinai to now, for "to be holy is to be like God; and *imitatio Dei* is the fundamental aim of humanity."[32]

At the heart of this sacred communion is the "cult of authenticity," which pursues the quest for the true vision of the nation. Here again is the central nationalist process of *authentication*, now conceived in theological terms. According to Smith, authenticity is the nationalist equivalent of holiness: "the distinction between the authentic and the false or inauthentic carries much the same emotional freight as the division between the sacred and the profane."[33] The authentic is the "irreplaceable and fundamental," that which is essential to the nation, separating "us" from "them" and making one's own nation singular and irreplaceable. It is the center of the "binding, ritually repetitive, and collectively enthusing" religion of the people, and its pursuit enables and effects salvation

---

30. Ibid., 47–49. Smith here briefly discusses the examples of early Dutch and English nationalism. He refers to the work of Liah Greenfield, whose study of early modern English nationalism identified Christianity as the "'lubricator' of English national consciousness," wherein the faith "had lost its role as the source of social values and had now to adapt to secular social and national ideals." Thus, "it was natural that religious creed . . . would be pushed aside when national identity became established as fundamental and the need for justification diminished." In this context of election, we should note Greenfield's finding that the earliest known use of the term *nationalism* in the English language was in the mid-nineteenth century, referring to the "doctrine of the divine election of a nation" (Ibid., 47). See Greenfield, *Nationalism*.

31. Smith, *Chosen Peoples*, 51.

32. Ibid., 59.

33. Ibid., 37.

in this world via the rediscovery and cultivation of the nation's true self. This is exemplified by various national heroes and messiahs, persons seen as particularly authentic—"pure, true, pristine, originary"—who provide models for emulation throughout the generations.[34]

Of course, the exemplar of this model is biblical Israel, in which Smith finds the quintessential formulation of divine election and covenant. Smith insists on the essentially voluntary nature of covenant as a corollary to its conditionality: "it is not an act of imposition by and submission to God, but rather one of offer and acceptance," such that "the whole community's observance of their part of the covenant is the critical factor in its making and unmaking, and hence in the fate of the people." The people "consented to be chosen, and to submit themselves to the law of goodness and justice."[35] This "active consent" is, for Smith, the key ingredient, since "this means taking on responsibility and becoming 'a people in the strong sense, capable of sustaining a moral and political history,' rather than just a people in so far as they share tribal memories and the experience of oppression."[36]

Appropriated elsewhere, this conditional obligation and destiny has inspired and empowered other peoples who felt they had been given divine favor, and it has provided the stimulus and reasoning for moral renewal among those who see themselves as chosen. Within Christian doctrine, Smith notes, chosenness is "transferred from a particular ethnic community to the universal Church of believers." However, we often find historically a certain tension between this universalism and the profession and practice of Christianity in particular communities. This characterizes most covenant-style Christian nationalisms,[37] such as those of the Gregorian Armenians, seventeenth-century Dutch and English, and the Puritan settlers of Ireland and, significantly for this study, North America.

The second major sacred foundation of nationalism is that of territory and the notion of the "homeland." For modernists, it is the state that, via census taking and mapmaking, creates the body of the nation

---

34. Ibid., 40–41.

35. Ibid., 57. David Novak, whom Smith appropriates here and at multiple points in this discussion, argues that Israel's choice is really only to confirm what God has already done, and that rejection would be unacceptable; but Smith prefers later rabbinical interpretations that tended to emphasize Israel's voluntary acceptance.

36. Ibid., 61. Quoted from Walzer, *Exodus and Revolution*, 76.

37. Smith, *Chosen Peoples*, 95.

and makes such an abstraction imaginable.³⁸ However, while the state certainly undertakes these activities, such an explanation alone overlooks a deeper, more profound process at work. Here, Smith refers to the "territorialization of memory," the "process by which particular places evoke a series of memories, handed down through the generations." It refers to the "tendency to root memories of persons and events in particular places and through them create a field or zone of powerful and particular attachments." This process is twofold, referring on the one hand to the "historicization of nature," by which various features of the land become essential to the community's evolution and history; and on the other, to the "naturalization of history," by which the people's history is shaped by land—where the terrain provides the setting for key events as well as resting places for ancestors, and where historical monuments become naturalized, that is, come to be treated as part of the natural setting. This sacred foundation also includes notions of promised lands and ancestral homelands.³⁹ Smith concludes that this conception of the meaning of territory differs importantly from that of modernists, emphasizing the role of values, symbols, and traditions of sacred lands over long periods of time within the discourse of nationalists, who subsequently politicize them.⁴⁰

The third sacred foundation is "ethnohistory" and the golden age, comprising a pattern of myth- and memory-formation. The golden age is the center of this narrative, acting as a model and source of inspiration. It is not limited to the exploits of a particular hero, but rather represents a period of the entire community's life together that is characterized by a "burst of collective activity" in political, military, economic, artistic, intellectual, and religious arenas. It is this golden age that "represents the 'authentic' spirit of the community and its moral core." Because it lies at the heart of a people's ethnohistory—because it provides a picture of the people's "true self"—the golden age is integral to the grounding and energizing of national identity; it is considered "canonical and sacred," central to the cult of authenticity.⁴¹

Within nationalism, golden ages act as "frameworks of interpretation" for the nation. First, they function to provide a sense of continuity

---

38. Ibid., 131.
39. Ibid., 134–36.
40. Ibid., 165.
41. Ibid., 171–72.

between the present and the past, as perceived through the nationalist lens. Earlier ages limit later ones in terms of hermeneutics for contemporary circumstances. Moreover, golden ages suggest an enduring identity underlying the ebb and flow of historical development. Second, golden ages also assist the "recurrent quest for collective dignity" over against opposition. While they do not themselves effect unity or cohesion, they are vital to the nation locating itself within a wider, international and historical context. Finally, golden ages provide "expression, and sanction, to the quest for *authentication*." It is in the process of selecting and describing golden ages that the cult of authenticity comes into sharp focus, for these eras are "models of the nation's 'true self,' uncontaminated by later accretions and unimpaired by corruption and decline." To this end, the nationalist must rediscover the nation's inherent goodness, and then mobilize the people "to 'realize themselves' by discovering and emulating the virtues of the nation" as envisioned. In this manner, the golden age acts as a blueprint for national actualization and collective regeneration.[42]

The final significant sacred foundation is that of sacrifice and destiny, and particularly their memorialization and retelling. National celebration and mourning are inherent in these processes:

> The self-sacrificing citizen, the fallen patriot-hero or heroine, the genius who contributed his or her work (and even life) to the nation, the mass sacrifice of the people, the glory of patriotic valor, the everlasting youth of the fallen, the overcoming of death through fame—these are the stock in trade of nationalist values, myth, and imagery. They have become standard actors and motifs in the national salvation drama, the agents and vehicles of the nation's deliverance and subsequent triumph.[43]

Elements of this "national salvation drama" can be found in multiple eras preceding modernity, and nationalism uses them "to weave the fabric of its own salvation myth, in its own very special manner."[44] This is particularly clear in the celebration of the "glorious dead," of self-sacrificing heroism, both individual and collective. As the notion of nation as "sacred communion" developed over time, there arose in these celebrations "a very public imagery of national communion," con-

42. Ibid., 212–15.
43. Ibid., 219.
44. Ibid., 219.

taining themes like national unity and autonomy, identity, authenticity, and the homeland. This imagery was "designed to encourage reflection and emulation," to provide a ritual—and by implication an entrée into the overall nationalist endeavor—with which "the citizen could identify and in which they could, eventually, participate."[45] Subsequent emulation then achieves the nation's glorious destiny.

In short, nationalists select and reinterpret elements of received traditions, including theological ones, for the purpose of formulating a vision of the "true nation" toward which they galvanize the populace. This vision incorporates compelling notions of community, territory, golden ages and subsequent decline, and the sacrifice necessary to reach the nation's destiny (a full recovery of the past golden age in the present). Through the process, the nation becomes true to itself (i.e., holy) by diligently cultivating these cultural resources that operate as sacred foundations of national identity, elevating them as "canonical and holy."[46] In this manner, nationalism acts as a salvation narrative entailing a particular political outworking in national community. That salvation narrative often relies on elements of preexisting, theological or "traditional" salvation narratives, which it then selectively fuses with a national narrative of history and myth to create a vision of the present nation that portrays it, in part, as a fulfillment of those traditional, theological narratives.

Smith provides an extensive and extremely helpful treatment of the role of religion in nationalism, as appropriated by nationalists and as received by the people. Presenting nationalism in theological terms as its own sort of religion, and particularly emphasizing the process of authentication—perpetuated by the "cult of authenticity"—as the standard of "holiness" in explicitly religious nationalism, helps immeasurably in understanding nationalism as a theopolitical project, the purveyor of a particular salvation narrative that becomes embodied in a particular politics. As such, Smith's account is perhaps the most helpful account in contemporary nationalism scholarship for addressing the theopolitical concerns discussed in the first chapter.

There are some discrepancies or inconsistencies in his schema, however; it is not always clear whether these are Smith's own, or are rather embedded in the nationalist patterns he describes—in either

---

45. Ibid., 223.
46. Ibid., 258.

case, there are important implications. To begin with, he states that the "sacred communion" of the nation—as imagined in an authentic sense—is the object of the "religion of the people," and that the nationalist movement is its church. But he later describes the people as a "holy congregation," and the nation, within a covenant context, as chosen by the divine. There seems to be some confusion regarding the role of the nation or the precise identity of the deity in question, though it seems the latter conception of nation-as-elect (rather than divine) ultimately wins out. Of course, one might resolve the ambiguity in the direction of the nation's worship of self, but he does not do that.

Second, there are discrepancies having to do with his description of the nationalist model as derived from biblical Israel. According to Smith, within the context of the "myth of ethnic election," a nation is singled out for special purposes by the divine, required to be separate from the other nations for the sake of its role in global salvation; in so doing, the people "become God's elect, saved and privileged through their obedience to His will and their identification with His plan."[47] However, logically, one does not *become* divinely elected by agreeing to be chosen: by definition, one is elect at the initial point of the divine act of choosing. This also means that one cannot "agree" to be elected; there is no human agency involved in the act of choosing. Rather, humans can only respond to election after the fact. (Participation in covenant, the *actualization* or *fulfillment* of election versus the initial divine act, is a different matter.) Perhaps more importantly, Israel's adherence to covenant was not the means by which it was elected or saved. Rather, according to the Exodus narrative, the covenant was established *subsequent to* Israel's salvation—its deliverance from Egypt—and its election at Sinai, and was justified by Yahweh *on the basis of* that salvific act. Salvation in that context was a means toward Israel's covenant identity and mission, not vice versa.[48] However, it would be correct to say

---

47. Ibid., 48–49.

48. Smith may want to argue from the historical-critical perspective he appropriates that the proper context is rather the exile, since (his sources would argue) that is where the concept of covenant originated, and salvation therefore refers to something yet to come. However, it is not the historical-critical conception of covenant and salvation being appropriated by nationalists; rather, it is the story of Israel as told in the Pentateuch and the historical books of the Old Testament, which emphasizes the priority of narrative sequence.

that Israel's identity and mission were a means toward global salvation. These narrative elements will be discussed in detail in chapter 4.

Third, there is the theme of voluntarism in Smith's interpretation of covenant and sacred communion. Not only is human agency the key effecter of election and covenant—a rather debatable theological and exegetical point—but salvation is achieved by means of emulating the holy. To reiterate one of his central claims, "The chosen people act as a model or *exemplum* of what it means to be holy, and hence like God. And to be like God is to be free of sin and death, and thereby to be eternally saved."[49] That is in the context of global salvation, where the nation fulfills its singular vocation before the world. Internally, emulation is the impetus behind the cult of authenticity and its careful delineation of the nation's golden age, and also celebrations of heroic individual and especially collective self-sacrifice. It is interesting to note the rather Pelagian character of this soteriology, emphasizing the centrality of human agency over against the initiation of the divine—particularly salvation by moral emulation—and therefore providing no real sense whatsoever of how the divine actually enables the salvation of the nation beyond merely providing the opportunity. If nations are appropriating theological models within the context of Christendom, what is the significance of reformulating them according to one of the most notable of early Christian heresies?

There are at least two explanations for these apparent discrepancies: either Smith has misconstrued the theological understandings that play such an important role in his own model, or he is describing nationalist mis- or re-interpretation of those theological tenets. If the former, then although Smith establishes the fact that nationalists often appropriate key elements of the religious traditions shared by their people, serious questions must be raised about whether or not he has adequately grasped the extent and manner in which they do so. There are obvious similarities between particular nationalisms and the faith

---

49. Smith, *Chosen Peoples*, 51. Smith's assertion here also seems logically suspect. In most theological understandings, to be holy *is* the equivalent of being free from sin, and particularly here where "sin" would be conceived as inauthenticity to the national ideal; that equation is therefore redundant. The other equation, between holiness and freedom from death, is a non sequitur as he presents it. The latter is not necessitated by the former, without some intervening explanation of how lack of holiness causes or equals death. Merely being "like God" is insufficient, since it would obviously be possible to be like God in one respect and not another.

traditions they appropriate, as his work reveals, but there are often important differences, too. Is Smith adequately accounting for nationalist behavior if he is not properly attentive to the theological moves inherent to it? This question is intensified when noting the dearth of Christian theological sources in his account, despite the fact that most instances of nationalism mentioned in his work occur within Christendom.

If these discrepancies are rather internal to the nationalist moves Smith describes, then he is surely correct to say that nationalism has historically "sought to challenge or co-opt" religion, and often "parallels and competes with traditional religions," constituting itself in great part "from key elements of traditional religions, duly sifted and reinterpreted."[50] But this then raises the question of his rather astonishing claims elsewhere that nationalism "heightened and sharpened" elements of traditional religion, politicized them, reinforced and revived religion in particular communities, and "did not generally disrupt, or abolish, pre-existing beliefs, sentiments, and symbols."[51] Or more specifically, that the cult of authenticity—in drawing upon the "spiritual power" of the conviction of the community's eminent descent— "complements, [and] does not supplant, the old ideas of the sacred in religious traditions."[52] How can what Smith conceives as a religion not in fact seek to supplant traditional religion, particularly when it advances its own conceptions of deity, soteriology, and ecclesiology? Could this be in part because Smith misunderstands the political nature of the Christian church? How can the national community not thereby supplant the faith community? As I have shown just with snippets of Smith's own explanation, there are necessarily incompatible elements at issue, and these merely scratch the surface. Thus, the nationalist duplication of religious categories for ulterior motives suggests not complementarity, but parody. Yet at no point does he explicitly address to what extent a particular nationalist message diverges from the theological traditions from which it derives its form and substance, and what the significance of such divergence might be.

50. Ibid., 255, 42.

51. Ibid., 6. As with Hastings, one must ask whether nationalism is a case of the politicization of religious traditions, or rather a *re*politicization of existing theopolitical frameworks.

52. Ibid., 205.

While these questions obviously have significant implications for a theological study such as this, they also have implications for Smith's own conception of nationalism. For if nationalism is in fact supplanting religious traditions, and actually contributing to alterations in those traditions over time, then any simply linear conception of traditions shaping nationalism and nationalist methods is put into question. If, over the *longue durée*, what we actually have is a cycle of nationalist (or proto-nationalist) appropriation of religious traditions such that later nationalist movements are actually appropriating earlier nationalized elements, then it is the reinterpretation—or perhaps, "reconstruction"—of those elements that is the definitive factor in the form and content of later nationalism. This then begs the question of whether the primary agents in nationalism are cultural traditions or the nationalists themselves. Again, this would likely vary case to case, but it is clear that Smith needs to attend further to the constructive side of the construction-constraint relationship within nationalism.

Conclusion

The work of these scholars brings forth the importance of religious elements and themes to nationalism and national identity, challenging not only modernism's narrow time line and tendency to dismiss early modern or even premodern manifestations of nationhood, but especially the modernist neglect of religion as the chief galvanizing element of many nationalist movements. This is particularly true of Smith, whose ethnosymbolic approach specifically demonstrates the significance of communal models rooted in religious traditions for nationalist development, and in so doing, he goes much further than most of the field in explaining the significance and the inner workings of the relationship between religion and nationalism. Smith does this by presenting nationalism as a sort of theological construct, with marked similarities to Christianity—some obvious, some not. Nationalism is itself a type of revivalist religion, driven by a particular "cult of authenticity"—a sort of prophetic movement seeking the holiness (authenticity) of the nation—toward enacting a particular "salvation drama" involving the nation as the divinely elected people of God, with whom God has instituted a unique covenant toward the end of global salvation (according to a particular conception). Members of the nation are bound together by various rites and symbols, exhorted toward the faithful emulation of various heroic exemplars, most importantly, the community itself at its historic best. Moreover, the exemplary form of the nation is marked by self-sacrifice leading to triumph and exaltation, a process that is not only recalled for emulation but is encapsulated in celebrations of "national communion" by which later generations may participate in that process. In this manner, the nation is actualized and regenerated.

It is here that we see significant implications for theopolitical scholarship like that discussed in chapter 1, for Smith's work suggests that nationalism is, at the very least, a necessary intervening variable or link in the state's reordering and unification of society. Without this link, it requires an inordinate leap to understand how the state is so successful at disassociating the people from each other via local communities and connecting them directly to the state apparatus. It is also possible, however, that nationalism presents a more significant challenge to these theologians, namely, an alternative explanation for the breakdown of ecclesial identity in modernity alongside those of state and market, and one that potentially broadens the scope of the problem back beyond merely the modern era. If, in most cases, it is nationalism that so directly parodies the symbols and practices of the church, and if nationalism must be distinguished—even separated in some cases—from state behavior, then a singular focus on state behavior is misplaced, and a deconstruction of such will only be partially successful at identifying reasons for historical and current challenges to ecclesial identity. This is especially true where nationalism is supported by or emanates from within the church itself.

Having said that, the theopolitical scholarship in turn brings up a significant question regarding the treatments of religion and nationalism in this chapter, namely, the dichotomy between politics and faith, often repeated in these works in a variety of ways. This is a false dichotomy. On the nationalism side, the politics espoused and practiced by elites and commoners alike are always concerned with ultimate matters of human existence, or there would be no need for an appropriation of religious elements. If Smith is correct regarding nationalism as an alternate religious system, and I believe he is, then one must recognize the inherent theological moves at work, even by those who are little concerned with religious faith and practice. On the other hand, within a Christian context, there is very much a politics at work in faith and practice, given the various Christian understandings of divine sovereignty, ecclesial social order, and mission vis-à-vis the political, economic, and cultural systems in the world. In either case, theology and politics are intertwined, and in very many elemental instances, one and the same. Scholars such as Marx, Hastings, and Smith are therefore missing the point if they perceive nationalism as the co-opting and politicization of previously *apolitical* elements of faith and practice.

As I will demonstrate in following chapters, given the political elements of the biblical narrative, Christianity cannot merely be considered a religious phenomenon, but must be considered a fully fledged, though alternative, social body. Nationalism scholarship does not yet appreciate the significance of this.[53] Nationalism is not merely appropriating the elements of a religious phenomenon—an "-ism," as it were—it is appropriating the features of an alternative political community. Nationalism is the fusion of narrative elements from distinct *peoples*. I believe misunderstanding this fact is what allows nationalism scholars who are rightly concerned about the role of religion in nationalism to misunderstand its inherent political and social forms and subsume it under the umbrella of "culture."

Therefore, notions of politicizing a heretofore apolitical faith tradition—such as Marx's, where "faith became politicized and increasingly relevant to state- and nation-building"—are erroneous. Rather, nationalism must be seen as a *re*-politicization of the faith community away from a previous politics. Indeed, as nationalism is inevitably theologized, it constitutes an alternative *theopolitical* system to that of the Christian ecclesia, which suggests points of significant tension where those two systems are made to coexist. Existing theopolitical scholarship accounts for this to an extent, though it tends to misunderstand the existence of biblical Israel as a theopolitical model for the church. This critique is the argument of the next chapter. Chapters 4 and 5 then take up the question of ecclesial theopolitics by looking at the stories of Israel and the church in the biblical narratives. There I examine what Israel was really meant to be, whether understandings and appropriations of it in typical modern political contexts are fitting or not, and what the implications are for the church—especially in relation to the

---

53. Smith's *Chosen Peoples*, for instance, provides no complete index entry for "Church," but redirects the reader to "Christianity, Catholicism, Orthodoxy, Protestantism" (320).

nations—as it is engrafted onto Israel's identity and mission. Chapters 6 and 7 then provide case studies of nationalism in popular Christian and academic theological discourse, fleshing out the present discussion of the relationship between theology and nationalism, and the nationalist misappropriation of the Christian theological tradition.

CHAPTER 3

Scripture in Theopolitical Scholarship

INTRODUCTION

In framing this study, I argued that current theopolitical scholarship is as yet unable to adequately account for nationalism as a challenge to Christian identity and mission today. The first two chapters addressed aspects of that question in terms of the nature of nationalism itself, particularly the relationship between theology and nationalism in certain cases. I also stated, however, that even if nationalism were properly understood, theopolitical scholarship is still not fully able to respond to it due to an inadequate appreciation of the theopolitics of Scripture, and in particular of Old Testament Israel, whose narrative plays such a central role in both Christian nationalism and faithful ecclesial mission. Christian nationalism, by which I mean those movements arising from within the church (or with its indispensible support), typically misappropriates the biblical narrative, portraying a given earthly nation as Israel's proper theopolitical extension. Within these movements, Israel's theopolitics is misread—for example, Yahweh is understood to bless Israel's efforts to secure itself through power politics rather than calling Israel to be an alternative people in the world—and Israel is subsequently and consequently co-opted for the nationalist agenda. Discerning where and how this occurs, and effectively resisting it, requires a robust understanding of biblical theopolitics: Israel is that theopolitical community called in the Old Testament to be a visible sign of God's salvation to the world, a vocation ultimately and definitively fulfilled by Jesus Christ. That fulfillment is to be embodied by the theopolitical community of the church, which is, through Christ, engrafted—organically attached—back onto Israel.

In this chapter, I flesh out my critique by examining the salvation narratives put forward in current theopolitical scholarship, and particularly its appropriation of the biblical texts. For each of the scholars discussed here, the salvation narrative of the Christian tradition is fundamental to ecclesial mission and identity. In all cases, it significantly marks, if not drives, their conceptions of the church as theopolitical community. The biblical narrative plays an important role for each scholar, but informs their work in somewhat different ways. One of the clearest differences is the degree to which the Old Testament is appropriated, and particularly the elements of Israel's election and covenant. While, as in the first chapter, I find much in this work that is normative for my own, I find its biblical accounts of Israel in relation to the church to be lacking in different ways and to different degrees, suggesting the need for further development. The work of Scott Bader-Saye, which is briefly surveyed at the end of this chapter but then brought into the discussion of the next two chapters on a constructive biblical theopolitics, assists in such development.

JOHN HOWARD YODER: THE JEREMIANIC TURN AND RECONCILIATION IN CHRIST

"That all identity is historical is a platitude, but not one that we can afford to leave unspoken."[1] This sentence, with which the Mennonite John Howard Yoder begins one of his better-known works, is indicative of his understanding of the ecclesia as contingent, even tentative. It is so because the vocation of the church is to be a movement through time, its faithfulness "realized in particular times and places, never assured and always subject to renewed testing and judgment." Such an approach is confident about God's ultimate project, but it is highly skeptical about human attempts to control history toward that end, and especially the exercises of power that have historically accompanied such attempts.

---

1. Yoder, *Priestly Kingdom*, 2.

For Yoder, the history of salvation is the story of how in the suffering of Jesus Christ, God has inaugurated the coming of God's kingdom and has effected the reconciliation of humanity, both to God and among peoples, and particularly between Jew and Gentile. Jesus, in his divinely mandated role, bore a new possibility for human sociopolitical community, one that was inaugurated in his baptism and culminated in the cross, "the punishment of a man who threatens society by creating a new kind of community leading a radically new kind of life." In the context of Jesus' temptation to either concede to empire or to subvert it through violence, Yoder views the cross, "not as a ritually prescribed instrument of propitiation but as the political alternative to both insurrection and quietism."[2] It is not merely the way to the kingdom of God, but "it is the kingdom come."[3] The communal outworking of this salvation history is thus "a visible social-political, economic restructuring of relations among the people of God," accomplished by divine intervention in the person of Jesus.[4]

Key to Yoder's understanding of salvation history is how God's intervention in Jesus Christ reordered the powers of the world. The New Testament makes clear three things about these powers: (1) as "a network of norms and regularities to stretch out the canvas upon which the tableau of life can be painted," the powers were created for humanity's good; (2) these powers have rebelled and are fallen, unwilling to accept their inherently modest divine mandate; and (3) despite their rebellion, they cannot escape divine sovereignty. If humanity is to be saved but still be properly human, the powers cannot be destroyed; rather, "their sovereignty must be broken." This Jesus Christ did, "concretely and historically," by living an alternative existence: he willingly submitted to them, but refused to endorse or participate in their self-absolutization.[5] Consequently, according to the Apostle Paul, the church's very existence is its foremost task, in that "it is in itself a proclamation of the lordship of Christ to the powers from whose domination the church has begun to be liberated." Christ has successfully and salvifically triumphed over the powers. The responsibility of the church, then, is to refrain from

---

2. Yoder, *Politics of Jesus*, 36.
3. Ibid., 51–53.
4. Ibid., 32.
5. Ibid., 142–45.

being seduced by them, that is, to maintain an existence that "demonstrates that their rebellion has been vanquished."[6]

As the outworking of this salvation history, the church is a political community by nature. In addition to its role in Christ's reordering of the powers, the church is a political reality in general terms because it is a "structured social body" with "ways of making decisions, defining membership, and carrying out common tasks." Indeed, "to be political is to make decisions, to assign roles, and to distribute powers, and the Christian community cannot do otherwise than exercise these same functions, going about its business as a body."[7] Its theopolitical "business" can roughly be characterized for Yoder in terms of a sacramentality of ordinary life. He rejects as unbiblical the notion that "there is a special realm of 'religious' reality—so that when you speak special prescribed words, peculiar events happen."[8] Instead, sacraments are understood biblically as those practices of regular life that manifest the reign of God in Jesus Christ in community.

For example, Yoder refers to "binding and loosing," rooted in passages like Matthew 18 and Acts 15 where God is active when Jesus' disciples, in community, determine a particular theological/ethical understanding or course of action, following a specified decision-making process that is constituted by the priorities of dialogue and reconciliation. In such a context, disciples can justifiably claim, "it seemed good to the Spirit and to us."[9] Another key sacrament is that of the Lord's Supper, which Yoder understands as a regular common meal taken together by Christians. This reorders social relations, extending the sharing of the common table into all areas of socioeconomic interaction. Indeed, "it demands some kind of sharing, advocacy, and partisanship in which the poor are privileged, and in which considerations of merit and productivity are subjected to the rule of servanthood."[10] A third central sacrament is that of baptism, which, according to 2 Corinthians 5, "introduces or initiates persons into a new people" in such a way

---

6. Ibid., 150. It should be noted that Yoder's understanding of "the powers" is operative for the present study as a whole.

7. Yoder, *Body Politics*, viii–ix.

8. Ibid., 14.

9. Ibid., 1, 6.

10. Ibid., 22.

that "all prior given or chosen identity definitions are transcended."[11] According to Ephesians 2, Christ brings peace between Jew and Gentile, thereby creating a new humanity; with Galatians 3, this peace is subsequently manifested in other areas of social, economic, and political division. Therefore, "the primary narrative meaning of baptism is the new society it creates, by inducting all kinds of people into the same people."[12] This new society is the church, which acts as exemplar for the world. All together, these insights clearly place the church at the center of Christian theopolitical identity. Despite Yoder's apparent eschewal of "religious" sacramentality, these points indicate at the very least certain extraordinary moments in the life of the church that are profoundly constitutive of ecclesial identity.

Yoder also draws on certain elements of the Old Testament narrative for understanding how the church should approach its mission. In particular, he relies on what he calls the "Jeremianic turn" (referring especially to Jeremiah 29) to argue that the church should embody an exilic identity. This is, according to Michael Cartwright, a sensibility stemming from Yoder's free church formation and concern for resisting the challenge of Constantinianism. As Cartwright explains, Yoder concentrates on the exile, "where 'the synagogues and the rabbis of Babylon' entered 'creatively into the Jeremianic phase of creating something qualitatively new in the history of religions.' According to Yoder's inductive reconstruction of the logic of this shift, 'living without a temple, while yet retaining the mythic memory of the temple and the hope of the return to the messianic age, enabled the creation of a faith community with a globally new gestalt . . .'" This new communal structure is marked by the centrality of a text that can be duplicated and read anywhere, as well as by identity defined in the common life of the community. No special hierarchy or liturgy is necessary; the texts ground worship, and ordinary, daily practices hold the community together.[13] The vocation of this diaspora is to seek the welfare of the community into which it is sent.

This vocation, explains Cartwright, is part of a counter-narrative Yoder uses to connect various developments: "The hermeneutical tra-

---

11. Ibid., 28.

12. Ibid., 32.

13. Cartwright and Ochs, "Editors' Introduction," 21. This is discussed by Yoder himself in *Schism*, 187.

jectory that Yoder ultimately discerns within the canons of Scripture in the Old and New Testament links the call of Abraham in Genesis 12 to the prophecy of Jeremiah 29. It then reads the latter texts through the lens of Ephesians 2–3, which provides the vision of reconciled humanity that Yoder sees dramatically displayed in St. John's visions in Revelation 5, 7, and 22."[14] Yoder thinks it especially important that the Deuteronomic history is remembered and then organized within a diasporic context, such that "it constitutes a document of the acceptance of the Jeremianic turn," one which acknowledges the divine disapproval of the Davidic project of state centralization and territorial security, and which approves in its stead an exilic communal life free of irredentism.[15] As such, the Jeremianic model prefigures the ecclesia both in terms of its mission and the character of its communal life as well as the potential challenges it might face in tending to become too settled or secure in one context.

In examining Yoder's approach to salvation history, I appreciate his messianic understanding of Jesus as the definitive presence, rather than merely forerunner, of the kingdom of God, and that in Jesus' death and resurrection (the latter of which seems relatively underexamined), the powers of the world are reordered. I also follow Yoder's argument that Jesus' mission inherently entailed a new social order, into which baptism initiates the believer. However, in doing so, Jesus was in part fulfilling Israel's own covenant identity and mission, an important point that Yoder does not dwell on, but that arguably provides additional important insight into the nature of that alternative communal life he advocates. For instance, Christ's reordering of the powers is, in significant ways, well in line with Yahweh's defeat of the Egyptian imperial system in the exodus, which then provided space for the alternative community of Israel. How might such a connection between Old and New Testaments be significant theopolitically? Additionally, with regard to sacraments, one sees in Israel that the social order Yahweh establishes through Torah is one in which the ordinary life of the people as a "royal priesthood" is sacramental in and of itself and vis-à-vis the world; but still within that ordinary life there were extraordinary moments of celebration and symbolism from which the people derived their identity. It would seem that both of these, in tandem, would constitute proper

---

14. Cartwright and Ochs, "Editors' Introduction," 22.
15. Yoder, *Schism*, 188.

sacramentality, and that any biblically informed treatment of sacrament and liturgy must take this into account.

While a diasporic model of ecclesial mission is both central and indispensible,[16] I think Michael Cartwright attends well to perhaps the most significant difficulty in Yoder's appropriation of the Old Testament. He suggests that Yoder may, albeit inadvertently, tend toward supersessionism when he appropriates exclusively the exilic model of Israel for the church, and that understanding this requires engagement with a key matter Yoder largely neglects, namely, that of Israel's election and covenant.[17] For Yoder, Jesus has restructured Israel's conception of peoplehood from what Israel had understood during the monarchy.[18] Yoder goes on to differentiate the "faith" of Abraham from "ethnic-political peoplehood,"[19] but as Cartwright points out, Yoder's understanding of what it means to be a "child of Abraham" verges on Christian supersessionism insofar as "faith" detaches Abrahamic identity from "historical embodiment in the people of Israel." Moreover, Yoder bypasses the notion of election in Israel, tending to "shift discussion of 'covenant' and 'election' toward a conception of Jewish missionary vocation in exile." Cartwright refers here to Douglas Harink, who argues that Yoder actually obstructs the doctrine of Israel's election by offering instead a "'moral history' of Israel's obedience through his reading of the Jewish diaspora history *since* the exile."[20] In short, Yoder neglects the theopolitically significant stage of Israel's election and covenant in Yahweh and locates its normative communal form much later in an existence that most directly resembles Yoder's own ecclesial background:

> The way that Yoder goes about affirming the "Abrahamic model" as constitutive for Jews and Christians alike involves narrating the history of Jewish peace witness in a way that is determined by the Anabaptist tradition. As a result, the very coherence of the vocation of the Jewish people turns out to be reliant upon "the free church vision." The immodesty of Yoder's

---

16. On this point, see especially Harink, *1 & 2 Peter*.
17. Cartwright, "Afterword," 206.
18. Ibid., 210. Cartwright refers here to Yoder, *Original Revolution*, 27–28.
19. Yoder, formed by free church theology, was concerned about the priority of voluntary over ethnic membership in the faith community. For him, Jewishness after Jeremiah required such freedom. See Cartwright, "Editors' Introduction," 23.
20. Cartwright, "Afterword," 210–11. Cartwright refers to Harink, *Paul among the Postliberals*, 201–2.

narrative can be measured by the fact that he virtually ignores the biblical vision of Israel as the elect people of God affirmed in the Scriptures of the Old Testament and reaffirmed in Romans 9–11 by the apostle Paul.[21]

For the present study, the problem with this move is not that diasporic mission is not normative for the church in significant ways, but rather that Yoder's argument for such an existence lacks the theopolitical grounding only a careful treatment of election and covenant can provide. The resulting picture for the church is incomplete, and inadequate for addressing nationalist discourse that plays upon those key themes.

Stanley Hauerwas: Ethical Formation in the Kingdom

For Hauerwas, a community of faith radically alternative to the politics of the world requires a people formed in virtue via Christian sacrament and discipleship, inculcated with the skills to resist formation by the powers, especially that of the modern liberal state. This is a community formed by story,[22] namely that related in the Hebrew and Christian Scriptures. This story "cannot be abstracted from those communities engaged in the telling and the hearing," since "as a story it cannot exist without a historic people, for it requires telling and remembering if it is to exist at all." Indeed, "the particularity of Israel, Jesus, and the Church must be taken up constitutively into what those who proclaim Jesus as Lord and Christ regard as true and good and right." The story of God as embodied in God's people is what makes God's kingdom visible in the world, lived out in a continually renewed community of faith and "embodied in a people's habits that form and are formed in worship, governance, and morality."[23]

While Hauerwas is clearly committed to the biblical history of salvation, he does not venture into much detail on the content of that narrative. As Jeffrey Siker notes, Hauerwas emphasizes the importance

---

21. Ibid., 229. Cartwright contrasts Yoder's approach with that of Scott Bader-Saye, whose work is discussed below.

22. Hauerwas, *Peaceable Kingdom*, 24–30. This "narrative mode" is important to Christian understanding, as it is a fundamental human way of talking about God, as well as presenting our existence as that of contingent, historical beings. Moreover, Christian convictions constitute themselves "a narrative, a language, that requires a transformation of the self if we are to see, as well as be, truthful."

23. Ibid., 97–98.

of understanding the story of Jesus in continuity with the story of Israel, yet, regarding Hauerwas's use of the Old Testament, "the reader senses that he simply does not know it all that well."[24] Hauerwas does go so far as to briefly sketch the continuity of the narratives of Israel and Jesus, particularly in the context of *imitatio dei*, and with special, albeit limited, attention to covenant faithfulness. Interestingly, he states that proper biblical reflection on this theme must begin with Israel, "'for Jesus brought no new insights into the law or God's nature that Israel had not already known and revealed.'" The content of the Sermon on the Mount, for instance, was a recovery of earlier "'habits of thought'" in Israel, cultivated through Israel's experience with Yahweh.[25]

With regard to this continuity, however, Hauerwas limits his attention to the theme of office: prophet, priest, king.[26] Hauerwas primarily focuses on the New Testament, preferring the Synoptic Gospels, particularly Jesus' ethical teachings—paramount among these, the Sermon on the Mount (Matt 5–7)—and the centrality of the cross, which for Hauerwas summarizes Jesus' whole life.[27] He also appeals to a number of Pauline writings, especially Romans, 1 Corinthians, and Ephesians, as normative for what the community of faith is to look like, and particularly, what type of habits it is to cultivate and manifest. Yet, Hauerwas misses key insights into the theopolitical nature of the people of God by focusing almost entirely on the New Testament—and more narrowly within that to snapshots of Jesus' ethical teachings and prescriptions for community life—to the neglect of biblical Israel and its theopolitics of covenant as a model for ecclesial politics. If Jesus is, in fact, the fulfillment of Israel's election and covenant calling, then a robust notion of

---

24. Siker, *Scripture and Ethics*, 98. Siker's portrayal of Hauerwas's use of Scripture in ethics is quite positive, acknowledging the centrality of the Bible in Hauerwas's conception of the church as ethical community. Here, though, he cites Hauerwas's own admission, "I really do not know the 'text' of the Bible well" (238n9; quoted from Hauerwas, *Unleashing the Scripture*, 9.). Siker goes on to mention, "In private correspondence, Hauerwas has written that 'when I started I simply did not know the Bible well enough to use it one way or the other'" (238n9; quoted from a letter to Jeffrey S. Siker, 17 March 1992). This may explain the relative dearth of specific biblical citations in a number of Hauerwas's own works (238n5). Hauerwas has, however, since published several works of biblical commentary, but again, his emphasis has been largely on the New Testament.

25. Ibid., 98. Quoted from Hauerwas, *Peaceable Kingdom*, 76.

26. Hauerwas, *Peaceable Kingdom*, 76–78.

27. Siker, *Scripture and Ethics*, 99.

the latter is necessary to more fully understand ecclesial identity and the problems posed to it by nationalism. Moreover, if there are, as I will demonstrate in chapter 5, multiple conceptions of Israel's identity vying against each other in the narrative, that could have significant implications for contested ecclesial theopolitics today.

Hauerwas sees Christianity as inherently political, its politics defined by the Gospels, wherein "the challenge of Jesus is the political dilemma of how to be faithful to a strange community, which is shaped by a story of how God is with us."[28] The Gospels proclaim that Yahweh proves himself king through the work of Jesus, in which we see God's continuing rule over nature and history, reclaimed and restored in Christ's redemptive order. Yet it is unclear what the significance of Yahweh's reign is given the lack of any robust treatment of Israel. Christianity is inherently political, for a people is presumed by the principle of the "kingdom of God,"[29] and in the Beatitudes, "we see nothing less than the order of God's kingdom, the charter of his commonwealth, as we are treated to a vision of life that can occur only when a people have been formed who know who the true Lord of the world is."[30] Christians are by definition engaged in politics, but a politics that finds its locus in servanthood rather than domination, thereby exposing the theological backwardness of any politics rooted in falsehood and coercion.[31] Truly, this is an ethic discernible in a study of the Sermon on the Mount, but again, one wonders how any robust theopolitics can be discerned from it without an understanding of the Torah, which forms the heart of Israel's covenant and which Jesus claims *in this very sermon* to be fulfilling (Matt 5:17).

In terms of the communal outworking of the biblical salvation history, and in partial contrast with Yoder's emphasis on the processes of regular communal life as sacramental (in lieu of special liturgical rites), Hauerwas emphasizes the role of the community in producing habits of virtue within the individual via liturgy and sacrament, and through the practice of moral mentorship. Particularly important to Hauerwas are the church's sacramental liturgies, chief among them baptism, initiating the believer into Jesus' death and resurrection, and the Eucharist as "the

---

28. Hauerwas and Willimon, *Resident Aliens*, 30.
29. Hauerwas, *Against the Nations*, 115.
30. Ibid., 116.
31. Hauerwas, *Peaceable Kingdom*, 102.

eschatological meal of God's continuing presence" that enables a peaceable people. Such rites "are not just 'religious things' that Christian people do. They are the essential rituals of our politics. Through them we learn who we are."[32] As such, they are not merely the basis for Christian social engagement, but actually constitute that engagement. As Hauerwas asserts, "The church does not have a social ethic; the church is a social ethic,"[33] and "these actions are our most important social witness."[34] I agree with Hauerwas on the importance of these practices for forming identity and enabling Christians to resist countervailing tendencies in the communities where they reside, but at least equally important are the narratives that give these practices theological meaning and import. Identity-forming practices for God's people did not begin with Christ, but with Israel. What Christ proclaims and practices is in continuity with Israel's story, albeit with Israel as it was meant to have been. Yet the theopolitical implications of this for the church today are largely absent from Hauerwas's account. Thus, when such narratives are appropriated by other entities with agendas antithetical to the church's, Hauerwas's theology cannot evaluate that move until it sees the ethical results. As stated in the previous section, this neglects some of the root problems facing ecclesial identity today.

William T. Cavanaugh: Scripture and Liturgical Politics

William Cavanaugh's work involves reading the stories of modern political development and theory against the Christian stories of creation, fall, and redemption. In so doing, he finds that modern politics tends to present itself as an alternative soteriology to that of Christianity. The Christian story begins with the "natural unity of the human race," a unity rooted in the *imago dei* and the source of catholic unity. This unity is disrupted by humanity's sin in the form of a "usurpation of God's position." The initial effect of this sin is the breaking up of the whole of humanity throughout the world, the "very creation of individuals as such, that is, the creation of an ontological distinction between indi-

---

32. Ibid., 108.
33. Ibid., 99.
34. Ibid., 108.

vidual and group." Redemption from sin in the person of Jesus Christ is thus the restoration of that primal unity.[35]

Key to God's redemptive activity in the world is the people of God called into political community. Both Israel and the church are clearly political entities in that they "give order through law and ritual to the social life and everyday practices of a distinctive community of people."[36] Cavanaugh argues for the church, in continuity with Israel, as a counter-model to the surrounding polities, embodying an alternative politics so that the world may see and be transformed. This mission is accomplished first through the sacraments of baptism and Eucharist, which "now become the center of the ritual fulfillment of the Law, enacting a liturgical drama that recalls the confrontation of Christ with the powers and calls the participants into the body of Christ."[37]

Cavanaugh brings biblical Israel into his theopolitical work at several points. It is through covenant, liturgy, and law that Israel embodies the drama of sin and salvation, and all three are distinctly political in nature. As he quotes Walter Brueggemann, covenant is the "'radical and systemic alternative to the politics of autonomy, the economics of exploitation, and the theology of self-indulgence'" from which Israel had been delivered in the exodus. Liturgy, moreover, "is the enacted drama of the different kind of power and the different kind of political order that YHWH wills over against the oppressors of Israel." Indeed, "'this distinctive community is invited to affirm that the world constructed in liturgy is more reliable and more credible than the world "out there."'"[38] Liturgy is definitive for politics in proclaiming Yahweh's sovereignty in the face of competing claims to lordship by worldly powers and in constructing an alternative way of life. It proclaims a particular salvation history, one that necessarily entails particular political outworkings.

Elsewhere, Cavanaugh explicitly addresses Israel's covenant identity and mission as normative for the church. He takes up the role of the Decalogue in Jewish and Christian theology and uses it to evaluate arguments by proponents of American empire. Focusing on the language of election (Exod 19:5–6), he challenges notions of American exceptionalism that appropriate the language of salvation for the American

---

35. Cavanaugh, "The City," 183–84.
36. Cavanaugh, "Church," 394.
37. Ibid., 396.
38. Ibid., 395. Brueggemann quotations taken from "Always in the Shadow," 48, 43.

nation-state as the eschatological fulfillment of Israel rather than the church, the latter being the proper communal locus of salvation.[39] He then takes the initial commandments of the Decalogue (Exod 20:2–6) to point out the inherent idolatry of placing the national god at the center of the salvation narrative, thereby effecting a system of self-worship. Finally, he addresses the commandment against killing (Exod 20:13) to note the inherent incompatibility of imperial expansion via military force with the biblical tradition of the people of God. He also touches on the Israelites' failure to rely on Yahweh in situations of threat, and their subsequent prophetic indictments for turning to the tools of statecraft for deliverance. While relatively brief, Cavanaugh's discussion here points directly to key elements of the biblical narrative and of Israel's politics that are essential for understanding the theopolitics of the church, and he does so, to his credit, much more explicitly than other theopolitical scholars. Nevertheless, such a discussion could and should be elaborated upon in order to more fully understand the significant appropriation of Israel's theopolitics for the church in the New Testament.

Elaboration could include a discussion of biblical Israel's theopolitical development at several key points. In another article, Cavanaugh helpfully points out that Israel's period of statehood—so often taken as normative for contemporary politics by certain Christian theologians—was not by itself definitive for Israel's political experience: "Israel's prior existence as a tribal confederation, and subsequent experience as a temple community and as a federation of synagogues, show that the nation-state is not by any means the most determinative analogue for Israel." As he rightly notes, "Israel is a people, one that stands in a unique relation to all the nations of the earth, because of its covenant with the God of Abraham, Isaac, and Jacob."[40] However, Cavanaugh's portrayal here tends toward merely a linear progression of political forms for Israel. Rather, what is dramatized in the biblical narrative is a contested theopolitics, a conflict between concurrent and opposed views of Israel's politics and its relation to Yahweh. As I will demonstrate in chapter 4, what the careful reader notes throughout Israel's experience, and especially as attested to by the prophets, is a struggle between a politics rooted in Israel's identity and mission given in election and covenant at Sinai, and a statist politics located in a misconstrual of the Davidic

---

39. Cavanaugh, "Empire of the Empty Shrine," 13–14.
40. Cavanaugh, "Messianic Nation," 276.

covenant. And it is this contested politics, not merely the multiplicity of political forms, that best foreshadows and informs the situation the church faces as its identity and mission are challenged by nationalism.

Scott Bader-Saye: Election, Covenant, and Engrafted Ecclesia

One scholar of theopolitics who has directly and comprehensively treated the Old Testament narrative is Scott Bader-Saye. Bader-Saye argues that the church has a "common covenant and common calling" with Israel, its identity and mission rooted in Israel's election. The church is thus "carrying forward Israel's covenantal politics."[41] The church has become depoliticized in modernity, having lost its politics through an inadequate understanding of election, "which sought to leave the Jews and their materiality behind."[42] The communal understanding of election in biblical Israel has, in many quarters, been replaced with an individualized conception of election focusing on the predestination of the individual soul. This, he argues, is a misconstrual of Israel's politics of election. Personal election, he argues, can only be understood as a corollary of communal election.[43]

While some of Bader-Saye's most important insights will be incorporated into my own discussion of Old Testament theopolitics in chapter 4, it is worth highlighting several key points for the sake of comparison with the preceding theologians. To begin with, Bader-Saye thinks the "polis" language of Hauerwas has helped challenge the problem of liberalism in the church, but it unnecessarily relies on "a political and moral discourse from outside the church's biblical idiom."[44] He believes that Hauerwas's emphasis on the polis also overlooks the tendency of that ancient form of community to be defined by struggle, by conquest of oneself and others and by defense from external threat. Even where Hauerwas alludes to a direct ecclesial continuity with Israel, his argument tends to look overly individualized, wherein "ecclesial practices threaten to become instrumental to the larger goal of the formation of

---

41. Bader-Saye, *Church and Israel*, 2.
42. Ibid., 3.
43. Ibid., 31.
44. Ibid., 6.

the individual person."⁴⁵ Bader-Saye responds with the priority of the communal and political in the Old Testament narrative, superseding any individual identity. Scripture emphasizes God's design for forming a covenant people, where the primary concern is the corporate obedience of the church. For Bader-Saye, the only feasible alternative to modern liberal individualism is not the classical polis, but "a return to Israel, into whose election the church has been graciously grafted."⁴⁶

For Bader-Saye, Israel's election and its outworking in covenant are not attachments to Israel as a preexisting political community, but actually constitute Israel as such.⁴⁷ Israel becomes a people through its "relationship of mutuality" with Yahweh, in which it freely responds to Yahweh's initiative.⁴⁸ This he contrasts with modernity, which "posited a political sphere outside of the covenant and within which the covenant had to be made intelligible."⁴⁹ The church, having accommodated to the latter conception, must return to the prior one, seeing itself as a continuation or extension of the biblical covenant community, which was intended to be a polity in its own right, though of a very different form than the nations.

Torah is central to covenant, both for Israel and by extension, for the church. Including "both the stories of Israel and the practices that correspond to these stories," Torah is the condition of possibility for the people's existence as God's people. For this reason, he states, "Torah obedience is not in opposition to freedom (a point Christians have long misunderstood) but rather is the ground of freedom. Freedom is the result of being trained by the practices of Torah."⁵⁰ Thus, Israel's divergence from Torah holiness places the people in bondage, from which they must be redeemed. This is accomplished in Jesus Christ, in whom "redemption includes the ingathering of the Gentiles to share the blessings of the peaceable kingdom."⁵¹ In this way, "the promised redemption

---

45. Ibid., 22.
46. Ibid., 25.
47. Ibid., 35.
48. Ibid., 38.
49. Ibid., 41.
50. Ibid., 43.
51. Ibid., 46.

of Israel and the inclusion of all creation in God's reign of peace is the unseen political and historical horizon of God's election."[52]

In this light, the "newness" of the "new covenant" in Jesus Christ is understood by Bader-Saye not in terms of a new people or new content, but rather that Torah will be definitively embodied. The church exists as part of the story of Israel, engrafted onto the same covenant beginning with Abraham, but in a different part of the story wherein the kingdom of God has indeed arrived and the church lives within that reality.[53] This is the messianic age, wherein Jesus and his disciples "carry with them the visible presence of God's reign." The powers are disarmed by the forgiveness of sins on the cross (the precise opposite of their logic of retribution), and the people are released from bondage. Christ's faithfulness in this endeavor transforms covenant expectations; Torah is not rendered obsolete but "Torah obedience is stamped by the cross of Christ, which becomes the definitive paradigm of faithfulness."[54] Gentiles participate in the new covenant, but not by being gathered separately from Israel. Rather "after reconstituting a community of Israel that would embody the ways of redeemed life, the Spirit moves to draw the Gentiles into the elect community."[55] Gentiles are thus gathered through Christ and in the Holy Spirit *into* Israel as "'fellow heirs' . . . *alongside* the original heirs of the covenant."[56]

In this manner, the church shares the same vocation as Israel to praise God through its formation as God's people. It is in this social and political form that the church embodies the "politics of election," which is understood not as a denial of freedom, but as its very ground: it is "freedom as the capacity to live faithfully," requiring both "freedom from sin and self-determination and freedom for risky engagement with the reign of God."[57] For Bader-Saye, "freedom within the covenant means faithfulness to one's identity before God." Such freedom is not found abstracted from the particularities of relationship and communal life; liberation requires covenant, identity requires common life.[58]

52. Ibid., 44.
53. Ibid., 97.
54. Ibid., 106–7.
55. Ibid., 108.
56. Ibid., 112.
57. Ibid., 118.
58. Ibid., 124.

Hence the sacrament of baptism, a political practice affirming Christ's lordship and reorienting the identity of the one baptized into covenant community.[59] Or, for that matter, the Eucharist, which, as a central act of covenant—a remembrance of Passover, a commitment to a life together in community, and enfleshing the new covenant via Jesus as the perfect embodiment of Torah—acts as the locus of Israel's extension to the Gentiles as well as "a place where the redeemed life of God's elect is recalled, embodied, and anticipated."[60]

I find Bader-Saye's treatment of biblical Israel compelling on many counts, particularly its central focus on covenant and Torah, as well as how covenant identity and mission carry forth into the church. I also appreciate his treatment of certain practices, such as baptism and Eucharist, as theopolitical in nature. For that reason, I appropriate a number of his insights in the biblical theopolitics discussions of chapters 4 and 5, and will not rehearse them here. I do find certain of his points overstated or unclear, however, which I will address specifically in those later chapters. Suffice it here to say that I believe he overstates the unconditionality of covenant with Israel, overlooking certain key passages that suggest this *realization* of election was always contingent. That is to say, enduring election does not equal enduring covenant, and even an enduring covenant does not necessarily mean a continuously active one. As such, he regards arguments about God's rejection of Israel, however temporary it might be, as arguments against God's trustworthiness. He does not note the possibility that Israel can hypothetically be rejected from a conditional covenant without impinging upon God's credibility in any way. He also does not dwell on the significance of divergence from covenant. Situations of conquest, say by the Assyrians and Babylonians, are put in terms of "threat" rather than "judgment";[61] nothing is said about how covenant is disrupted in such contexts, or about how judgments upon Israel by Yahweh are more often than not direct consequences of Israel's own covenant violations. Bader-Saye admits that "without Israel's decision to live in accordance with its election, however, God's work would remain de facto irrelevant in history despite being de jure a reality."[62] However, most of his argument

59. Ibid., 130.
60. Ibid., 139–41.
61. Ibid., 138.
62. Ibid., 35.

seems to revolve around the "de jure" dimension and not nearly enough around the "de facto" reality that in any given context of divergence from covenant, election is simply not being realized. Yet, this is one key place where the biblical narrative of Israel is particularly helpful to the church: it shows the church the all too typical ways in which theopolitical identity and mission are compromised and even rendered inactive by pursuing embodiments—social, political, economic—incongruent with the kingdom of God.

Conclusion

In this chapter, I endeavored to examine selected works of theopolitical scholarship with attention to how the scholars conceived of Christian salvation history and its attendant political embodiment, especially in light of the biblical narrative. I found their accounts to be helpful in certain respects, but ultimately inadequate in terms of what role a biblical theopolitics plays in resisting contemporary challenges to Christian faithfulness, especially with attention to the theopolitics of biblical Israel. Within the theopolitics of Israel, what seems especially overlooked is the nature and significance of Israel's election and covenant. This question is central both to ecclesial identity and mission, as well as to resisting the biblical narrative's misappropriation in nationalist contexts.

The chapters that follow aim to account for just these considerations. The next two take up a constructive biblical theopolitics, discerning the theopolitics of the Old and New Testaments respectively as they describe Israel's identity and mission and then engraft the church onto those elements through Jesus Christ. In these chapters, I will show not only that understanding biblical Israel is essential to the church's faithful witness today, but that a properly understood biblical theopolitics effectively undermines Christian nationalism by defying the ways in which the latter defines and appropriates Israel on the one hand, and supplants the church on the other. The following two chapters then examine particular cases of such nationalism, as found within popular, pastoral, and academic contexts.

CHAPTER 4

Old Testament Theopolitics

INTRODUCTION

In chapter 1, I laid out those theopolitical schemas that have been most formative in my own development, and with which I approach this project. At the same time, I delineated two significant gaps in their treatments. The first is their inadequate attention to the problem of nationalism as distinct from state and market, often emanating from within the church itself. Chapters 1 and 2 portrayed nationalism as a phenomenon entailing among other things a process of authentication, that quest by nationalists to craft an image and narrative of the "true nation" in order to galvanize the public behind them. Insofar as nationalism involves the reinterpretation and appropriation of various Christian symbols, and particularly the interweaving of the biblical narrative with the national, it becomes a "political religion"—an alternative theopolitics and salvation history—that alters ecclesial identity and practice, often from within. However, I also noted in those chapters that nationalism scholarship tends to suffer from a lack of attention to the theology involved in nationalist discourse and its propagation.

The second oversight I identified in theopolitical scholarship relates directly to the nationalist project of authentication, namely, attention to the significance of Israel's theopolitics for the church as expressed in the biblical narrative. I argued in chapter 3 that part of what was missing was a robust account of the nature and significance of Israel's election and covenant, particularly in relation to the church. In order to evaluate nationalist discourse, especially when it emanates from within the church, it is essential to establish theological criteria of assessment. That is the purpose of this chapter and the next, in which I trace within the biblical narrative a comprehensive theopolitical account of the people of God in Israel and the church. These two chapters are the theological core of this study, delineating my chief norm of understanding both for theopolitical identity in the church and for evaluating the important challenge of nationalism.

Story is central to identity, and discerning the ways in which the Christian salvation narrative is syncretized with the national story toward a new narrative of theopolitical identity is critical for discerning where and when the church mistakenly subscribes to a theopolitics not properly its own. Biblical theopolitics is located in the stories of Israel and the church. Israel is given a particular mission in the world, a singular identity that is remarkably alternative to the ways of the nations surrounding it. Later, the church is engrafted onto Israel's identity and mission through Jesus Christ. This understanding is critical to my larger project since, juxtaposed with nationalist discourse—particularly that emanating from within the church, which interweaves biblical and national narratives—it draws out those elements of the theology and the story of the people of God that have been misappropriated for the nationalist agenda, thus distorting the understanding of those elements and fundamentally altering the theopolitical understanding and identity of a significant portion of the church.

Furthermore, this chapter reinforces the essential unity of the theological and political in a proper understanding of the people of God. In some scholarship, both theological and social-scientific, these phenomena may be understood to affect each other, but in the end they operate in autonomous realms and can be separated for analysis. This is true even in biblical scholarship. I argue, on the other hand, that for Israel as the covenant community of Yahweh, politics and cultic life ("religion" or "theology" included) cannot be treated separately, as they typically operate not only in tandem, but as *one* entity. This is not only evident in Israel's establishment in covenant, but in the prophetic critiques as well. One can therefore conclude that the church, engrafted onto covenant through Jesus Christ, exists in a similar *theopolitical* framework. Also, part of the purpose of this chapter is to demonstrate that for the people of God in Israel and the church, practice and identity are correlated. The locus of the people's self-understanding is in election by God, and in the mission inherent in that election. Practicing that mission, that is, covenant faithfulness, is therefore constitutive of its identity. If that mission is not in practice, if covenant is not being actively kept, it is not sufficient to say that the people is not acting according to its identity; rather, it is *altering* its identity. It is *being* other than what it is called to be, though not without the possibility of repentance and return.

With these thoughts in mind, this chapter proceeds to relate a theopolitical understanding of the people of God, beginning with the centrality of election and covenant in Israel's national identity, with the aim of Israel being a visible sign of salvation to the nations. It moves from there to narrate the ways in which Israel gradually abandoned that identity for the theopolitical practices of its neighbors, resulting in an adulterated outworking of Yahweh's plan of redemption. It delineates key prophetic indictments of Israel's practices, and then ends with the prophetic promise that will set the stage for the next chapter on the church's identity in Jesus Christ. In addition to direct engagement with the biblical texts, I draw upon the work of other theologians and exegetes to construct a reading of Israel and the church's story such that the theopolitical nature of their identity can most clearly be seen.

Election and Covenant in Israel

According to the biblical narrative, the theopolitics of biblical Israel is rooted in election and covenant, initiated by Yahweh, that constitute Israel as a singular people, a nation established to be a visible manifestation to the world of the reign of God on earth, and of what human community looks like under that reign. Election is the divine action by which Israel is given identity and purpose, its mission in the world. Covenant—revolving around Torah—is the outgrowth of election, the social, economic, and political framework by which Israel's communal life is ordered. Election and covenant are therefore inherently political, and given that they originate from Yahweh and are bound up in Yahweh's actions in the world, are inherently *theo*political. This section spells out the theopolitics of election and covenant in Israel, how that theopolitics was an alternative to that of the surrounding kingdoms and empires, and how Israel abandoned its theopolitical commitments as it attempted to be conformed to the ways of its neighbors.

Exodus and Election

> Now the Lord said to Abram, "Go from your country and your kindred and your father's house to the land that I will show you. I will make of you a great nation, and I will bless you, and make your name great, so that you will be a blessing."[1]

In the first few chapters of Genesis, the reader finds the story of God's creation and ordering of the known world, particularly the place of humanity as caretaker. Humanity subsequently sins, obstructing the original divine intent and initiating an age wherein the peace and unity of creation are disrupted, as is humanity's fellowship with the creator. This begins the era wherein the powers rebel against their divine mandate, placing creation in bondage to their self-absolutization. Nevertheless, these texts also indicate a furtherance of God's creative intent, that is, the multiplication of the human race and the dispersion of diverse human ethnicities and languages throughout the world (Gen 10).[2]

In Genesis 12, though, the reader encounters a man, heretofore unknown except by genealogy, elected by Yahweh and called out from among his neighbors for particular service. That man is told he will become a great nation, a blessing to the world. The language used here is important for our understanding of the covenant people. In the Hebrew Scriptures, the word *am*, or "people," is usually used to refer to Israel. However, in this passage, one finds the word *goy*, or "nation," a term normally referring to the rest of the world outside of Israel, and usually used negatively when applied to Israel. Here, however, the term indicates the universal significance of Israel's calling. W. J. Dumbrell posits that these verses actually contain a "theological blueprint for the redemptive history of the world." Not only the "fact" of redemption is found herein, but the purpose as well: "the restoration of kingdom of God rule, divine

---

1. Genesis 12:1–2. Unless otherwise noted, or unless comprising a quotation in a secondary source, all biblical citations are New Revised Standard Version.

2. I am indebted to Doug Harink for this reminder that Genesis 5 and 10 are also creation texts, not merely subordinated to narratives of human decline (Douglas Harink, e-mail message to author, April 7, 2011).

dominion established once again over the world in which [humanity] functions once more as the completely recovered divine image."[3]

This promise is passed on through subsequent generations, until some 450 years later, as the exodus narrative relates, the reader finds Abraham's descendents held in slavery by the Egyptian empire. This is not merely an unfortunate turn of events, but the prelude to a major theopolitical conflict. Nations throughout the ancient Near East adopted any number of gods representing their material world, "earthly forces and powers that represented ultimate realities for human beings; their perceptions did not extend beyond these elemental realities to which they had subjected themselves." Not only were these powers of nature but "ultimately also the powers that shape history and society: knowledge, domination, violence, money, rivalry, war, life, death."[4] While political communities of the ancient Near East saw their gods as creators of nature, if only indirectly (e.g., through theomachy or sexual intercourse), these gods and their activities were nation-specific. There was little thought that one nation's deity or deities could lay claim to any other nation, except perhaps where one kingdom conquered another. Yet that is precisely what Yahweh claims in the face of Egypt, and it is precisely to substantiate that claim that he delivers Israel from the empire's midst and into a new theopolitical order.

So in the first chapters of Exodus, we find, in Jon Levenson's words, "two masters, two lords, are in contention for the service of Israel." One master embodies human pride and imperial hubris, smug in a sense of security natural to "an ancient and settled regime which has lasted for millennia."[5] Within this regime, "society, state, culture, nature, cosmos, religion, rule, wholeness, and salvation were melded . . . into a grandiose unity, and the unity of all these areas was visible in the person of the Pharaoh."[6] Pharaoh, in turn, is backed by an imperial pantheon, "immovable lords of order. They call for, sanction and legitimate a society of order, which is precisely what Egypt had." In this order "there were only the necessary political and economic arrangements to provide order, 'naturally,' the order of Pharaoh."[7] Thus, the pharaoh is

---

3. Dumbrell, *Covenant and Creation*, 65.
4. Lohfink, *Does God Need the Church?*, 1–2.
5. Levenson, *Sinai and Zion*, 22.
6. Lohfink, *Does God Need the Church?*, 68.
7. Brueggemann, *Prophetic Imagination*, 17.

presented as overseeing a "totalizing system" of politics and economics that, by its very nature, necessitates absolute allegiance, and in this case, oppression.[8]

The other lord is the "unpredictable deity himself," whose own authority and power transcend those of the ruler of Egypt, "reminding the Pharaoh of the limits of his power, which he and his subjects regard as infinite and, in fact, divine."[9] In the midst of the turmoil of this contest, God commissions Moses as his human representative in the famous burning bush scene in Exodus 3, and it is here that we witness an "apocalyptic" moment, in the term's proper sense of revealing a heretofore hidden reality: God gives the Israelites his name. He is "I AM WHO I AM" or "I WILL BE WHO I WILL BE," which is to say, Yahweh (YHWH), the self-existent One, the God who defies all definition, all categorization, all human attempts at order. This Yahweh is the God who comes from no other source, requires no other legitimation than God's very self. He is "the sovereign one who acts in his lordly freedom, is extrapolated from no social reality, and is captive to no social perception but acts from his own person toward his own purposes." Yahweh sets himself over against the pretender Pharaoh and his counterfeit pantheon. Pharaoh represents the world's zero-sum game of resource competition, while Yahweh provides a non-zero-sum paradigm by virtue of his infinite provision and power of initiation. Thus, the reader is given a "Yahweh vs. Pharaoh" dichotomy, which Brueggemann characterizes as a contest between the "alternative religion of the freedom of God" and its "politics of justice and compassion" on the one hand, and the "religion of static triumphalism" with its "politics of oppression and exploitation" on the other. Within such an order, there was no rest, no "breaks for freedom."[10] Hence the impossibility of even a "leave of absence" to worship in the wilderness and the necessity to impose further constraints (Exod 5:1–9). Not only can the Pharaoh's economic system not handle any halt in productivity, but there can be no consideration of an alternative way of life. Such would constitute a clear and present danger to the empire. Note that with each of these contending entities, theology and politics are inseparable; this is a contest of theopolitical paradigms.

8. Brueggemann, "Scripture: Old Testament," 10–12.
9. Levenson, *Sinai and Zion*, 22.
10. Brueggemann, *Prophetic Imagination*, 16–17.

In the end, as the narrative relates, Yahweh delivers his people through mighty works that Pharaoh's court is ultimately unable to counterfeit (Exod 7–12), and the "mythical legitimacy of Pharaoh's social world is destroyed."[11] The exodus is "nothing less than the dismantling of the empire both in its social practices and in its mythic pretensions."[12] It is Yahweh now, not Pharaoh, who "stands front and center in the political process and is the defining factor and force around which all other political matters revolve . . ." Yahweh has decisively demonstrated sovereignty over the natural order, over empire, and over Israel's own fate. The story of Yahweh's people, both during and following the exodus, is thus a "*theological politics* in which the defining presence of Yahweh, the God of Israel, impinges upon every facet of the political; or conversely, Israel's self-presentation is inescapably a *political theology* in which Yahweh . . . is intensely engaged with questions of power . . ."[13] Both the political and theological are intertwined, even melded together, as Yahweh concerns himself directly with Israel's destiny, and with its very identity.

In Exodus 19 the reader finds Israel safely delivered from the Pharaoh, and encamped at the foot of Mt. Sinai, where, like Abraham before it, it is elected for a particular purpose: "Now therefore, if you obey my voice and keep my covenant, you shall be my treasured possession out of all the peoples. Indeed, the whole earth is mine, but you shall be for me a priestly kingdom and a holy nation" (Exod 19:5–6). This declaration is critically important for several reasons. First, the nature of Yahweh's statement is key, as it is not merely a promise of blessing but an assertion about Israel's divinely oriented identity. As Jo Bailey Wells explains, the Exodus 19 pericope constitutes a "new description of Israel's function and character." The call to obey Yahweh, that is, holiness, is directed at embodying Israel's new identity, and "it is not the call to obedience, but the identity which it creates that receives the emphasis."[14]

Second, Israel's identity is in a very important sense a conditional endeavor. Key to this understanding is a distinction between election as an act of Yahweh, and the realization of that election in the covenant life

---

11. Ibid., 16.
12. Ibid., 19.
13. Brueggemann, "Scripture: Old Testament," 9.
14. Wells, *God's Holy People*, 211.

of Israel, both of which are required for Israel to realize its identity. As to the former, Yahweh has acted in his own sovereign grace to liberate Israel from its previous condition of bondage, and into a new freedom to be other than it was in Egypt; Israel is incapable of accomplishing this. Likewise, Yahweh makes a claim of his own initiative upon Israel at Sinai, freely electing the people for a singular role in history. Only Yahweh is capable of providing such a condition of possibility; Yahweh's act of election is the free act of a sovereign and autonomous God.

However, it is not sufficient in a theopolitical context to speak of identity from the standpoint of Yahweh's act alone; the question of the *realization* of Israel's election is equally integral. Notice that Wells refers to obedience as identity-creating: it is not Yahweh's act of election alone that constitutes Israel's identity, but also Israel's practices. Its ongoing life as the chosen people is therefore a cooperative endeavor: while it is impossible without the call of the sovereign God, it is realized only insofar as the people's practices are in sync with that call. In this sense, Israel is *actualized* as Yahweh's treasured possession—with all that entails in regards to fulfillment of its specific purpose—only insofar as it is faithful to covenant. To be clear, this is not to say that election is canceled out by a failure of covenant obedience, as though Yahweh's free action is subject to undoing by human action; it is rather to point out that election cannot be fully realized in the absence of said obedience.

Certainly this assertion could be contested. For instance, Scott Bader-Saye argues that Israel's election—which he equates with "Israel's status before God"—is "eternal and unconditional" and its covenant "enduring," in no way dependent upon Israel's faithfulness for its continuation. In passages such as Leviticus 26, where it seems that *covenant* is made conditional, Bader-Saye argues that the promises of judgment for disobedience actually operate within the stipulations component of a surviving covenant framework. If Israel is faithful, it will be blessed; if not, it will be cursed. Even where the passage predicates the promise "I will walk among you, and will be your God and you shall be my people" (v. 12) upon the previous statement, "if you follow my statues and keep my commandments and observe them faithfully" (v. 3), it does not make election conditional, for God never threatens to reject Israel as his people. Rather, God promises, "I will remember in their favor the covenant with their ancestors whom I brought out of the land of Egypt in the sight of the nations, to be their God: I am the Lord" (v. 45).[15]

Recalling the aforementioned distinction between election and covenant, I affirm Bader-Saye's reading of election, but Israel's identity in covenant—which I would argue is at least equally indicative of its existential status before Yahweh as its election—is clearly conditional in the biblical text. For instance, in the above example, Bader-Saye neglects the most fundamental assertion of Israel's identity in Exodus 19:5–6, where the status of Israel as treasured possession is clearly conditioned upon obedience to the soon-to-be-disclosed covenant. And his reading of the almost identical assertion in Leviticus 26 is rather strange. If "I will be your God and you shall be my people" is qualified by "if you follow my statutes," etc., does that not essentially condition Israel's identity as Yahweh's people upon its obedience? It is not clear what else it would mean. Moreover, in his mention of Yahweh maintaining covenant even in the midst of judgment (v. 45), Bader-Saye inexplicably neglects verses 40–41, where Yahweh remembers covenant "if they confess their iniquity and the iniquity of their ancestors . . . if then their uncircumcised heart is humbled and they make amends for their iniquity . . ." According to that caveat, Israel's status and covenant remain active only in the context of repentance and reparation. In short, Israel's fulfillment of its calling—its realized identity as the chosen people—which is as equally constitutive of its "status before God" as Yahweh's act of electing, is neither enduring nor unconditional, but is rather contingent upon its orientation toward covenant, whether in obedience or repentance. While Yahweh's act of electing Israel as his people is itself a free act of grace unconditioned by anything Israel does in any way, and while that call may be held open for Israel in an "eternal and enduring" manner, election is not actually brought to fruition without obedience on Israel's part. This is a crucial point, for if Israel's theopolitics is pertinent to the church, then the church must recognize when it is no longer *being* church and is acting in some other communal form, a divergence that nationalism necessarily entails.

The third significant aspect of the Exodus 19 declaration is that all three descriptors for Israel—"my treasured possession," "priestly

---

15. Bader-Saye, *Church and Israel*, 33–34. Again, despite disagreement on this point, I am overall quite appreciative of Bader-Saye's book, which proves quite helpful to this study.

kingdom," and "holy nation"—indicate a sort of *separateness* from the rest of the world. The Hebrew word for "possession" is derived from an Akkadian reference to "what is owned personally or what has been carefully put aside for personal use."[16] Yahweh has called Israel out of all of his creation to be his special possession for a particular purpose, and "confers upon Israel the status of royalty" if it is faithful to the covenant. In this call to covenant, "the suzerain establishes the vassal as the royal figure in a larger community which is itself under the great king's suzerainty."[17] The term "priestly kingdom" or "kingdom of priests" can also be understood as "a kingdom, namely priests" who will exist to mediate God's grace. Interestingly, the word *goy*, previously seen in Yahweh's promise to Abram, appears once again in "holy nation," prompting the following conclusion from Dumbrell: "Sinai in a very obvious sense marks an advance in the Abrahamic promises but now particularizes them to operate through Israel." Israel's distinctive role as a nation is to "provide, under the direct divine rule which the covenant contemplates, the paradigm of the theocratic rule which is to be the biblical aim for the whole world."[18] Notice that as opposed to the empire from which Israel is delivered, as well as the kingdoms among whom it is brought to reside, Yahweh's act of election moves well beyond the ancient Near East notion of national gods. Rather, this is a God who is sovereign over the world order, and who in Israel chooses a people to manifest that sovereignty before the nations.

Furthermore, Israel's election is not for its own sake. Consider Lohfink's insight:

> [I]t is part of the biblical concept of election that it is always combined with a mandate. God's choice fell on Israel for the sake of the nations. God needs a witness in the world, a people in which God's salvation can be made visible. That is why the burden of election rests on the chosen people. Israel's being chosen is not a privilege or a preference *over others*, but existence *for others*, and hence the heaviest burden in history.[19]

Election does not elevate Israel above all other nations toward the end of Israel's own aggrandizement or exaltation, but rather "crystallizes

---

16. Dumbrell, *Covenant and Creation*, 85.
17. Levenson, *Sinai and Zion*, 31.
18. Dumbrell, *Covenant and Creation*, 87.
19. Lohfink, *Does God Need the Church?*, 37.

Israel's knowledge that God desires to liberate and change the entire world but for that purpose needs a beginning in the midst of the world, a visible place and living witnesses."[20] The election of Israel, and therefore Israel's identity, is a means to the end of liberating the rest of the world to come under the creation-restoring reign of Yahweh. Israel will "embody a politics of blessing," demonstrating that election, covenant, and redemption "are related such that election founds the covenant community in God's choice and redemption extends the covenant community to include all the world."[21] Its separateness is necessary to the degree that it must faithfully and continually embody that politics of blessing amidst the surrounding kingdoms.

It is worth pausing here to note the character of God's activity. As Lohfink observes, part of the uniqueness of Yahweh's project is that, although certainly a revolution, it is not the rapid, violent upheaval so often witnessed throughout human history. God is far more subtle—and patient. God is free and creates human beings who can freely be in relation to God. How can God transform the world while protecting this freedom? According to Lohfink, "it can only be that God begins in a small way, at one single place in the world. There must be a place, visible, tangible, where the salvation of the world can begin: that is, where the world becomes what it is supposed to be according to God's plan."[22] Thus, the story of the people of God begins with one man, in one place, at one moment, and will unfold in that people, not as a series of responses to the exigencies of the moment, but as the manifestation of human freedom enlivened by and in response to Yahweh's patient sovereignty.

Fourth, Yahweh's *power of initiation* is manifest in Israel's election, for prior to Sinai, the Israelites, as indicated by their name, could perhaps be considered at most an ethnic group, related biologically with some rather low-lying shared cultural traits. However, through election, this loosely associated people-group is given form and purpose:

> In and by this election God *constitutes* the Jews as a people. Israel did not arise out of a collection of autonomous individuals who agreed that their self-interest would be furthered by entering into a political alliance. Nor did the people qua peo-

---

20. Ibid., 38.
21. Bader-Saye, *Church and Israel*, 31.
22. Lohfink, *Does God Need the Church?*, 27.

ple exist as a prior political entity which God then elected as God's own. Rather, Israel became a people by God's action . . . Chosenness *calls forth* existence."[23]

This is indicative of the decisive break with world empire that Yahweh achieves. With this newly chosen people, we witness the unprecedented: "the appearance of a new social reality" created "ex nihilo."[24] As O'Donovan writes, "The power which God gave to Israel did not have to be taken from Egypt . . . first. The gift of power was not a zero-sum operation. God could generate new power by doing new things in Israel's midst."[25] Indeed, it is worth noting that Yahweh does not give the covenant to Egypt, even a chastened one, as though by means of its superior culture or military and economic might it could effectively propagate Yahweh's reign. Israel is not called to transform Egypt from within for the sake of Yahweh's reign, nor does Yahweh need Israel to access or commandeer Egypt's power in order to fulfill its vocation.[26] Rather, Yahweh removes Israel from the empire's midst and gives Israel, by his own power, a different identity and vocation, which can only be corrupted by Israel's return to the old.

In short, as Dumbrell reminds us, "the biblical plan of redemption does not finally focus upon a saved people so much as it does upon a governed world."[27] Toward this end, Yahweh liberates and elects a people to embody Yahweh's reign on earth, to act as the decisive alternative to the ways of empire and domination, in whatever form. Israel's redemption and election are never intended for Israel's own sake, but are really about restoring worldwide submission to the reign of the Creator God, which results in creation's own fulfillment. To understand what such an embodiment of Yahweh's reign looks like, that is, Israel's prescribed theopolitics, the discussion turns to covenant.

---

23. Bader-Saye, *Church and Israel*, 35.
24. Brueggemann, *Prophetic Imagination*, 16.
25. O'Donovan, *Desire of the Nations*, 95.
26. This point is particularly pertinent when evaluating the nationalism discussed in chapters 6 and 7.
27. Dumbrell, *Covenant and Creation*, 66.

Israel as Covenant Community

Covenant, according to Bader-Saye, is the "correlate of election that, through Torah and the land, determines the material and political shape of Israel's free and holy life in mutual relation to God."[28] In other words, the Sinaitic covenant is the form of Israel's fulfillment of election. This covenant proceeds directly from Yahweh's sovereignty as Yahweh founds a society to embody his reign in the world. While this treaty form has precedents in the ancient Near East,[29] it is Yahweh's sovereign initiative that lends to the Sinaitic covenant its utter uniqueness. For one thing, as Israel's election calls forth a people into existence, the Sinaitic covenant actually *establishes a political community*. Yahweh does not enter into covenant with a preexisting political community, that is, a nation that already has an identity previously derived from within the normal political life and experience of ancient Near East kingdoms. Rather, a new and unprecedented political community is founded, whose politics consists of those disciplines, practices, needs, and distribution of powers ordering life together as derived from its essential purpose of embodying the international and even cosmological reign of Yahweh on earth.

A necessary corollary of Yahweh's sovereignty is the totalizing exclusivity of Israel's allegiance. The exodus and Sinai were God's self-revelation to the whole of Israel, not as an end unto itself, but a means to "a new kind of relationship, one in which the vassal will show fidelity in the future by acknowledgement of the suzerain's grace toward him in the past." Deliverance from Egypt adequately justifies Israel's entering into covenant with Yahweh, and as such forms the historical prologue of the Sinai covenant (Exod 20:2; Deut 5:6b). While this prologue is important, Levenson argues, what is crucial in this covenant is "the observance of the stipulations in the present and the sort of life that such observance brings about."[30] Of all the aspects of the suzerain-vassal covenant model, exclusive faithfulness by the vassal to the suzerain is paramount: "although a suzerain may have many vassals, a given vassal

---

28. Bader-Saye, *Church and Israel*, 37.

29. See McCarthy, *Treaty and Covenant*, 3, 28–29; Kline, *Treaty of the Great King*; Weinfield, ברית; Mendenhall, "Covenant Forms in Israelite Tradition," 48–57, 88; and Levenson, *Sinai and Zion*, 26–36.

30. Levenson, *Sinai and Zion*, 43.

must recognize only one suzerain."[31] If the vassal were allowed to submit to other suzerains, the first suzerain's claim would be compromised, the covenant undermined.

What Yahweh does through the covenant at Sinai is to consecrate for special service not just Israel's cult, but its entire national life, including its internal political organization and its relations with other nations. O'Donovan writes that for Israel to declare that "Yahweh reigns" is to assert three aspects of Yahweh's sovereignty: (1) Yahweh ensures the stability of the natural order; (2) Yahweh is in control of international politics, "the restless turbulence of the nations and their tutelary deities and could safeguard his people"; and (3) Yahweh orders Israel domestically as a political community.[32] As the first of these is established in the exodus, let us look in particular at the second and third of these elements.

Regarding Israel and ancient Near East international politics, a central feature of covenant is the suzerain's pledge to care for and protect the vassal in return for exclusive faithfulness. As such, "[Yahweh's] suzerainty does place a limitation upon the potential for a human counterpart. If there can only be one suzerain, how can Israel enter a covenant with any other lord? Hence, we find, especially in those books in which the covenant idea is prominent, an unqualified rejection of *Realpolitik*, since all (human) alliances are equated with apostasy." In the historical prologue, Yahweh's claim to suzerainty is that he has delivered Israel from bondage. By relying on other suzerains to deliver Israel from various threats, Israel disgraces that claim. Thus, according to Levenson, the Sinai covenant is given as an "alternative to conventional political relations." Israel must make a choice, "for the divine suzerain will not tolerate a human competitor any more than he will a divine one."[33] And this is not merely a matter of one suzerain over another, but

---

31. Ibid., 28.

32. O'Donovan, *Desire of the Nations*, 32. I appropriate this important description from O'Donovan, but take it in a very different direction than he does, concentrating on how Yahweh's kingship precludes human kingship in a proper Torah society. While O'Donovan finds the explicit enthronement formula of "Yahweh reigns" in the Psalms in a monarchical context, he still notes that the sentiment would likely have been understood in pre-monarchical Israel, a position I take much more strongly than he. I find O'Donovan's account theologically and exegetically profound, but I take issue with him in this chapter on specific points regarding key elements of Israel's theopolitics.

33. Levenson, *Sinai and Zion*, 72.

of one *politics* versus another, that is, a particular way of being in the world as a human community.

Israel, as a nation, is to mediate Yahweh's grace to the world, which requires it to be holy—consecrated and set apart for its singular purpose. Hence Dumbrell's crucial insight: "Israel is thus withdrawn from the sphere of common international contact and finds her point of contact as a nation in her relationship to Yahweh."[34] As Levenson states, "this proscribing of international politics is thus the political equivalent of covenantal monotheism. In each case, Israel's special identity demands a radical separation from the ways of the nations."[35] Israel's political identity is not derived in the typical political fashion as yet another player in the international political system, a competitor for scarce resources and relative power, only with its own divine sanction. Rather, its identity is theopolitical, derived directly from its election by and mission from Yahweh, and is radically alternative to conventional international politics.

As to Israel's internal political and social order, Lohfink correctly reminds us that in light of the narrative, "the fact that all around Israel there were reigning monarchs while Israel itself for two hundred years had no king must be taken seriously in theological terms."[36] Israel's tribal configuration and lack of a human king, he argues, was not merely preliminary or a "precursor to the state," but was a "deliberate countermodel" to the surrounding kingdoms.[37] Indeed, Exodus 19:6 introduces "the concept of Israel as the domain over which God rules. The theology of the kingship of God is here prominently displayed. But kingship and covenant are . . . co-ordinates since the presupposition of covenant is divine rule, while covenant in and through Israel is the implementation of divine kingship in national polity."[38] With Yahweh's kingship a clear corollary to covenant, Israel existed initially as a tribal league without a centralized government. Society revolved around the clan, but even between clans there was strong community. Compared with the social hierarchies found in neighboring nations, the tribal confederation was

---

34. Dumbrell, *Covenant and Creation*, 87.
35. Levenson, *Sinai and Zion*, 72.
36. Lohfink, *Does God Need the Church?*, 107.
37. Ibid., 108.
38. Dumbrell, 90.

"passionately egalitarian" in both political and socioeconomic terms, a political community of a decidedly new form.[39]

As an important side note, discussion of Israel as a counter-model brings up the question of conquest and settlement as narrated in the books of Joshua and Judges. There is not space to adequately treat this important question here, but it is worth noting the very particular circumstances under which Israel is called to war against the tribes in Canaan. Beginning in Genesis 15, allusion is made to the residents of Canaan, who are guilty of some "wickedness" to which the reader is not made privy; for this reason, Abraham's descendants will not be allowed to occupy the land until that wickedness has run its course, which according to the pericope will be at the point of their leaving some future situation of oppression (Gen 15:16). By Leviticus, the reader knows that situation is four centuries of slavery in Egypt, and upon the exodus and the giving of the law, the Israelites are directed to Canaan, where Yahweh is going to drive out the present residents for engaging in practices of such wickedness that Israel is not to emulate them at any cost (Lev 20:23). In Deuteronomy 9, the Israelites are further warned that it is not their righteousness that has in some way earned occupation of the land, but rather the wickedness of the Canaanites has rendered the land forfeit at the very point in time when Israel required settlement (Deut 9:4–6). This suggests a particular convergence of events: (1) a story of Yahweh's dealings with other nations that Yahweh does not share with Israel in the text, including an extended period of wickedness that has warranted dispossession of the land by those nations; (2) an exodus and migration of a people who, according to the narrative, were elected by God and promised in the form of their ancestors a land to dwell, which is even now being stipulated as a specific covenantal blessing; (3) and Yahweh's personal direction of the campaign (including personal engagement with its human instruments), as noted in all three of these passages and elsewhere. The narrative strongly suggests that this was a historically singular convergence, having to do with the nations being dispossessed for reasons not made known, rather than with any practice of violence that Israel was to retain as part of its covenant identity. Therefore, references to this period as justification for violence in any subsequent context are rendered untenable.

---

39. Lohfink, *Does God Need the Church?*, 57–58.

The form of Israel's new community is located in what Lohfink calls the "social project" of Torah. "Torah" denotes not only the law of this new people, but names Israel's new social order, the product of Yahweh's sovereign power of initiation. As the narrative is presented, "Israel's being led out of Egypt and immediately afterward being given the Torah shows that God alone is the founder of the new society. By human strength alone this new thing could not be accomplished."[40] According to Bader-Saye, "Torah is at the heart of the covenant because it names the ways in which Israel is to be set apart in its life of holiness . . . Torah names the kind of people God is forming." The objective of the covenant for Israel is that it becomes "a holy people, a people who live Torah-shaped lives . . . for only such a people can be capable of dwelling with God in joy."[41]

At the heart of the Torah is the Decalogue, the Ten Commandments, the first two of which demand unequivocal and exclusive worship of God alone and in proper manner (Exod 20:3–17; Deut 5:7–21). They form "the crystallizing core and focus of meaning of all the layers of the Pentateuch." If the Torah is about the embodiment of the reign of God, these commandments locate the sovereignty of God at the heart of Israel's identity, for they constitute a claim of absolute authority requiring absolute allegiance. Moreover, they also require total formation: "Having Yahweh alone as Lord and serving only Yahweh also means orienting every aspect of life to Yahweh."[42] The many ordinances put forth spell out the ways the Israelites are to appear toward and interact with each other and with the world. Offices are formed, a priesthood established, a tabernacle designed, all to provide an appropriate setting for Yahweh to dwell with his people. And in a sense, even these are a means to an end. In the Torah, "the people of Israel are called to imitate God's relationship with the world both in terms of *tsedaqah*—God's transcendent graciousness toward creation—and *mishpat*—God's immanent ordering of the cosmos, conformity to which is justice."[43] Yahweh dwells with Israel so that Israel might mediate Yahweh's grace and justice to the world, so that the world may in turn dwell with Yahweh.

---

40. Lohfink, *Does God Need the Church?*, 73.
41. Bader-Saye, *Church and Israel*, 43.
42. Lohfink, *Does God Need the Church?*, 78–79.
43. Bader-Saye, *Church and Israel*, 37.

According to Lohfink, the rule of God over Israel is developed in three aspects of the Torah: (1) concern not only for the "inner side" of the human being, but the "external side" as well—the material aspects of human interaction with each other and with other elements of creation; (2) concern not only with space but with time—rhythms of time, festivals, centralization of worship at the temple in Jerusalem—feasts became pilgrimage festivals, the Sabbath central; (3) the cultivation not merely of righteous individuals, but of a righteous society—hence meticulous systems of laws "meant to prevent the existence of classes of poor and enslaved people in Israel," a situation that would cause deep dissension within the people of God.[44] Indeed, O'Donovan notes, "as Israel is situated among the nations, so are the poor and defenseless situated within Israel. He who cared for the welfare of a servile nation in Egypt cares for the welfare of a servile class in Israel."[45]

All this, writes Lohfink, is connected with the exclusive worship of Yahweh. If there is oppression and exploitation occurring within Israel, Yahweh is not being properly worshipped, a violation of the second commandment: "For all worship only brings to expression in words and concentrates in symbols what is to be done constantly throughout Israel: being a just society in the world, to the honor of God."[46] For this reason, "not only must the human heart be holy, so must the conditions of life, the social structures and the forms of environment in which the person lives and into which he or she is constantly moving."[47] The life of the people of God, in all its manifestations, must reflect the reign of Yahweh. To the degree that Israel is faithful in this, it is shaped by, and finds its identity in, the Creator God, an identity that ultimately extends beyond itself:

> Israel's faith is always about "the world." Its desire is to bring more and more of the world under the rule of God. Its wish is to transform the world entrusted to it by living the Torah, God's social order, so that it will be clear to everyone how the will of God intends the world to be.[48]

---

44. Lohfink, *Does God Need the Church?*, 79–83.
45. O'Donovan, *Desire of the Nations*, 33.
46. Lohfink, *Does God Need the Church?*, 84.
47. Ibid., 87.
48. Ibid., 106.

This is the heart of Israel's theopolitical identity, to be formed as a unique theopolitical community with its theological vocation determinative of its politics, and to universalize that community by means of a compelling and transformative social order. Theirs was not to decide whether to accept the covenant as one choice among others for social embodiment; rather, they had to decide whether to be faithful to their divine calling, whether to submit to Yahweh's sovereignty and be formed by the Torah. Thus, Israel's identity as a political community is born in Yahweh's gracious action and realized in Israel's acknowledgement of Yahweh's reign and in its submission to his social order of Torah, so that in the covenant and its faithful implementation, the created order of Genesis 1–2 would begin to be restored.

Prophetic Critique and Prophetic Promise

Having established the norm of Israel's identity, it is necessary to examine the ways in which Israel gradually abandoned that identity, according to the biblical narratives. In particular, it is necessary to examine prophetic discourse to determine precisely what in Israel's behavior was being indicted and judged. In short, the covenant nation of Israel came to adopt institutions of power politics in order to secure itself among the surrounding kingdoms, as a viable counterpart to those kingdoms. This required the gradual adoption of a theopolitics antithetical to covenant with Yahweh, and in so doing, Israel altered its singular identity and mission given at Sinai. Subsequently, its new identity became something requiring security through the same coercive politics of its neighbors, resulting in a spiral of anti-covenantal theopolitics that would divide the nation and culminate in its partial destruction and exile.

Insofar as the church is engrafted onto Israel's identity—a subject of the next chapter—prophetic critique provides crucial insights into the problem of nationalism for the church, in that it points out the inherent dangers of theopolitical syncretism, the interweaving of one theopolitical identity with another such that a new form is created in the process. Recall that nationalism involves on the one hand the formulation and inculcation of a particular national identity in a given people group, and on the other a pursuit of power in order to institutionalize that identity either in the existing state or in a new one. To the degree that Christians residing in various nations seek to (1) identify themselves according to a syncretized theopolitical narrative of identity, and (2) secure that national identity through the political ways of the powers, they participate in a form of Israel's own error, directly altering their identity in the church of Jesus Christ.

In order to draw out the theopolitical issues at contention in Israel, I have chosen to focus on two prophetic books in particular: Hosea and Jeremiah. Hosea son of Beeri prophesied in the northern kingdom during the reign of King Jereoboam II in the mid-to-late eighth century. Jeremiah son of Hilkiah prophesied in the Southern Kingdom from some time during the reign of Josiah (640–609) through the next four kings, ultimately witnessing the conquest of Judah by the Babylonians in 587/586. In this chapter, the book of Hosea is appropriated for its examination and evaluation of Israel's practices of *realpolitik*, the conventional politics of the surrounding kingdoms, which Yahweh finds abhorrent and antithetical to Israel's election. Jeremiah is appropriated as an insight into Israelite civil religion (specifically that operating in the Southern Kingdom of Judah), which misinterpreted the Davidic promise to underwrite the monarchical state that the southern Israelites considered central to their collective identity, constituting an alternative and ultimately erroneous and unfaithful theopolitics. Before discussing the prophets, however, it is important to note the political developments in Israel over the course of its history as narrated in the Old Testament.

Covenant Gives Way to State

In 1 Samuel 8, one finds what is arguably the first major institutional departure from covenant, as the elders of Israel appear before the prophet Samuel and demand a human king. The previous chapters indicate a combination of factors contributing to this move, not least the corrupt leadership of Samuel's sons as judges and increasing pressure by the Philistines nearby. Even though Yahweh continues to prove faithful to his covenant promises—a faithfulness demonstrated some years before, as the narrative in the previous chapter indicates—the elders of the various tribes gather together and demand that Samuel set a human king over them. Samuel is displeased and goes to Yahweh with their petition. Yahweh's immediate response is key: the elders' demand is to be met, as a function of the freedom Yahweh extends, but such a development is to be unequivocally understood as a rejection of Yahweh as king over

Israel. Indeed, Yahweh sets their demand within the context of idolatry, a problem that has plagued Israel since the exodus from Egypt.

Yet, the demand is not to be met without qualification; Samuel is to "solemnly warn" the elders of the consequences of usurping Yahweh's role in this fashion (1 Sam 8:6–9). This Samuel does, predicting royal conformity to the norms of empire and the surrounding kingdoms: the seizing of person and property for the royal estate and for military security, the tithing of the people's produce for the royal court and retainers, even the enslavement of the people (8:11–17). If their demand is met, Samuel warns, "you will cry out because of your king, whom you have chosen for yourselves; but the Lord will not answer you in that day" (8:18). The obligations of the covenant upon the suzerain will no longer be binding because in replacing Yahweh with a human counterpart, covenant has been nullified. The elders reject the warning, responding, "No! But we are determined to have a king over us, so that we also may be like other nations, and that our king may govern us and go out before us and fight our battles" (8:19–20). Whether the threat to Israel's security would be exacerbated by *realipolitik* and a centralized state, or even manufactured by the monarchy for self-aggrandizement, goes unconsidered by the elders. Thus Samuel, at Yahweh's concession, anoints Saul as king.

However, Saul is from early on a failure as king, and Yahweh directs Samuel to replace him with David.[49] Power is eventually centralized under David into state form, and a "sacral kingship" is established under Solomon, who takes on the role of high priest for the kingdom. With the expansion of empire and its attendant utilization of foreign alliances, slavery, and a standing army, *realpolitik* becomes institutionalized in the state, and Israel becomes that from which it had been delivered in the exodus.[50]

As the kingdom breaks apart, dynasties are established and overthrown, kings are assassinated, and political maneuvering further un-

---

49. The Davidic covenant, along with the erroneous understandings thereof that become institutionalized in the divided kingdom, will be discussed below.

50. As this is a brief theopolitical overview aimed at identifying Israel's overall trajectory, I do not take up certain notable, yet individual and isolated, instances where God favors these kings and their actions or where it seems that certain Abrahamic promises are fulfilled in some limited extent (e.g., 1 Kings 10; Douglas Harink, e-mail message to author, April 7, 2011). The important exception of the Davidic covenant as described in 2 Samuel 7 is addressed below.

dermines the covenant people. As Blenkinsopp explains, "by the eighth century B.C.E., the two kingdoms were moving inexorably toward a situation in which the coercive power of the state, supported by a class of nouveaux riches parasitical on the monarchy and court, legitimated by state cults exercising their own forms of hierocratic coercion, and resting on a broad basis of peasant serfdom and slavery, was reaching out into every sphere of social life."[51] This mention of state cults is especially noteworthy, for as the monarchy assumed greater sacerdotal authority, "YHWH became a state god" legitimizing *realpolitik*, rather than Lord of the nations, of whose reign Israel was to be a manifestation. "For the first time there appeared and established itself within the people of God what later Europeans called the 'union of throne and altar.' Israel now resembled the Near Eastern systems of government."[52] This last sentence is key, for here we have the reversal of the original covenant orientation described by Dumbrell:[53] now Israel is effectively withdrawn from its proper relationship to Yahweh and instead locates its identity in the "sphere of common international contact."

Covenant and Identity in the Prophets: Hosea and Power Politics

The book of Hosea is a trenchant critique of Israel's corrupted embodiment of Torah. In graphic language, we find statement after statement of condemnation for practices antithetical to Israel's election, practices that themselves constitute, not religious *and* political sin, as though these were separate realms of behavior, but *theopolitical* sin, namely, the abandonment of *hesed*, or covenant faithfulness. Of particular interest are Hosea's treatments of human kingship and foreign alliances. Both are corollaries of state centralization, the cornerstone of power politics, and each works to secure the other.

Hosea targets human kingship in Ephraim at two significant points.[54] First, in 8:4, Yahweh protests that Israel has "made kings, but

51. Blenkinsopp, *Sage, Priest, Prophet*, 150.

52. Lohfink, *Does God Need the Church?*, 110.

53. To reiterate, "Israel is thus withdrawn from the sphere of common international contact and finds her point of contact as a nation in her relationship to Yahweh" (Dumbrell, *Covenant and Creation*, 87).

54. Within this chapter, I use "Ephraim" to refer specifically to the northern kingdom and its state apparatus, "Judah" for the southern. This is to distinguish from references to the whole people of Israel as established in covenant.

not through me; they set up princes but without my knowledge. With their silver and gold they made idols for their own destruction." Clearly, there is at minimum a willful neglect of seeking Yahweh's will, of relying upon his provision of leadership. As Hans Walter Wolff states, Yahweh's intent was not considered, nor did he select or approve the kings; rather, "lies and treachery" mark the enthronements.[55] Dumbrell characterizes this as Yahweh's "condemnation of political intrigue."[56]

At this point, Wolff argues that Hosea does not reject the monarchy per se, nor even the northern kingship, but simply the manner of establishing kings. By 13:9–11, however, the magnitude of the indictment is clear. Yahweh declares, "I will destroy you, O Israel; who can help you? Where now is your king, that he may save you? Where in all your cities are your rulers, of whom you said, 'Give me a king and rulers'? I gave you a king in my anger, and I took him away in my wrath." In verse 10, "it becomes quite plain that the roots of Hosea's criticisms of kingship go deeper than the present grievances. Almost like the Baal cult . . . kingship from the outset was in opposition to Yahweh's lordship." Indeed, the imperfect verbs used in verse 11 "refer to all the kings from Saul to Hoshea ben Elah, whom Yahweh in his wrath has just stripped of his royal office."[57]

Peter Machinist, also, inquires as to the scope of Hosea's critique of kingship. The critique is somewhat ambiguous, he suggests, with precedents throughout the Old Testament for either a specific critique of the northern practice, or a fundamental critique of the institution itself. That said, the latter seems more fitting. Hosea 9:15—"every evil of theirs began at Gilgal"—is arguably a reference to 1 Samuel 11:14–15, where Saul is publicly made Israel's first king at Gilgal, and this on the heels of 1 Samuel 8:7b, where Yahweh observes his rejection at the hands of the elders. Moreover, Hosea 8:4a reiterates the sentiment running through 1 Samuel 8–12, such that "we have the same problem framed in the same way, about the people's demand for a new political form, kingship, against the intention of Yahweh, and the reaction to their demand." Hosea also echoes 1 Samuel 8 in linking the demand for a human king with the worship of other gods. Machinist therefore concludes, "Hosea 8:4a looks as if it may well be calling up the problems of the very in-

---

55. Wolff, *Commentary on Hosea*, 139.
56. Dumbrell, *Faith of Israel*, 178.
57. Wolff, *Commentary on Hosea*, 227.

troduction of kingship . . . in order to make sense of the kings and cult of Hosea's period." Hosea 13:9–11 reinforces this conclusion, in that Yahweh acquiesced in anger, then became doubly disgusted at the evil kings that followed. Regardless, "it is not only individual kings of the North who are going to be punished by Yahweh; it is the entire monarchy, and so the state, that Yahweh is to end because of its crimes."[58]

It therefore seems that the internal political process of state centralization, located chiefly in the institution of human kingship, lies at the root of Israel's covenant failure. In seeking to be like the neighboring kingdoms, Israel has forsaken its covenant calling. State centralization necessarily undermines the openness to other nations that is required for mediating Yahweh's grace. Instead, it defines the other as potential threat or active enemy, and in the name of security, closes Israel off. Israel thus becomes a threat to the other, and its own military conquest then becomes a real possibility.

Of course, this conclusion contrasts with that of other theologians and biblical scholars, who see in the biblical texts rather considerable support for the monarchy. One such scholar is O'Donovan, who presents an affirmative though considerably nuanced view of the institution in his effort to derive "true political principles" from Scripture that might prove useful to reversing the listlessness of post-Christendom Western politics.[59] O'Donovan asserts that "David's dynasty was the form in which earthly political authority had been given most decisively to Israel."[60] O'Donovan sees this monarchical role as an essential component of the biblical narrative, a narrative by and large supportive of the institution: "Those who argued against monarchy that where Yhwh was king there was no place for any other (1 Sam 8:7; Judg 8:23) did not, of course, challenge the idea of human mediation of divine kingship. They challenged the erection of an image of Yhwh, one whose mediation held all Yhwh's kingly functions together, so that he, too, was a king."[61] In other words, it was the concentration of all these aspects that was actu-

---

58. Machinist, "Hosea and Kingship," 167–74.

59. O'Donovan, *Desire of the Nations*, 15. It should be noted that O'Donovan conceives of the monarchical role to be in conjunction with the prophetic office in Israel, the latter being the more significant (62). However, he nevertheless considers the human monarchy to be inherent to Israel's founding identity, a view that is resisted at key points in the biblical narrative.

60. Ibid., 24.

61. Ibid., 52.

ally problematic. Elsewhere, he argues, one can see entire story-cycles with leanings in either direction regarding the institution: the narrative of David's decline is quite critical of "the monarch's incapacity to control events," but earlier stories show how David came to replace Saul, ultimately in a way that legitimates the Davidic throne. Even the prophetic movement he reads to acquiesce, leading him to conclude, "in the end nobody opposed the monarchy."[62] Indeed, O'Donovan claims, "there are no anti-monarchist voices among the scriptural witnesses." Hosea, for instance, is responding to the corrupt practice of the institution in his day, and "even the narrative of 1 Samuel 8 is in fact an apologia for the monarchy addressed to its natural antagonists; it intends to leave no doubt that the monarchy came to existence by Yhwh's decision. The principle, therefore, that the monarch could provide unitary representation of Yhwh's rule was an accepted one."[63]

According to O'Donovan, the key function of the monarch as Yahweh's representative was the exercise of judicial functions. While this had more or less been the purview of the judges in pre-monarchical times, "it was a crucial element in the case for a monarchy that they had failed to provide not only the security necessary for Israel's identity but even a consistent standard of justice itself." The monarchy offered the "function of continuity" to Israel, "ensuring an unbroken tradition in the occupation of the territory and the perpetuation of the national identity." The monarchy was not a substitute for the law as the principle of continuity, but reinforced the law in that capacity: "It afforded the prospect that the statutes and law which Yhwh had commanded would no longer be flouted in future generations as they had in the past. Yhwh's 'covenant' with David . . . provided a defense against the instability of the covenant with Israel." In this way, the monarch acted as a double representative, representing Yahweh's rule to the people and ensuring their obedience, and representing the people to Yahweh, ensuring his favor.[64]

The arguments by Lohfink and Dumbrell arguably refute O'Donovan's claims regarding the monarchy as the most decisive form

---

62. Ibid., 53.

63. Ibid., 61. O'Donovan states on the next page that within the Deuteronomic perspective, the monarch could not replace Yhwh but only act as a safeguard. Nevertheless, the central theopolitical *necessity* of the monarchy is clear in O'Donovan's schema.

64. Ibid., 61.

of political authority for Israel, and the exposition above addresses in a general way his understanding of Hosea, which is in the end inadequate. Others of his claims warrant more direct challenge here. First, in his mention of contending story-cycles, he misconstrues the narrative of David's decline as critiquing "the monarch's incapacity to control events." In fact, the narrative criticizes David's incapacity to control himself! What is key in that incapacity is its relation to human kingship: his tendencies toward excess and abuse were inherent in his monarchical power and in the power politics by which he secured his throne, which provided the context for his particular sins. Moreover, one must consider the narrative sequence. Even if the story of David's replacement of Saul reads in such a way as to legitimate the Davidic throne, the fact that it is followed in the chronology by a narrative of David's decline means the overarching narrative should likely be considered, contra O'Donovan, as a theological indictment of kingship—not an endorsement—even a potential reconsideration of the foregoing "legitimation."

Additionally, O'Donovan's reading of an "apologia" for the monarchy in 1 Samuel 8 is inexplicable. Certainly, the story leaves no doubt that the institution was allowed by Yahweh, who set stringent terms upon it that, if followed (which they were not), would ironically rob it of most of what the elders sought. That said, Yahweh's statement that "they have rejected me from being king over them" is much more the central and definitive assertion of the pericope, but goes practically unaddressed in O'Donovan's account.[65] First Samuel 8:7 is an unequivocal assertion that human kingship is contrary to Yahweh's original intent for Israel and a fundamental alteration of Israel's theopolitics.

O'Donovan also seems to miss the point when he argues that the monarchy as an institution defended against the "instability of covenant." While he qualifies this by saying that it reinforced the law rather than replaced it, he fails to recognize that the very institution itself tended toward the covenant's nullification in that it established an alternative sovereign. Moreover, and as Lohfink would likely respond, to suggest that centralized institutions of power are necessary to secure Yahweh's word goes directly against the very essence of Israel's election and its calling to be a counter-model to the nations. Recalling Dumbrell, Israel's national identity was located in its relationship to Yahweh, rather than the conventional politics of the day. That must include political in-

65. It is mentioned only in passing on pp. 35 and 52.

stitutions, and the notion of a "circumcised" (or in our day, "baptized") worldly power was simply not in the picture.

Conservation of the law goes hand-in-hand with the maintenance of Israel's national identity, which, for O'Donovan, requires "security" provided by the monarchy. Indeed, the monarchy's role was to safeguard the continuation and perpetuation of identity. Yet, as I will shortly demonstrate with Jeremiah, the question at hand is precisely *which* national identity is being secured. In fact, multiple identity discourses are at work at various points in Israel's national experience, and what the prophets help bring out is that those perpetuated by the monarchy were often quite contrary to those of the covenant.[66] The monarchy, rather than defending Israel's covenant identity, more often worked to undermine it.[67]

Israel's internal political order is not the only problem for the prophets, however. The proliferation of foreign alliances in the Old Testament, that is, covenants with suzerains alternative to Yahweh, is a major theme of general prophetic critique in Israel, and Hosea indicts the northern kingdom for this practice at multiple points. In the aftermath of the Syro-Ephraimite War, Hosea condemns Ephraim for going to Assyria, even though "he is not able to cure you or heal your wound" (Hos 5:13; cf. 2 Kgs 16:3). Lind links the war itself to "power politics" on the parts of both Israel and Judah, but also their behavior afterwards: "To heal their wounds, they did not repent of their act of warfare . . . but extended their violence by appealing to an international politics quite foreign to Yahwism. Each against the other appealed for help from the king of Assyria."[68] This critique continues in 7:11, where Hosea says of Israel's strategic vacillation, "Ephraim has become like a dove, silly and without sense; they call upon Egypt, they go to Assyria." To put it in other words, "Ephraim herds the wind, and pursues the east wind all day long; they multiply falsehood and violence; they make a treaty with Assyria and oil is carried to Egypt" (Hos 12:1). In 8:8–9, he observes Israel's abandonment of purpose and loyalty: "Israel is swallowed up; now they are among the nations as a useless vessel. For they have gone up to Assyria, a wild ass wandering alone; Ephraim has bargained for

66. This points to the possible relevance of certain understandings of nationalism—e.g., contested narratives and symbol competition—even back into antiquity. See Grosby, *Biblical Ideas of Nationality*.

67. Indeed, arguably the most basic objection to O'Donovan's schema regarding the monarchy as mediator of divine rule is that it simply did not work.

68. Lind, "Hosea 5:8—6:6," 400.

lovers." As Wolff remarks, "Israel's surrender to the enemy makes it despicable among the nations . . . Israel is a precious, desirable, notable people among the nations only as her God's free covenant people."[69]

Yahweh's judgments are unequivocal: "Though they bargain with the nations, I will now gather them up. They shall soon writhe under the burden of kings and princes" (8:10). This last phrase, "kings and princes," can be read as "king of kings," which is to say, "suzerain," that is, the king of Assyria.[70] Ephraim has traded covenant for alliance, so "they shall not remain in the land of the Lord; but Ephraim shall return to Egypt, and in Assyria they shall eat unclean food" (9:3). And again, "They shall return to the land of Egypt, and Assyria shall be their king, because they have refused to return to me" (11:5). Note that Yahweh's judgments—conquest by Assyria and deportation there or to Egypt—are not arbitrary or unrelated to Israel's transgressions; rather, they are the theopolitical extensions of Israel's own actions, Israel's particular acts of unfaithfulness carried to their logical conclusion.

What are the theopolitical implications of Israel's *realpolitik*? Among the biblical scholars discussed here, Machinist puts the question best: "Is it, for example, a public renunciation of YHWH in favor of foreign deities, or a pursuit of a foreign policy that Hosea believes YHWH regards as mistaken, even if the perpetrators try to invoke YHWH's support?"[71] Perhaps the answer cannot be bound to either on its own, not because it is simply both, but because in this case of *realpolitik*, they are one and the same. This becomes especially clear if we conceive of Yahweh's covenant project in terms not just of Israel's religion and/or politics, but in terms of Israel's very identity. Again, the themes of (1) inseparability of the religious and political for Israel, and (2) identity as constituted by practice, return to the fore.

The theopolitical emphasis of this study, if correct, must bring into question the differentiation made by some scholars between Israel's religious and political practices. In the matter of kingship, for instance, Dumbrell argues that the covenant breach addressed in 8:4–6 was evident at the "political level" in that the people had established their own form of kingship, usurping Yahweh's authority to install his own choice; "their real allegiance, however, was exhibited at the religious level," in

---

69. Wolff, *Commentary on Hosea*, 142.

70. Ibid., 144. See also Machinist, "Hosea and Kingship," 159.

71. Machinist, "Hosea and Kingship," 164.

their setting up a calf at Samaria (8:5–6).[72] He goes on to describe the religious and political in Israel as "interrelated," but this is more of a passing comment, as he continues to state that "Israel's corruption manifests itself in its idolatrous worship."[73]

If my analysis is correct, Dumbrell's is a false dichotomy, for if Yahweh is usurped as king, there is already a corruption of covenant, already a violation of a system inherently both religious and political, that is, theopolitical. As Lind states, "In ancient Israel, religion and politics were one. Yahweh as political leader to whom the people committed themselves in obedience made his will known through the prophet. Thus torah and word of Yahweh through the prophet, rather than kingship as an institution representing violent power . . .were at the center of Yahwistic politics."[74] By supplanting Yahweh's position as king, and thereby subverting the divinely instituted theopolitical system, the human king becomes an idol. Political behavior directly constitutes cultic corruption. By centralizing the state, Israel compromises its covenant vocation, another direct affront to Yahweh, and therefore a transgression simultaneously religious and political. Dumbrell mentions the calf at Samaria as an example of religious disloyalty, but if the calf is set up to secure the political power of the northern king(s) (1 Kgs 12:26–30), is it primarily a religious or political offense? Again, one must conclude that this behavior is theopolitical, both political and religious at the same time, refusing to draw a sharp distinction between the two aspects or to subordinate one to the other.

The same is true for Israel's practice of foreign alliances, where the problematic differentiation by some scholars between Israel's religious and political behavior is even more pronounced. To begin again with Dumbrell, who seems almost solely concerned with "religious deviations,"[75] Israel's waywardness is due to "incorrect theology, which is indicated clearly by the national dependency on the Canaanite fertility cult and on other apostasies."[76] Prophesying against the divided people,

72. Dumbrell, *Faith of Israel*, 179. Overall, Dumbrell's insights are helpful, especially concerning the centrality and scope of covenant. It is unclear why he seems to become so singularly focused here.

73. Ibid., 181.

74. Lind, "Hosea 5:8—6:6," 401.

75. Dumbrell, *Faith of Israel*, 171.

76. Ibid., 177.

> Hosea 11:12—12:2 takes up a new reproach against Israel and Judah as faithless and unrepentant, because of their Canaanite idolatry. Judah is on view (11:12b), where Judah still roams with Canaanite El and keeps faith with the 'holy ones' (i.e., of El's Canaanite court) by their policy of foreign alliances. Israel is on view at 11:12a and 12:1 as the inveterate liar. It is extreme folly for Ephraim (12:1) to seek security from any other source than Yahweh.[77]

Through prophetic critique, "Israel is reminded of the first commandment. The survival of the nation depends on their keeping it, for polytheism denied Yahweh's uniqueness." Finally, "Hosea sees clearly that it is Israel's spiritual adultery . . . which has undermined and drained the nation's moral fiber."[78]

It is not that Dumbrell is incorrect *per se* in identifying Hosea's referents, but rather that he too narrowly interprets Hosea's critique. The Israelites did not wake up one morning and think to themselves, "We feel religiously unsatisfied. Let's go to our neighbors and experiment with their cultic practices."[79] Nor was cultic idolatry merely the by-product of political maneuvering in the international realm. Rather, such power politics actually *constituted* idolatry. Since Israel was in covenant with not just any suzerain, but with the divine Yahweh, vassalage to another would be synonymous with idolatry. Indeed, it could be argued that were Israel's cultic practices to have remained the same (against all odds, of course), Israel would still have been guilty of idolatry. Dumbrell overemphasizes the cultic problem at the expense of the political, and more importantly at the expense of the unity of both.

Wolff also misses this in a minor way, when he relates the mention of silver and gold in 8:4b to idols only in the cultic sense, even though the immediate context is political.[80] He goes on to note Hosea's decrial of Israel having to pay her "lovers" to take her (8:9), mentioning that Tiglath-pileser III reported Hoshea's gift of one thousand talents of silver in tribute.[81] Considering the immediate context, and with the theology of covenant in mind, could not the "idols" in 8:4b also refer to

---

77. Ibid., 182.

78. Ibid., 184, 185.

79. Whether this could describe various phenomena among church attendees in the United States I will leave for another discussion.

80. Wolff, *Commentary on Hosea*, 139.

81. Ibid., 143.

alternative suzerains? Meanwhile, Pentiuc inexplicably shifts gears from the political to the cultic where Hosea complains in 7:8 that "Ephraim mixes himself with the peoples"; despite this reference occurring in a section titled "Failed International Politics," Pentiuc writes that Hosea "probably refers to religious syncretism" with Assyria and Egypt.[82] Such assertions fail to note that the religious and political are, at all times, interwoven to an almost indistinguishable degree. Under the Sinaitic covenant, where religion is inherently political and politics inherently religious; where I AM, creator of all and redeemer of Israel, reigns as sovereign and as suzerain; where the very purpose of Israel as a political community is the embodiment of Yahweh's reign on earth and the mediation of Yahweh's grace to the world; here, there cannot be religious faithfulness apart from political faithfulness, nor proper politics without proper theology. They are symbiotic; indeed, in a very strong sense, they are one.

Hosea's prophetic critique of Ephraim can therefore be read not merely as a critique of Israel's political "promiscuity" or cultic idolatry, nor as the former leading to the latter, but ultimately as an indictment against Israel for adulterating its covenant identity before Yahweh, for worshipping "the projection of its own national ego into the world of the divine."[83] As Levenson compellingly asserts,

> In covenant theology, Sinai serves as an eternal rebuke to man's arrogant belief that he can govern himself. The state is not coeval with God. Rather, it was born at a particular moment in history and under the judgment of a disappointed God. In a better world, one in which man turns to God with all his heart, it would not exist . . . For the theological tradition maintained that Israel had been a people before she was a worldly kingdom, a people to whom laws and even a destiny had already been given. She owes neither to the state.[84]

By forgetting Yahweh as deliverer and provider, protector and king, Israel seeks to secure itself by the same means as the rest of the nations before whom Israel is supposed to be embodying Yahweh's transformative kingdom, and to whom Israel is supposed to be mediating Yahweh's

---

82. Pentiuc, *Long-Suffering Love*, 108.

83. Lind, "Hosea 5:8—6:6," 400. Lind's line here is a neat encapsulation of the theme of this entire project.

84. Levenson, *Sinai and Zion*, 74.

grace—and these, in the ultimate hope that the nations will join Israel in submission to Yahweh's reign.

Not only are religion and politics melded together as one phenomenon, but they act as one in the formation—or deformation—of Israel's identity. Identity is a continuous phenomenon, wherein theopolitical practices do not merely reflect, but constitute it. Of course, for Israel, it is *both* a "founding act" (Yahweh's act of election) *and* a "regulated process of repetition" (Israel's realization of election in Torah) that contribute cooperatively to identity. The point remains, however, that stability of identity is directly related to stability of practice. Note the significant shift in Hosea 8:8, the change in Ephraim's very identity. The northern kingdom is no longer part of the special possession of Exodus 19:5, put aside by Yahweh for special purpose, but is now "useless." Rather than being understood as merely "ineffective," this can be read as a sort of anti-election, albeit temporary; it is a judgment that the northern kingdom is at this moment, and of its own volition, completely *other* than the community Yahweh established at Sinai. If this seems too strong an interpretation, consider the progression of names of Hosea's children conceived with Gomer (1:4–8). The first is Jezreel, named after the location of a bloody coup d'état under Jehu and undoubtedly condemning the political violence rampant in the north, as well as foreshadowing the site of Yahweh's impending judgment. The second is named "Lo-ruhamah," or "not loved," for Yahweh will "no longer have pity on the house of Israel or forgive them."[85] The third child, whose name is the culmination of this movement toward Ephraim's condemnation, is named "Lo-ammi," or "No-kin-of-mine," for "you are not my people and I am not your God." It is clear that covenant with the northern kingdom is no longer in force, as it has been broken by Ephraim's own theopolitical practices and then officially annulled by the covenant suzerain. That said, hope remains, for the people will not forever be estranged from their Lord (1:10).

---

85. This statement is in contrast to Yahweh's next, namely that he will have pity on the southern kingdom of Judah, and save it. Yet, it is significant that Yahweh rejects in 1:7 the use of typical military means to achieve Judah's salvation; instead, "I will save them by the Lord their God."

Covenant and Identity in the Prophets: Jeremiah and Civil Religion

A century later, the prophet Jeremiah is commissioned to declare Yahweh's judgment over the southern kingdom of Judah, which during his career increasingly succumbed to the same tendencies as its former northern counterpart. What we find in Jeremiah is a critique of *realpolitik* similar to that of Hosea, but specifically over against a particular understanding of the Davidic covenant that adulterates Judah's theopolitical identity in covenant with Yahweh. Examining Jeremiah in this manner sheds light on the significance of the theological-political symbiosis in Israel, and within that, the particular element of national story. The discussion must begin, however, by discussing the Davidic covenant itself.

In 2 Samuel 7, King David, sitting back after achieving a measure of stability and contentedness, notices the disparity between his own residence and that of the ark of the covenant, the seat of Yahweh. He proposes to build a more prestigious structure for Yahweh, but Yahweh intervenes, reminding David through the prophet Nathan that he (Yahweh) has never requested such a structure, that he has freely moved about with his people (7:1–7). The reader senses a resistance on Yahweh's part to any move that would attempt to make Yahweh's presence static, to anchor or constrain him amongst his people and in the world. Note also that Yahweh's desired tent dwelling does not prompt David to question the luxury of his own accommodations; the latter is merely assumed as appropriate, by which David then evaluates the former. But in a move that reverses the initiative and surprises both David and the reader, Yahweh tells David that *he* will make *David's* name great, and shall provide a permanent place for Israel. Moreover, with a metaphorical twist, Yahweh will establish David's "house," with particular attention to David's offspring, upon whom Yahweh will bestow attentive care and "steadfast love" (*hesed*, covenant faithfulness). In short, "your house and your kingdom shall be made sure forever before me; your throne shall be established forever" (7:12–16). In this passage, there is no mention of conditionality upon Yahweh's promise; permanence, not contingency, is the theme. Note also that nothing is mentioned of David having earned this "house" by his previous behavior. This is simply a gracious act of Yahweh's own initiative, for the sake of the people of Israel (7:10–11), interpreted later in the Christian tradition to be preparation for the Messiah, rather than glorification of David. We find an almost identical telling of the story in 1 Chronicles 17. David then charges Solomon to build the temple, and makes preparations since Solomon is still young (1 Chr 22).[86]

Eventually, Solomon builds the grand temple and proceeds to dedicate it. Of great interest, however, is the discourse of that dedication, in which Solomon alludes to Yahweh's promise to David, "There shall never fail you a successor before me to sit on the throne of Israel," but with the caveat, "if only your children look to their way, to walk before me as you have walked before me" (1 Kgs 8:25; 2 Chr 6:16). The seemingly unconditional covenant with David has been, within a generation, conditioned by his "children's" covenant faithfulness. Whether "children" refers to royal heirs or to the whole people, it is clear that by Solomon's reign, ongoing allegiance to Yahweh's covenant is understood as necessary for the continuity of the dynasty. Second Chronicles 7 reinforces this qualification. Here, Solomon receives a vision in the night, wherein Yahweh affirms his own covenant *hesed*, reminding Solomon that when he punishes Israel, he will also forgive, "if my people who are called by my name humble themselves, pray, seek my face, and turn from their wicked ways" (7:13–14). Yahweh affirms his consecration of the temple as a permanent dwelling for his presence, and reaffirms his establishment of the Davidic throne, *but only* "if you walk before me, as your father David walked, doing according to all that I have commanded you and keeping my statutes and my ordinances" (7:16–18). Moreover, Yahweh warns, "if you turn aside and forsake my statutes and my commandments that I have set before you, and go and serve other gods and worship them, then I will pluck you up from the land that I have given you; and this house, which I have consecrated for my name, I will cast out of my sight, and will make it a proverb and a byword

---

86. It is interesting, in light of the Davidic covenant passages above, to note David's remark to his son regarding his own desire to build the temple: "But the word of the Lord came to me saying, 'You have shed much blood and have waged great wars; you shall not build a house to my name, because you have shed so much blood in my sight on the earth'" (22:8). In this confession of a father to his son, we see Yahweh's displeasure at the violence inherent in the centralizing state. Equally interesting is Solomon's own explanation to Hiram of Tyre when ordering cedar from Lebanon: "You know that my father David could not build a house for the name of the Lord his God because of the warfare with which his enemies surrounded him, until the Lord put them under the soles of his feet" (1 Kgs 5:3). Not only does this directly contradict 2 Samuel 7:1, where *prior to* entertaining the notion of a temple, David "was settled in his house, and the Lord had given him rest from all his enemies around him," but it more significantly puts the onus for the violence upon David's enemies rather than himself.

among the peoples" (7:19–20). When passersby ask why Yahweh has destroyed his own temple and the land of Israel, "they will say, 'Because they abandoned the Lord the God of their ancestors who brought them out of the land of Egypt, and they adopted other gods, and worshiped them and served them; therefore he has brought all this calamity upon them'" (7:22)—in short, because Israel has forsaken covenant.

What sense do we make of this in conjunction with the promise to David? Certainly, it is possible for the Solomonic caveats to be later insertions into the texts by redactors concerned to explain the exile and to justify a renewed sensitivity to Torah. However, that would beg the question of why the insertion was made only later in the narrative (1 Kgs 8; 2 Chr 7) and not in the original, most problematic passages (2 Sam 7; 1 Chr 17). Surely, if a redactor is motivated by such profound concerns and is bold enough to change the text in this dramatic a fashion, he would go right to the source of the problem and adjust the original pronouncement; but the earlier passages are left alone. Therefore, I believe it more reasonable, exegetically and theologically, to read the narrative to say that within a generation—if not from the beginning and simply taken for granted—an understanding existed with divine confirmation that the continuation of the Davidic throne was contingent upon the continued obedience of Israel. Yahweh will, as promised, hold faithful to his own covenant obligations, and will even allow Israel to be restored with proper repentance; but the heirs of the covenant must abide by their own obligations for the covenant to remain active. Thus, the Davidic covenant is firmly situated within the expectations of the Sinaitic, where Yahweh's election is always open to Israel, but must be realized in Israel's own covenant faithfulness.

Jeremiah grapples with such contested interpretations of the Davidic covenant to the point of great personal suffering, as is well known. Of course, Jeremiah's career might not have been expected to go in the dismal direction it did, as it began in the midst of a major project of reform initiated in 625 under the auspices of King Josiah. It was during the various stages of reform, which included the purging of the Assyrian cult from Judean territory (2 Kgs 22:1–7; 2 Chr 34:3–8), that the temple in Jerusalem was being refurbished and a copy of the book of the law was found (2 Kgs 22:8ff.; 2 Chr 34:14ff.). As the narrative relates, Josiah and the people of Judah repented upon hearing the words of Torah, and pledged themselves to further measures for purification, "for great is the wrath of the Lord that is kindled against us, because our ancestors did not obey the words of this book, to do according to all that is written concerning us" (2 Kgs 22:13; 2 Chr 34:21).

The work of John Bright is very helpful in relating the theopolitical backdrop of Jeremiah's ministry. By the mid-to-late seventh century, Assyria's power was on the wane, and the kingdom of Judah saw an opportunity to finally reassert its independence. The Josian reforms, while no doubt aimed at correcting genuine problems in cult and politics, were likely motivated in part by nationalist desires to reassert Judean autonomy over against a weakening imperial rule.[87] Bright notes "oscillation between syncretism and reform coincident with shifts in the national policy" over time, with Josiah reversing Manasseh just as Hezekiah had Ahaz. And since any Assyrian-initiated cult would have symbolized "national humiliation," a nationalist independence movement would certainly have moved to eradicate its elements. Josiah's incorporation of former territories of Ephraim would likewise have contributed to the twofold vision of a free Israel united under the Davidic throne in Jerusalem. Additionally, this process occurred during a period of considerable tension and unease in the ancient Near East as the great empires of the era were dissolving: "Side by side with the excitement of newly found independence, and the optimism implicit in the official dynastic theology, there walked a profound unease, a premonition of judgment, together with the feeling . . . that the nation's security lay in a return to ancient tradition."[88]

Within this context, "the Deuteronomic law fell like the thunderclap of conscience." The finding of the Book of the Law catalyzed this reform program like nothing else could, and though found while reform

---

87. Bright, *History of Israel*, 319. The first part of 2 Chronicles 34 tells of some of Josiah's measures, including a campaign throughout Judah and in the lands of Manasseh and Ephraim in the north to destroy remnants of the Assyrian cultic system. This included the taking up of funds for the refurbishment of the temple in Jerusalem, money acquired in part "from all the remnant of Israel" (34:9). Clearly, Josiah's reforms aimed at reconsolidating the kingdom of Israel, concentrating on the royal court and temple in Jerusalem.

88. Bright, 320. There is no need to appropriate this statement by Bright in a merely sociological sense. It is consistent with the theological schema of covenant as well, though the faith in "official dynastic theology," as we will see, is misplaced, and notions of "security" require redefinition. Certainly insecurity and listlessness would have been expected after a long period of disregard for Torah, and a return to covenant would be viewed as necessary.

was already in progress, arguably provided its core motivation. In this context, the Law would have been understood to say that "the nation's very life depended upon a return to the covenant relationship in which the national existence had originally been based," and until then, it was "living in a fool's paradise in assuming that Yahweh through his promises to David was irrevocably committed to its defense." Reform, on the other hand, "called the people back behind the official theology of the Davidic covenant to an older notion of covenant, and committed nation and people to obedience to its stipulations."[89] For his acts of faithfulness, Josiah is informed that while judgment upon Judah is now inevitable, he will himself be spared the experience (2 Chr 34:23–28).

It is within this context that Jeremiah arises as prophet, one who "stood in a yet older tradition reaching back through Hosea to the Mosaic covenant itself."[90] While Jeremiah undoubtedly supported Josiah's measures of reform and purification, Bright suspects that this support likely waned as the measures became institutionalized, for in that process a priestly monopoly along with the attendant temple bureaucracy was established in Jerusalem. This likely contributed to a certain "secularization" of other aspects of society, "a separation of cultic and common life never known before." Moreover, the reforms tended toward external measures over against more "spiritual" ones, creating "a false sense of peace that nothing could penetrate."[91] Bright's conclusion regarding the reform proves telling for our own discussion:

> The very reform law that imparted a note of moral and religious responsibility to the national theology fortified that bogus sense of security against which Jeremiah battled in vain. Since the law demanded reform as the price of national security, the popular mind supposed that by making that reform Yahweh's demands had been satisfied (chs. 6:13f.; 8:10f.). The Mosaic covenant, its demands supposedly met, became the handmaid of the Davidic covenant, guaranteeing the permanence of Temple, dynasty, and state. The theology of the law had, indeed, been made into a caricature of itself: automatic protection bought by external compliance."[92]

---

89. Ibid., 321–22.
90. Ibid., 321.
91. Ibid., 323.
92. Ibid.

Ultimately, under the reign of Jehoiakim, reform collapses altogether. Whether it was simply a lack of attention, or whether Josiah's death and subsequent national humiliation galvanized opposition to and resentment of Deuteronomic covenant, "pagan practices crept back ... and public morality deteriorated." Those who spoke out against this deterioration were met with scorn, persecution, and even death. Thus, as Bright suggests, "one senses that the official theology with its immutable promises had triumphed in its most distorted form, and that the people were entrenched in the confidence that Temple, city, and nation were eternally secure in Yahweh's covenant with David—for so prophet and priest assured them . . ."[93]

It is against this larger backdrop that Jeremiah conducts his long and dramatic prophetic ministry in Judah. At the outset of the book, Yahweh appoints Jeremiah "over nations and over kingdoms, to pluck up and to pull down, to destroy and to overthrow, to build and to plant" (Jer 1:10). This commission is significant even at first blush because it suggests that the prophecy to follow is going to be global in character, with direct implications for international politics of the day. Moreover, Yahweh is clearly claiming international sovereignty, the singular authority to control the fates of kingdoms, and to appoint a prophet as mediator of that authority. What is also clear, though, is that in claiming such sovereignty, Yahweh is through Jeremiah directly repudiating his reduction to state god in the days of the early monarchy. This God is not in service to the state, but rather is Lord of the nations, and he has appointed a spokesperson to proclaim his world sovereignty in the face of a people who would not.

Similarly to Hosea in Israel, Yahweh makes clear through Jeremiah his displeasure with Judah's *realpolitik* of foreign alliances. Yahweh complains, "They did not say, 'Where is the Lord who brought us up from the land of Egypt?'" He then asks, "Has a nation changed its gods, even though they are no gods? But my people have changed their glory for something that does not profit. Be appalled, O heavens, at this, be shocked, be utterly desolate, says the Lord, for my people have committed two evils: they have forsaken me, the fountain of living water, and dug out cisterns for themselves, cracked cisterns that can hold no water" (Jer 2:11–13). These complaints are noteworthy for their covenant allusions, namely to the historical prologue (Exod 20:2a; Deut 5:6a) and

---

93. Ibid., 326.

to the covenant witness of the heavens (Deut 30:19; 31:28). Yahweh asks specifically why Judah has appealed to Assyria or Egypt for help (Jer 2:18), as opposed to the suzerain who has already proved himself, namely, Yahweh. Jeremiah seems to specifically target the ruling elite in Judah, warning them that on the day of the Lords' judgment, "courage shall fail the king and the officials; the priests shall be appalled and the prophets astounded" (4:9). Like Ephraim before it, the leadership of Judah has committed theopolitical apostasy, and judgment is imminent.

With such a fate in view, Jeremiah 27 relates that a number of foreign dignitaries gather in the court of Zedekiah to devise a common strategy against Babylon. In the midst of this summit, Jeremiah declares that they are all to submit to Babylon, according to the word of the sovereign Yahweh, and that any prophet or other official proclaiming that their god—even Yahweh—will save them is a liar, a false prophet (Jer 27:8–10). As Pixley writes,

> This is a truly remarkable historico-theological assessment of the geopolitical situation of that time. It can only be understood when we realize the royal theology that Jeremiah meant to undercut. This theology claimed that God had an eternal commitment to David and to the Jerusalem temple, God's resting place, and that its security was assured, regardless of greater geopolitical developments. Jeremiah's ministry was devoted to destroying that false security, a security based on a theology that was not faithful to the Torah . . .[94]

Two elements of Pixley's observation are particularly interesting. First, he underscores the very different and even competing views of Israel's national identity at play. One view, rooted in a distorted understanding of the Davidic covenant, confuses the *state* for the *covenant community* of Israel as Yahweh's vassal. Its propagators, operating out of their own institutional interests, attempt to secure themselves through a theology that conforms to their political practice and that ensures their survival. Jeremiah resists this vehemently, and his sharp response later in chapter 46 to notions of allying with Egypt illustrate his confidence in Yahweh's word. This alternative empire, in whom the small kingdoms of Palestine consider placing their trust, is no match for Babylon as Yahweh's instrument of judgment: even as Egypt projects its power against an imperial competitor, it meets a grim fate in the day of the

---

94. Pixley, *Jeremiah*, 87.

Lord's judgment (46:3–12). The Judeans are not to listen to those prophets who proclaim otherwise.[95]

Jeremiah's view is rooted in the Sinaitic covenant, and his is a "theology of uncompromising Torah loyalty."[96] Of course, in fulfilling his prophetic vocation, he becomes "a traitor to his nation at a grave moment of national crisis,"[97] or more precisely, Jeremiah has subverted one national identity in favor of another, more fundamental one. Opposed to him are all the kings, prophets, priests, and others who "believe that God crowns the Judean king and is loyal to him [notice the direction of this loyalty], elects Jerusalem as a resting place and will defend it, and chooses a people and protects them in the land given to their ancestors."[98] Here, a national identity rooted in the claim of divine mandate for humanly constructed political institutions is cast aside by Jeremiah for the sake of a covenant identity rooted in Yahweh and his sovereignty.

The second intriguing element in Pixley's quote is the emphasis on security, especially security based on false theology. Arguably, the theology Jeremiah resists is not simply the Davidic covenant and the promise of the house of David restored,[99] but rather the notion that Yahweh would somehow bless the *realpolitik* of the nations as practiced within and by the nation of Israel. As Hosea made clear for Ephraim, kingship and alliances, state centralization, and the foreign policy of state interests all contradict Yahweh's intent for Israel to be a nation mediating his grace to the world. Recall Lohfink's description of ancient Near East national deities, those "earthly forces and powers that represented ultimate realities for human beings," and particularly human powers and powers that shaped history: "knowledge, domination, violence, money, rivalry, war, life, death."[100] To this list we may add security, which became the ultimate reality for Israel, in both the North and the South. Security drove the people to demand a king of Samuel. Security, both national and personal, prompted David to centralize the state and es-

95. Huwyler, "Jeremia und der Volker."
96. Pixley, *Jeremiah*, 83.
97. Ibid., 12.
98. Ibid., 83.

99. This is not to mention that any concept of "restoration" would be foreign to the establishment interpretation since it conceived of the *actualization* of the Davidic promise as enduring and unable to be broken.

100. Lohfink, *Does God Need the Church?*, 2.

tablish a professional army, Solomon to expand the empire and institute slavery, Rehoboam to maintain conditions of servitude, Jeroboam to set up calves at Dan and Bethel, and the subsequent dynasties to take land, oppress the poor, kill the innocent and the prophets, enter into myriad foreign alliances, and seek alternate suzerains. Security was the god of the northern and southern states, of their civil religions, and thus of their national identities; and though they may name that god Yahweh, declares Jeremiah, the Yahweh of the covenant will not bless them, but will bring an end to their apostasy.

If this assessment is correct, then what we find advocated by Jeremiah and other prophets is an alternate notion of national identity to that held by the monarchy and ruling elite. The latter portrays the Davidic covenant as an unqualified guarantee of state survival, such that no threat can be seen as a potential act of discipline or judgment, but rather can be resisted according to the means and methods inherent in the monarchical institutions Yahweh has ostensibly sanctioned. This, according to Redditt, ultimately constitutes Israel's "civil religion," revolving around a "national story," the height of which is the monarchy, and Yahweh is the ever-forgiving god who endorses it.[101] Note that this story is an amalgam: an interweaving of certain aspects of Israel's covenant narrative, selectively sifted and reinterpreted, with a national narrative of Yahweh blessing and securing the monarchical state. In some ways, it is a departure from the Josian understanding that prompted repentance in his day; but it is also consistent with the Josian emphasis on centralization of power as key to continuity. In short, the existence and success of the monarchy is the central element of national identity. On the other hand, Hosea, Jeremiah, and other prophets represent an earlier, covenantal view of Israel's national identity. According to this view, the monarchical state is an inherently corrupt institution, its existence and practices inevitably constituting an adulteration of covenant. Their prophetic critiques aim in part to galvanize the leaders and people toward recapturing the previous period of covenant *hesed*, and the judgments they prophesy are part of that revitalization process.[102]

101. Redditt, "When Faith Demands Treason," 231.

102. O'Donovan argues that only at the point of Jehoiachin's reign, immediately preceding the exile under King Zedekiah, has the prophetic office essentially "taken over the mediatorial role, a sign that the monarchy, which was to mediate Yhwh's rule to his people, has been set aside" (*Desire of the Nations*, 77). Later, in his discussion of the convergence of mediatorial and representative roles in Christ, he identifies the pro-

These competing views are manifested throughout the prophetic critiques, but especially in pericopes relating confrontation between the prophets and representatives of the ruling establishment. As Jeremiah declares early in the text, the nation has been corrupted, as "the prophets prophesy falsely, and the priests rule as the prophets direct; my people love to have it so"; for this reason, Yahweh will bring retribution (5:29–31). In chapter 6, where Yahweh complains that "from the least to the greatest of them, everyone is greedy for unjust gain; and from prophet to priest, everyone deals falsely." These leaders have taken seriously neither the sin nor the suffering of the people, "saying 'Peace, peace,' when there is no peace." Consequently, they will not be spared in the coming judgment, for "they acted shamefully, they committed abomination; yet they were not ashamed, they did not know how to blush" (6:13–15).

Along these lines, we see in Jeremiah 28 an encounter between Jeremiah and another prophet, Hananiah, who addresses Jeremiah in the midst of the latter's proclaiming Judah's fate via visual demonstration. Hananiah publicly contradicts Jeremiah's message with a proclamation of assurance: Yahweh will "break the yoke of King Nebuchadnezzar of Babylon from the neck of all the nations within two years" (28:11). Hananiah then removes the yoke Jeremiah has been wearing, thereby symbolizing Yahweh's rejection of Jeremiah's message. As Redditt writes, the audience was now confronted with two diametrically opposed visions of the nation's future: "Whom should they believe? It would be easier to believe Hananiah, because his version suited the belief that God would defend God's people and return them to God's land and God's temple."[103] While Jeremiah agrees that Hananiah's word would be good news if actually borne out, he ultimately returns to Hananiah with a word of judgment: "the Lord has not sent you, and you made this people trust in a lie." For this transgression, Hananiah will die within the year (28:15–16).[104]

---

phetic role as "representative individual" who dramatized "the tradition of the isolated sufferers in Israel's liturgy," over against the "Davidide monarch" as "mediator of God's rule" (123). However, given the account I have presented, it is more reasonable to understand the prophet as the proper mediator of Yahweh's rule all along, a role necessitated once that rule had been usurped (albeit with Yahweh's reluctant acquiescence) by the monarchy.

103. Redditt, "When Faith Demands Treason," 238–39.
104. Cf. a similar scene of competing theopolitical narratives in Amos 7:10–17.

This confrontation helps illustrate the opposed viewpoints of Yahweh's "outsider" prophets versus priests and prophets in the employ of the state. For the monarchical understanding of national identity, it is inconceivable that Yahweh would allow, not just the nation but the state to fall. For the covenant view, nothing is unimaginable given the sovereignty of Yahweh; his word is to be obeyed. The survival of Yahweh's plan in and for the people of Israel is simply not synonymous with the survival of the state.

Moreover, it is interesting to note how the people's relationship with Yahweh is conceived within these opposing viewpoints. In the first, it is not simply the covenant nation of Israel, but the *state* of Judah that is elected and blessed by Yahweh. The monarchy's politics, both its internal political ordering and its foreign policy, are assumed to be sanctioned by Yahweh for the expansion of the state, since the state itself is the manifestation of Yahweh's blessings and intent for Israel. Here, Yahweh is again god of the state, the securer of the state's survival, or more precisely, the divine underwriter of the state's own pursuit of security. In the second, Yahweh's name is not to be taken in vain, as it was with Hananiah. Yahweh is Lord of all the nations, and it is a manifestation of Yahweh's sovereignty as well as his compassion that the nation of Israel is chosen to mediate grace to the world. To reiterate Lohfink's helpful point: "Israel's being chosen is not a privilege or a preference *over others*, but existence *for others*, and hence the heaviest burden in history."[105] The exigencies of state survival preclude other-oriented existence, undermining Israel's calling; hence the judgment. Yahweh knows the world simply cannot afford the continuation of an Israelite state, whether united or divided, for that is not what it means to be the people of God.

Prophetic Promise

Yet even in the face of certain judgment, the prophets do envision a "future with hope" (Jer 29:11) in which a new nation is complete, in perfect obedience to covenant. Amos foresees a day when Yahweh will "raise up the booth of David that is fallen, and repair its breaches, and raise up its ruins and rebuild it as in the days of old," when he will "restore the fortunes of my people Israel" (Amos 9:11, 14a). Hosea promises that

---

105. Lohfink, *Does God Need the Church?*, 37.

upon Israel's return to the Lord, Yahweh will "heal their disloyalty" and "love them freely"; he will be the "dew" that nurtures Israel to again "blossom like the lily." In that day, "they shall again live beneath my shadow, they shall flourish as a garden" (Hos 14:1–7). The severing of covenant is undone in Yahweh's mercy, when Hosea's children will be renamed Ruhama, "shown mercy," and Ammi, "my people" (21:1, 23). Indeed, exile has been described as a new stage for Israel's mission to the world (Jer 29), in which by contrast with the centralized monarchy and its distorted national identity, Jews would live in diaspora, amongst the nations as dispersed and sent out witnesses. Here, Torah would became more central than it ever had been for them when they enjoyed the land, becoming in certain ways written on their hearts as Jeremiah suggests (Jer 31:33–34).[106]

And of course, there are Isaiah's prophesies of a restored Jerusalem with a glorious future (Isa 2:2–5; 4:2–6; 26:1–4), as well as a future creation-wide kingdom of peace under the rule of an heir to the Davidic throne (9:1–7; 11:1–9). This leads to Waldemar Janzen's discussion of the Suffering Servant in Isaiah. According to Janzen, Isaiah's first Servant Song in 42:1–9 portrays the elect people of Israel as God's servant, who by the power of the Spirit will bring justice to the nations awaiting Torah. However, Israel fails in this mission, and in the second Servant Song of Isaiah 49, a new servant is chosen, one who, as an individual elect of God, will shoulder Israel's calling. Here, the task is not transferred away from Israel to this person, but rather Israel is *incarnated* in this person who will fulfill its divine mandate. This person will simultaneously restore Israel and accomplish Israel's mission of being a light to the nations.[107]

In the final Servant Song of Isaiah 52:13–53:12, this servant is described further. The servant will experience suffering but will be exalted before the world (52:13–15). This one, supposedly struck down by God, is now viewed differently. He is seen as innocent, bearing the sins of the people Israel for their own salvation, and is therefore exalted, a truth to which the people witness and confess. This person "shoulders the calling of Israel and extends this calling to address both the nations and his

---

106. I am indebted to Doug Harink for this reminder (Douglas Harink, e-mail message to author, April 7, 2011). See also his discussion of this in Harink, *1 & 2 Peter*, 35–36.

107. Janzen, "Suffering Servants," 22.

own renegade people." This servant has suffered at their hands, but at the same time suffers vicariously for their sins. Thus "God's new move" is to not ultimately reject the people of Israel despite their sundering of covenant, but rather "'reducing God's expectation' of Israel to the obedience of *one* person and accepting it as vicarious for the people."[108] The onus for the fullfilment of election and covenant is placed upon this one person, who will not fail. The people can therefore be comforted even in the midst and aftermath of judgment. Now the discussion of election and covenant is further nuanced: Yahweh's faithfulness, never in doubt, is extended in grace to include the restoration of the covenant vassal. This is not Yahweh's obligation under covenant, since the covenant was conditioned upon Israel's faithfulness. Rather, Yahweh acts outside of covenant for Israel's sake. This is an initiative of Yahweh's freedom and grace, to overcome Israel's failure to realize its own election by incarnating Israel in a Servant who will suffer on its behalf and thereby definitively fulfill Israel's identity and mission.

Conclusion

This chapter has had the very important purpose of laying out the theopolitics of biblical Israel as normative for the church, whose relation to it will be made clear in the next chapter. Here, I have explained the significance of Israel's election and covenant, which were given by Yahweh to Israel for the express purpose of embodying a theopolitics in the midst of the nations that would be a visible sign of God's reign, and thus of God's salvation, inviting the nations to join Israel in submission to and praise of that reign. I also delineated the ways in which Israel gradually syncretized its divinely ordained theopolitics with the politics of the nations and of empire, and how that syncretism led necessarily to an abandonment of covenant. I also pointed out that in freedom and grace, Yahweh did not likewise abandon Israel but promised through the prophets to restore the singular people to its election-and-covenant identity. How Yahweh accomplishes this is the subject of the next chapter.

---

108. Ibid., 23–24. According to Janzen, the historical identity of this person is deliberately kept hidden, so that "the emphasis falls fully on the servant-role, a role marked not only by proclamation in words, but by suffering unto death."

What is important here is to note that nationalist appropriations of Israel as the forebear of the current nation are off base from the start, given that Israel's identity is theopolitically unique and constituted in contrast with the world's political systems. Moreover, given that nationalism essentially entails the acquirement of power and the securing of its identity in political institutions—often through the use of violence—its necessary *realpolitik* cannot be made continuous with biblical Israel properly understood. Thus, any nationalist narrative presenting the present nation and/or state as rooted in Israel—whether the historical examples from the previous chapter or the contemporary examples discussed in chapters 6 and 7—must be considered false. Israel cannot be appropriated in this fashion. Rather, continuity works in the other direction: a people must be engrafted onto Israel. And as will be made clear in the next chapter, the only people so engrafted is the church. This is only made more clear in light of the incarnation of Israel in Jesus Christ, Christ's definitive fulfillment of Israel's election and covenant, and the church as the theopolitical embodiment of that fulfillment. The next chapter will therefore demonstrate how the biblical theopolitics of Israel, and then of the church, is critical for discerning nationalism as a problem for ecclesial identity and practice and for correcting it.

CHAPTER 5

New Testament Messianic Theopolitics

INTRODUCTION

The previous chapter presented a theopolitical understanding of Israel's identity and mission as constituted in its election by Yahweh and the outworking of that election in covenant. It argued that Israel was called to be a singular theopolitical community, an embodied witness to God's reign on earth, a vision of what the world would look like under that reign. The chapter also narrated how Israel gradually abandoned that vocation by breaking covenant in various ways, was subsequently indicted by the prophets for doing so, and was judged accordingly. It also indicated, however, that even the most strident prophetic indictment was not without the hope that Yahweh may act, in spite of covenant stipulations, to restore Israel by fulfilling Israel's vocation vicariously. That vicarious fulfillment of Israel's election and covenant in Jesus the Messiah is the subject of this chapter, as is the church's call to embody that fulfillment in the world. By relating these core elements of the New Testament salvation narrative, I hope to demonstrate that it is the church that is uniquely engrafted onto Israel's identity and mission, such that no state and no other nation can be considered divinely chosen to this end.

This chapter picks up where the previous one left off, namely with the promised definitive fulfillment of covenant in the one, chosen

Suffering Servant. The Christian tradition understands this servant to be Jesus of Nazareth, who brings to Israel—and then to the nations—a "new covenant" that will not fail. Jesus is the Messiah, the Christ, the one anointed as king of Israel who will be for Israel the "Way" toward finally realizing its election. In this manner, Christ proclaims a social order fulfilling and transcending Torah, inviting the world to come into the kingdom of God. Christ, in his lordship, establishes the church to embody the covenant as he has fulfilled it. This ties the church uniquely and inextricably to Israel—thereby making Israel's theopolitics relevant to the ecclesia—and inaugurates the messianic age wherein the kingdom of God is present alongside the passing age of the powers, and wherein the church awaits the day of that kingdom's final consummation.

Covenant in Jesus Christ

The incarnation of the second person of the Trinity in Jesus Christ, his life and ministry, his crucifixion and resurrection, and finally his exaltation, constitute the central point and pivot of Christian salvation history, and the perfect embodiment of God's reign on earth. In Christ, covenant is restored and a people he calls his own is given identity as the definitive political community in the world. What is the nature of the "new covenant" Christ brings? In what ways is it derived from the Mosaic covenant and yet different, and *why* is it different? How does it affect the direct relationship between God's sovereignty and the political identity of the people of God? This section will attempt to answer these questions, with the goal of demonstrating that the covenant with Israel has not changed in its intent and effect, but has been secured in and through Christ, and extended to all the people of the world. Through Jesus, a theopolitical community is established in the form of the ecclesia, whose purpose, like Israel's, is to proclaim and embody God's reign on earth.

The "New Covenant"

In Old Testament prophecy as well as New Testament gospels and epistles, the reader is told that there will be a covenant between God and humanity, even after Israel has failed to uphold the one made at Sinai.[1] We

---

1. See Jeremiah 31:31; Matthew 26:28; Mark 14:24; Luke 22:20; Hebrews 8.

find in Jeremiah 31 that the nation of Israel (represented by Judah) had come to a point of no return in its rebellion against Yahweh and Torah, and had refused to repent and receive Yahweh's forgiveness. Therefore, writes Scott Hafemann, "what is needed . . . is nothing less than a new beginning, a 'new covenant,' in which Israel will be decisively changed in her relationship to God."[2]

But what is the nature of this new covenant? How does it differ from the "old" covenant? Hafemann points to the contrast made between the two by the prophet Jeremiah as read in 31:32, wherein "the essential difference between the new covenant and the Sinai covenant is not that a new *type* of covenant or a new *content* within the covenant will be established, but that the new covenant will not be broken like the previous one, in spite of the fact that under the Sinai covenant God was faithful to his covenant commitments . . ." The new covenant is therefore one that will not be forgotten.[3] In the new covenant, according to Jer 31:33–34, God will place his law in the minds and hearts of the people of Israel, who, from the greatest to the least, will know the Lord. The law—the Torah—will be "inculcated by God within the heart of the people," resulting in continuous faithfulness and fellowship with Yahweh. This "law" is "the Sinai Law itself as the embodiment of the will of God." What distinguishes the new covenant from the old is that the people, given transformed natures, will be able to obey the Torah: "the contrast between the two covenants is a contrast between the two different *conditions of the people* who are brought into these covenants and their correspondingly different responses to the *same Law*."[4] Jesus, as the fulfillment of the law (Matt 5:17), is the perfect embodiment of Torah, and through the Spirit, will enable believers to embody it as well. The people will know the Lord directly and personally (which is not to say merely individually); because their hearts are transformed, they will be able to maintain covenant.[5]

Lohfink provides a helpful note of caution here, reminding the reader to not dichotomize the Old Testament and the New. It is a mistake, he argues, to think the New Testament is about new inner spirituality or about love in contrast to wrath and punishment in the Old

---

2. Hafemann, *Paul, Moses and Israel*, 129–30.
3. Ibid., 130, in reference to Jeremiah 50:5.
4. Ibid., 132–33.
5. See Lohfink, *Does God Need the Church?*, 122–23.

Testament. It is also a mistake to think the New Testament is about the individual as opposed to the "collective" in the Old Testament. In fact, the Old discusses individual responsibility, and the New emphasizes the people of God: "Of course the people of God in the Bible are more than a 'theme.' This idea is the basis, the ground of all biblical theology in both the Old and New Testaments." Indeed, as Hans Urs von Balthasar comments, "Christ did not annul everything in the Old Testament that depended on law and on form; rather, his achievement was to make these things transparent to the light of love and to live them as the expression of the Old Testament's covenant-fidelity (*fides* in the fullest sense), now brought to perfection."[6] How, then, did this definitive fulfillment take place?

Jesus as Messiah

Christian theology, as formed by the gospels and epistles of the New Testament, holds that Jesus of Nazareth is the Messiah foretold in the prophetic promises of the Old Testament, the Suffering Servant of Isaiah, the one definitively to hold David's throne. Jesus is presented in the royal line as heir to David (Matt 1:1–17). At the moment of Jesus' birth, a celestial announcement is made to the shepherds in the fields nearby that this child is to be the Messiah (Christ), Savior, and Lord (Luke 2). Through various events of his own life, Jesus recapitulates the story of Israel. Matthew 1–4 tells how he goes to Egypt to escape death in Palestine, as Jacob's family did. He is then brought back up from Egypt as Israel was delivered from slavery. After a time, he is baptized in the Jordan, reminiscent of the Israelites' crossing of the Red Sea, and then he proceeds immediately into a forty-day period of testing in the wilderness, as Israel did for forty years. During this testing, as John Howard Yoder explains, Jesus is presented with multiple ways of being king,[7] reminiscent of the many ways in which Israel was tempted to the practices of domestic and international *realpolitik* in order to secure its position vis-à-vis its neighbors. Where Israel succumbed to temptation, Jesus does not, and as the incarnation of Israel successfully fulfills covenant in this regard. Jesus' fulfillment is extended in the Sermon on

---

6. Balthasar, *Glory of the Lord*, 218.
7. Yoder, *Politics of Jesus*, 24–27.

the Mount, among other places, where he declares unequivocally that he has come to fulfill Torah (Matt 5–7, esp. 5:17).

Jesus Christ is the "Way" by which the new covenant can be fulfilled. Lohfink explains that in Jesus, Israel is gathered together; he represents Israel as a whole, even echoing Israel's historical experience.[8] Instead of having the people of Israel go into the wilderness again, Jesus goes himself, but then returns and enters into their towns and homes, into the context of their daily lives.[9] Lohfink pairs up Mark 1:15 with Isaiah 52:7 in order to show what is happening in and through Jesus. In the former passage, Mark prefaces his entire Gospel with Jesus' statement, "'The time is fulfilled, and the kingdom [*basileia*] of God is at hand; repent and believe in the gospel.'"[10] The "gospel" or "good news" mentioned here refers back to the latter passage in Isaiah, wherein it is an announcement of salvation, encapsulated in the proclamation to Zion, "Your God reigns." This statement, he writes, was probably a confessional formula, as it is found throughout the Old Testament. Its use in Isaiah, however, indicates a new level of meaning, that is, that God's reign is being manifested in the world even now as an act of salvation.

Not only is redemption about the reign of God (a la Dumbrell), but God's reign *is* humanity's redemption. While God's sovereignty had long been celebrated in Israel's worship, the radical new idea is that his reign is "now being proved victorious in history."[11] This irruption of the kingdom of God into the world is not something abstract. The *basileia* is real, material, tangible. These passages declare that in the person of Jesus Christ, the people of God is beginning to be gathered together again, a sign to the world of the reign of God: "With the disciples begins the eschatological re-creation of Israel, and in the re-creation of Israel the reign of God is revealed . . . for Jesus the coming of the *basileia*, that is, the acquisition of a space for the reign of God in the world, was the center of his existence."[12]

A new kingdom has arrived, out of which flows true justice (Mark 1:15; Luke 4). This kingdom is neither fully consummated nor entirely

---

8. Lohfink, *Does God Need the Church?*, 128.

9. Ibid., 129.

10. This statement is paralleled in Luke 4:14–30, wherein Jesus makes the declaration after reading from Isaiah to worshippers in the synagogue at Nazareth.

11. Lohfink, *Does God Need the Church?*, 129.

12. Ibid., 130–31.

future, its nearness defined not so much by chronological imminence as by actual proximity. In Christ, it is present fully, though it remains to be manifested fully throughout the world. The proclamation of this gospel, of course, is a threat to the established orders (Matt 2, 3, 21, 23), who eventually seek Jesus' destruction. Jesus, as the second person of the Trinity having emptied himself (Phil 2; Col 1), does not resist their violence, but absorbs it despite the ever-present nationalist temptation, of which Judas Iscariot is merely the agent.[13] In the narrative of John 18–19, we see Jesus, as both Israel and Yahweh—Yahweh assuming the throne of Israel once again—standing before a people who, goaded on by the Jewish temple and political leadership, declare their allegiance to one king alone: Caesar (19:15). And so Jesus is killed, an enemy of the Roman Empire, but even more so, an enemy of the continuing *realpolitik* cherished by powers even within the Israelite community.

But that is not the end of the story. In utter vindication by the Heavenly Father, Jesus is resurrected from the dead. He had spoken truly. He had practiced truly. He had believed truly. And in definitively fulfilling covenant for the sake of Israel—and thus for the sake of the world—Jesus is exalted by the Father, triumphing over the powers arrayed against him, and putting them in their places for all time (Col 2:8–15). This is the good news he commissions his disciples to tell to the nations in word and in deed, which is largely to say, in communal life (Matt 28:18–10). All authority in the cosmos has been given to Jesus. The kingdom has arrived. True justice has come. Go make disciples to that new reality, conforming the world to its truth.

Jesus and Israel

In addition to Yoder's work mentioned above, Lohfink is again quite helpful for a theopolitical understanding of Jesus Christ's relationship to his people, Israel. As he explains, "Jesus directed his efforts to Israel. He sought to gather it in view of the coming reign of God and to make it into the true people of God. What we now call church is nothing other than the community of those ready to live in the people of God, gathered by Jesus and sanctified by his death." Therefore, "it is very meaningful to ask how Jesus gathered Israel and how he envisioned the community

---

13. Yoder, *Politics of Jesus*, 43.

of the true Israel, because right here we reach the ultimately decisive question of *what the church should look like today*."[14]

The fact that Jesus did not simply institute a school of discipleship, but rather first instituted *twelve* disciples, constitutes for Lohfink a "symbolic prophetic action": "The Twelve exemplified the awakening of Israel and its gathering in the eschatological salvific community, something beginning then through Jesus." This was a sign, something that was already present "in an anticipatory manner" but simultaneously pointing toward a fulfillment in the future, and which even now indicated what was to come.[15] Everything Jesus did, even healing, was directed toward gathering the people of God in Israel from across all their various social, political, economic, and cultural divisions.[16] And it is in God's re-creation of Israel that the kingdom of God arrives. The Gentiles are never precluded from salvation, but Jesus' attention is directed at Israel. The imagery in Scripture—particularly the pilgrimage of the nations—suggests that the Gentiles, "fascinated by the salvation visible in Israel, are driven of their own accord to the people of God." Their belief is not so much the result of missionary activity, but rather "the fascination emitted by the people of God draws them close."[17] While God aims at and provides for the salvation of the nations, "the pagan peoples achieve participation in salvation by achieving participation in Israel."[18]

Yet, this can happen only when Israel becomes such a recognizable sign, "when God's salvation transforms his people recognizably, tangibly, even visibly."[19] Lohfink argues that "people of God" refers to something other than the monarchical national structure, and it is not "equivalent to the state of Israel." Neither is it "merely the spiritual community of the pious." Rather, it is "the Israel which knows itself to be chosen and called by God in its entire existence—which includes all of its social dimension."[20] Consistent with the earlier discussion of elec-

14. Lohfink, *Jesus and Community*, xi.

15. Ibid., 10.

16. Ibid., 11–14.

17. Ibid., 17–19.

18. Ibid., 19. This argues against O'Donovan's attempts to abstract political principles for application elsewhere, as though God's politics can be emulated without participation in God's salvific activity and community.

19. Ibid., 28.

20. Ibid., 122.

tion, Israel is to be a holy people on two grounds: the "electing love of God," and also "whether [Israel] really lives in accordance with the social order which God has given it, a social order which stands in sharp contrast with those of all other nations."[21]

Yet, as the gospels attest, Israel as a whole did not accept Jesus' mission and message, at which point the function of Jesus' Jewish disciples became "the task of representing *symbolically* what really should have taken place in Israel as a whole: complete dedication to the gospel of the reign of God, radical conversion to a new way of life, and a gathering unto a community of brothers and sisters." In the Sermon on the Mount as presented by Matthew, Jesus' demands "presuppose from the perspective of salvation history that Jesus has announced the reign of God and made it present both in word and in mighty deeds on behalf of the afflicted members of God's people." Jesus proclaims the new social order of God's people before the whole of Israel, just as Torah was proclaimed on Sinai, only here it is proclaimed in the context of Jesus' perfect embodiment. What is key for Lohfink is that "the addressee of Jesus' ethical instruction was neither the individual as such nor humanity in general. The addressee of his teaching was Israel, or the circle of disciples which represented Israel."[22] The will of God in Jesus is the arrival of the kingdom and the "gathering of the true Israel." Within this context, "the ones who do the will of God are those who believe Jesus' message of the nearby reign of God and let themselves be gathered into God's eschatological people."[23] This is the renewed people of God, consisting, writes Paul (Gal 3), of the heirs of Abraham, all those who believed as Abraham did and now believe in Christ. According to Lohfink, the task of the church in relation to Israel is to "prefigure eschatological Israel, to represent symbolically what really should have taken place in Israel as a whole." The church "cannot exist without Israel"; it is a branch engrafted onto "the power of the ancient olive tree, Israel (Rom 11:17)." The ecclesia learns from Israel "to recognize both the danger of arrogance on the part of those chosen and the irrevocability of God's electing love."[24]

---

21. Ibid., 123.
22. Ibid., 34–38.
23. Ibid., 43.
24. Ibid., 80–81.

Jesus' ethical teachings in the Sermon on the Mount must therefore be understood in light of the gospel of the coming reign of God.[25] Lohfink argues that "'Jesus' yoke' replaces the Torah; his word, his teaching take the place of the Law of Sinai."[26] It might be more accurate to say that Jesus' teaching *fulfills* the Law of Sinai, or reiterates and fully embodies it according to its original intent, whose obfuscation had been critiqued by the prophets. Nevertheless, within the community according to Matthew, "the place of the Torah is taken by the order of life and of society which is proclaimed by Christ." It is into this new order that the disciples are called to go throughout the world and call the nations (Matt 28:19–20).[27]

What Jesus calls for is tangible in the here and now, even if it is yet to be globally consummated. When Jesus says, "My kingship is not of this world," (John 18:36), we must carefully note the phrasing, argues Lohfink: "there is no reference to *heaven*."[28] Jesus' kingdom is *in* this world, but it is not *of* this world, "that is, it does not conform to the structures of this world." Rather, it is the community of the family of God, counter to the "structures of domination" that characterize the world around it (Matt 23:8–12). This community is thus marked by peculiar virtues, such as a "radical ethic of renouncing violence." It is barred from the use of coercive power, either within itself or in contact with any other community. Fighting for one's rights with conventional means is out of the question; rather, Jesus' followers should suffer injustice over asserting their rights through violence.[29] In this manner,

---

25. And so Lohfink asserts, in contrast to those who would portray Sermon ethics as "heroic" and therefore not realistic, that "the question is whether the gospel of the reign of God imposes intolerable demands, or whether the rule of God exerts a fascination which removes the burden and the difficulty from all the demands which it implies" (ibid., 59).

26. Ibid., 61.

27. Ibid., 65–66.

28. Ibid., 49. This has implications for soteriology as well. When Paul says in Galatians 1:4 that "Christ died in order to 'rescue from the present evil age' all who believe," he is not referring first to an assumption of believers into heaven so much as "the profound separation from the world which takes place through faith and baptism. The baptized person is rescued from the world to the realm of Christ's rule" (127). This should in no way negate the eventual direct presence of believers with God (2 Cor 5:1–8), but it should reframe our understanding of that destiny as a function of the more direct activity of Jesus within the world, i.e., toward a more holistic understanding of salvation.

29. Ibid., 54–55.

> Jesus understood the people of God which he sought to gather as a *contrast-society*. This in no way means that he envisioned the people of God as a *state* or a *nation*, but he did understand it as a community which forms its own sphere of life, a community in which one lives in a different way and treats others in a different way than is usual elsewhere in the world. We could definitely describe the people of God which Jesus sought to gather as an alternative society.[30]

The ecclesia "lives a social order which is plausible to humanity (Matt 5:16)" and is "anything but an elitist community." However, it fulfills its mission "precisely by not becoming the world or by being dissolved in the world; it rather achieves this effect by preserving its own contours."[31] If anything, this connotes the "separateness" of the new covenant community: it is partly by maintaining its own singularity vis-à-vis other theopolitical communities, while welcoming the world into it, that the ecclesia fulfills its own mission. That said, such singularity is not deliberately pursued in itself, but is rather the byproduct of a theopolitical order—identity and mission—thoroughly defined by Christ.

The Sovereignty of God in Jesus Christ

Yahweh proves through Israel that he is the Lord of all nations, indeed of all history. In Jesus Christ, God continues to manifest his sovereignty, as beautifully demonstrated in the incarnation. As von Balthasar describes it, "the whole affair proceeds in the sovereign freedom (and so in the power and majesty) of the God who has the power to 'empty himself, in obedience, for the (eventual) taking of the form of a servant, and from out of the divine form itself.'"[32] As we are told in Philippians 2, the second person of the Trinity did not consider his power something to be retained at the cost of the Father's will for humanity. Therefore,

---

30. Ibid., 56. While in his later writings, Lohfink distances himself from the language of "contrast society" so as to present the church as something constructive in its own right rather than existing only over against some other entity, there is no doubt that the constructive community envisioned in this quotation would be, by definition, alternative to empire and the sociopolitical ways of the nations. His use of "nation" here should be understood within a context of conflict and security, a political community defined, like state, according to a supposed necessity of violence.

31. Ibid., 66.

32. Balthasar, *Mysterium Paschale*, 26–27.

becoming incarnate in Jesus, God becomes one of us, or rather, as we were originally intended to be. The result of Jesus' perfect obedience to the Father—"obedience to the point of death, even death on a cross" (Phil 2:8)—is his exaltation to the position of sovereign over the nations of the earth.

The New Testament is filled with allusions to this exaltation. Not the least of these is the "Great Commission" text of Matt 28:18–20, which contains Christ's rather startling yet often overlooked claim, "All authority has been given to me in heaven and on earth." This claim hearkens back to the prophecy in Daniel 7:13–14, wherein Daniel relates,

> I kept looking in the night visions, and behold, with the clouds of heaven One like the Son of Man was coming, and he came up to the Ancient of Days and was presented before him. And to him was given dominion, glory and a kingdom, that all the peoples, nations and men of every language might serve him. His dominion is an everlasting dominion which will not pass away; and his kingdom is one which will not be destroyed.

Jesus Christ, the Son of Man, incarnation of the second person of the Trinity, through obedience to the Father (even to death on a cross), is exalted to the position of sovereign over the world. O'Donovan interprets the fulfillment of Daniel 7 as the role of a "Davidic heir," such that there is envisioned "a structured form of political leadership for authority to be exercised by 'the people and the saints of the Most High' (7:27)." In this sense, Christ, as "Son of Man," is placed in a "clearly representative role," namely, that of representing a restored Israel, which would mediate God's rule.[33] This is a consequence of O'Donovan's presumption that "if the Davidides were the vessel by which political authority was given to Israel in the first instance, then they must be the vessel by which it would be restored. The coming of the Kingdom must at least *satisfy* the lack in Israel's life created by the long disappearance of Judah's monarchy."[34] Such a "lack" is important to O'Donovan, since he believes that a major part of later Israel's inability to adequately serve Yahweh is its "depoliticization," or the "political difficulties which have arisen from a lack of power, or from its excessive diffusion" following the collapse of Judean state.[35]

33. O'Donovan, *Desire of the Nations*, 116.
34. Ibid., 117.
35. Ibid., 94.

However, O'Donovan does not account for the possibility that Israel's problem might have been earlier in origin, and in actuality an *alternate politicization* than called for in its election and covenant. Certainly, Jesus is a Davidic heir; the genealogies in Matthew 1 and Luke 3 make that abundantly clear. However, if the foregoing theopolitical account is correct, then what we see in Christ as Lord is not a continuation or extension of the Davidic monarchy as such, nor is it the legitimation of the institution as properly exercised, but rather *Yahweh's reassertion of divine kingship* over against human usurpation. It is in this reassertion of divine kingship that the sovereign Christ "precedes the people and elects and creates the people," constituting not only the ecclesia but every person in it via incorporation into the people of God. As Harink states, "The mystery of the ages apocalyptically revealed in Jesus Christ the king is not the salvation of individual Jews and Gentiles. It is the reconciliation of Israel and the nations in Jesus Christ (cf. Rom 15:7–13), the creation of a new humanity the reality of which is anticipated in the new theo-socio-political entity, the church (cf. Eph 2:11–3:12)."[36]

If this is accurate, then it must mean that Christ alone is given such authority in the messianic age, that "already/not yet" era existing between Christ's exaltation and second advent. Thus, I believe O'Donovan misreads the Daniel pericope when he claims that in it, God confers his authority upon "mankind" as an extension of Israel, such that "mankind is now free to interpret God's law in a way that realized God's purposes for mankind's welfare."[37] While in Daniel 7:27 authority is given to the saints to reign in place of the pretenders, this is clearly a reference to a consummated eschaton, a fulfillment that no one in the New Testament claims to have accomplished. Jesus, on the other hand, clearly claims to have fulfilled 7:13–14, and so it is more reasonable to understand that "Son of Man" is more properly a direct reference to God's kingly rule manifested fully in Christ as Lord. Jesus Christ alone rules in the messianic age. None of this, however, takes away from O'Donovan's arguably more solid claim:

> The kingly rule of Christ is God's own rule exercised over the whole world . . . St. Paul declared that God has 'disarmed the principalities and powers and made a public show of them in Christ's triumphal procession' (Colossians 2:15). That must be

---

36. Harink, *1 & 2 Peter*, 73.
37. O'Donovan, *Desire of the Nations*, 104.

the primary eschatological assertion about the authorities, political and demonic, which govern the world: they have been made subject to God's sovereignty in the Exaltation of Christ . . . this awaits a final universal presence of Christ to become fully apparent.[38]

While this "eschatological assertion" indeed awaits its consummation, God's reign through Christ is present even now. Christ's sovereignty in the messianic age is of the same scope as that of Yahweh's sovereignty in the Old Testament. As with "*Yhwh malak*," it is a sovereignty over the created order, including over the international political system. And it is to be humbly embodied (as opposed to triumphalistically mediated) by the ecclesia—around the world and throughout time—which invites the world to join it in worship and service to the sovereign God of the universe.

Yet the capacity of God cannot be acknowledged without paying heed to the character of God, especially as demonstrated in his sovereignty. As von Balthasar reminds us, "God is not, in the first place, 'absolute power', but 'absolute love', and his sovereignty manifests itself not in holding on to what is its own but in its abandonment—all this in such a way that this sovereignty displays itself in transcending the opposition, known to us from the world, between power and impotence."[39] Harink agrees, explaining that the sovereignty of Christ is cruciform, and the church participates in that cruciformity. Thus, "the church enacts and makes visible its 'lordly' freedom in the patience, suffering, and 'witness' (*martyrion*) it shows in the face of enmity and oppression." Martyrdom is the church's witness to the character of the Messiah's theopolitical rule, "the bodily, visible sacrament of the church's participation in Christ's sovereignty among the nations, for the nations—the manner in which it is a 'royal priesthood.'"[40]

Covenant and Church: The Significance of 1 Peter

That essential core of the covenant—unconditional love of God and neighbor—does not change from the Old to New Testaments, from the old to new covenants. And if that comprises the essence of the pur-

---

38. Ibid., 146.
39. Balthasar, *Mysterium Paschale*, 28.
40. Harink, *1 & 2 Peter*, 72–73.

pose of election and Torah, then the shape and form those claimed for Israel's theopolitics is normative for the church even today. This connection is made strongly in the New Testament book of 1 Peter, which, for Douglas Harink, exhorts the church to "take up, dwell in, and live out of its identity as 'the elect, the exiles of the Diaspora' [1:1], a chosen people called out from the wider social and political orders to embody and display God's transforming holiness and love as its peculiar mission among the nations."[41]

The Church in the Messianic Age

The *ekklesia* addressed is the community of Jesus the Messiah, who "enacts in his concrete historical life and death, within the concrete historical conditions of his time, an *alternative sociopolitical messianic life*" and calls his followers to imitate that life "as their baptismal share in his own being and act as the incarnate Word, crucified, risen, exalted, and coming again in glory."[42] This means that the church in no way requires the security of conventional politics in order to be faithful to its identity and mission; all that is necessary has been accomplished in Christ.

As with Israel, 1 Peter 1:1 indicates that the church is constituted by God's own choosing, and that its existence is intrinsic to its character as God's people.[43] As opposed to nations throughout history that have constituted themselves by self-assertion, territorial control, and violence—"such peoplehood is at best an approximation, at worst a simulacrum or parody of true peoplehood"—Israel and the church are constituted by God in "grace and peace" (1:2). In this way, the church can actually "refuse self-assertion" and its attendant coercion and violence, since its establishment is rooted in "the Father's sovereign love and election constituted in the life, death, resurrection, ascension, and intercession of the Son."[44]

The initial salutation of the letter also indicates the church's exilic status, which Harink interprets as synonymous with separateness. God's election of his people necessarily sets that people apart, making it a holy people to witness "with the whole of its life" to God's very nature. Thus,

---

41. Ibid., 19. Translation of 1:1 by Harink.
42. Ibid., 20.
43. Ibid., 28.
44. Ibid., 30.

Israel and the church—including their "praise, politics, social and economic order, personal responsibility"—belong to God and God alone. They are "strangers among the nations" whose citizenship is in heaven (Phil 3:20), "rooted in God's own triune being and action." And what makes God's people foreign or separate is the fact that God's reign is being actualized here and now; this means that the church can be vulnerable, living "out of control" of the world's processes.[45]

Diaspora is something different, however. Diaspora has to do with dispersion, or the deliberate "sowing abroad" of the people of God among the nations of the world as seeds of the gospel, witnesses to God's grace and reign. This is the Jeremianic model, where a people sent into exile is separated from its home but flourishes in its present location, and does so as itself, that is, without needing to conform to its surrounding systems. In this way it may participate in society from a distinctly ecclesial standpoint; while it may often be an "irritant" in its society of residence, critical and even subversive of that society's way of life (for the sake of its members), it can also become in their shared life a "witness of cultural, social, and political order obedient to the Lord of the universe, an icon through which the wider society, by God's grace, might behold its own true form and destiny."[46] This is diaspora for the nations.

The chief underlying theme operating in 1 Peter is the messianic age of Jesus Christ, and by believing in, loving, and following Christ in every sense, "the church now shares in the divine power (the 'grace' 1:10)" of this age. The manner of the church's sharing in divine power is that of sharing in Christ's suffering, for this "Jesus Messiah" is the Suffering Servant of Isaiah, in whose suffering and glorification is revealed "God's way of making history." This is the "apocalypse" of Christ, the revealing of what was only alluded to in the prophets. It is this sort of "retrospective messianic hermeneutic" of the Old Testament that is operative throughout 1 Peter, and that helps tie the church so firmly to biblical Israel.[47]

The messianic hermeneutic of 1 Peter, especially as it addresses both hope and holiness in 1:13–16, is manifested as well in a certain account of time. According to Harink, "messianic time is the time of God's

---

45. Ibid., 31–32.
46. Ibid., 35–36.
47. Ibid., 51.

invasive and decisive reign." We still await the fullness of that reign, but it is present here and now in the "comprehensive alteration of reality already brought about through the crucifixion, resurrection, and ascension of Jesus Christ." The powers have already been subjected to Christ (3:22) and the people of God are already destined for his own glorious inheritance (1:4). While it may seem, especially in persecution, that the powers of this world still reign and are definitive of the age, messianic time declares otherwise: "In the face of often seemingly powerful evidence that the powers are victorious ('Be realistic!' as they say), what is called for from the church is an act of hopeful resistance," in which the messianic age—both already present and not yet fully so—"is grasped in thought and action as the all-determining truth of the church's life, and indeed of the life of the world."[48]

Hence the centrality of holiness for the church, what is commonly recognized as the chief theme of the epistle. Holiness is an attribute of God, which means that the church's holiness stems from God's very being and in God's initiative in constituting a people reflective of that being. The holiness of the people of God is therefore "a matter of being transformed by, conformed to, and sharing in the prior action and character of God," which entails obedience and proper orientation of desire. Unholiness, by contrast, is a refusal to be thus formed, and is furthermore an epistemological failure in which we are incapable of properly perceiving God and our true ends.[49] Holiness and messianic time are brought together in 1 Peter 1:17-21, where the people are called to live in "reverent fear" of God,[50] reverence that liberates the church from anxiety about marginalization or even death in the cultures in which it resides. Christians are prepared to be witnesses—that is, martyrs—for the sake of the gospel of Christ, the inherent righteousness and justice of the kingdom of God.

---

48. Ibid., 53–54. As will be shown in the final chapter, this conception of messianic time contradicts the understanding of time and future espoused in certain nationalistic academic theologies, for whom time is inescapably bound to tragedy and violence, requiring the "realistic" politics to which Harink here alludes.

49. Ibid., 55–56.

50. Ibid., 58.

The Church and Israel

This church, rooted in Christ, is then given its purpose in the world, namely that given to Israel at Sinai in Exodus 19. Here we reach the crucial passage of 1 Peter 2:4–10, and particularly verses 9 and 10, which appropriate the calling Yahweh gives Israel in Exodus 19:5–6 for the church: "But you are a chosen race, a royal priesthood, a holy nation, God's own people, in order that you may proclaim the mighty acts of him who called you out of darkness into his marvelous light. Once you were not a people, but now you are God's people; once you had not received mercy, but now you have received mercy."

It is well known that biblical authors wrote their works with earlier texts or traditions in mind in order to more effectively communicate their messages. Here, as Joel Green puts it, "Peter has studied the past with an eye to serving the present and especially to showing the continuity between followers of Jesus and Israel of old." Peter focuses on the theological unity between Israel and the church, not to preclude their historical differences, but to root this "'elect clan' in the antiquity of the relationship between God and Israel."[51] Robert Wall and Eugene Lemcio explain that such "sub-texts" reflect the later author's own Scriptures as well as their strategies for appropriating those Scriptures for the crises of the day. Ultimately, a "hermeneutical environment" emerges wherein the biblical author's Scriptures interact with his story of Jesus or the early church to "bring focus to the theological meaning of 'the events that have been fulfilled among us'" and to define more clearly the theological dimensions of the people of God. Thus, the direct appropriation and reiteration of Exod 19:5–6 in 1 Pet 2:9–10 indicates a deliberate theological analogy at work.[52] Like Israel, the church "takes its place among the nations as a people among peoples, but with its own distinct political *raison d'être*, authority, calling, and practice," its political character "decisively and critically embodied in and given to it by its own sovereign, the crucified and risen Jesus Christ."[53]

It is important, explains Jo Bailey Wells, to recognize the structural role that the Old Testament material plays in 1 Peter, especially the theological role: the material is "drawn together for the purpose of pre-

---

51. Green, *1 Peter*, 63.
52. Wall and Lemcio, *New Testament as Canon*, 17.
53. Harink, *1 & 2 Peter*, 71.

senting the gospel of Jesus Christ in the light of the Hebrew Scriptures." It is clear that those Hebrew Scriptures are considered authoritative, and thus "we find them re-read from a new perspective, and scoured for their themes of promise, election, and covenant which are found to come together and make sense in the person of Jesus Christ."[54] As the previous chapter demonstrated, Exodus 19:5–6 establishes the unique identity of the people of God, and while it is a call to obedience, the identity that obedience fosters is the central point.[55] Appropriating that Exodus pericope, the declaration of 1 Peter 2:9–10 functions as "'the fundamental indicative for the entire epistle,'" reminding God's people of their identity and compelling them to live holy lives even in the midst of crisis (2:11—5:14).[56] As already indicated in Harink, the Exodus pericope clearly plays a hermeneutical role in 1 Peter, as the material is "drawn together for the purpose of presenting the gospel of Jesus Christ in the light of the Hebrew Scriptures," which are considered authoritative and are here "re-read from a new perspective, and scoured for their themes of promise, election, and covenant which are found to come together and make sense in the person of Jesus Christ."[57] In this manner, the entire story of Israel's election is appropriated for the church, or perhaps more properly stated, the church is brought into Israel's story of election.

The appropriation of the Exodus pericope in 1 Peter is significant, not least because of the nature of the church as perceived in the non-Pauline epistles, namely as a "pilgrim community." This motif entails four primary themes: (1) separation from former allegiances; (2) travel to a certain destination; (3) hardships faced along the way; and (4) reception of blessings upon completion of the pilgrimage. In particular, "the two primary elements of the . . . letter's ecclesiology are its sense of community and its transcendence of a competing society."[58] Hence the understanding that the church's identity, derived in part from Israel as reinterpreted in Christ, necessitates a similar sort of "separateness" to that which Dumbrell attributes to Israel's calling. In this calling of the church, the "theological blueprint" cited by Dumbrell is applied to

---

54. Wells, *God's Holy People*, 211.
55. Ibid., 40; Levenson, *Sinai and Zion*, 43.
56. Wells, *God's Holy People*, 210–12. Here, Wells quotes J. H. Elliott.
57. Ibid., 211.
58. Wall and Lemcio, *New Testament as Canon*, 202.

the Christian community, that is, the divine dominion resulting in the restoration of creation to its original intent. The ecclesia therefore has a "common covenant and common calling" with that of Israel; it is "carrying forward Israel's covenantal politics."[59]

Implications of Biblical Theopolitics for Ecclesial Identity

If the church is indeed a continuation of Israel's covenant politics, as radically fulfilled in Jesus Christ, then there are a number of significant implications of the biblical narrative for the church's theopolitics. First, there is no division between the church's life of faith and the church's politics. As Yahweh stood at the center of Israel's politics following the exodus, so does Jesus Christ stand at the center of ecclesial politics upon his crucifixion, resurrection, and exaltation. As with Yahweh over Egypt, Jesus has demonstrated sovereignty over the powers and therefore "impinges upon every facet of the political" not only for the covenant community but for the world. Consequently, the necessary corollary of Christ's sovereignty is the total exclusivity of the church's allegiance. The church's self-understanding and self-presentation is therefore inherently theopolitical, with Jesus Christ "intensely engaged with questions of power." The political and theological become one, and there is no politics that escapes from the theology of Jesus Christ and his reign. Moreover, neither the church nor segments thereof can behave in such a way as to compartmentalize its liturgical practices from its political identity: each is a function of the other, and neither can function independently.

Second, as identity is in part performatively constituted, the church is only fully and actively the church to the degree that it faithfully practices its vocation and mission. On the one hand, the election of the church is a divine act, securing forever the conditions of possibility for the church's fulfillment of its mission. In this sense, as with Israel, identity is first of all *received*, rather than generated, by the people. On the other hand, that election is, subsequently, only realized in practice. The ecclesia finds itself liberated from the powers through Jesus Christ, with the calling to embody God's reign in the world. Insofar as its practices correspond to this calling, to its divinely revealed purpose(s), the ecclesia can properly consider itself as such. Where it diverges in prac-

---

59. Bader-Saye, *Church and Israel*, 2.

tice from its election, whether through a more overt substitution of the powers as sovereign, or more subtly via altered teaching and practices, the ecclesia (or parts thereof) alters its identity, acting as something other than the true (new) covenant community of faith. Liturgy, doctrine, and political practices are all interwoven, all part and parcel of ecclesial identity.[60]

Third, as Israel's calling is appropriated for the church, the descriptors contained therein make claims upon the church as well. The connotations of separateness contained in "chosen race," "royal priesthood," "holy nation," "God's own people" are part and parcel of ecclesial identity. The church is set apart for particular use by God in the world, namely to mediate the grace extended via Christ, but it is also to act as the definitive (though not only) embodiment of God's reign through Jesus Christ, reflecting in its practices the attendant subjugation of the powers. It does this not primarily for its own sake, but as a "visible place and living witnesses" of God's desire to "liberate and change the entire world." Thus, separateness is not conceived as a quest for purification so much as a necessity for furthering the mission, for "embodying a politics of blessing." Or as Harink nicely puts it, the "politics of doxology, that is, the people of God making history and discerning its 'progress' through the crucified, risen, and exalted Christ whom it worships."[61]

Closely related to the third implication is a fourth: the church is unique in its identity and mission. What Yahweh does in Israel is a singular, unique endeavor. While some would present Israel as an exemplary political community whose principles of governance can be abstracted and universalized,[62] Lohfink corrects that by emphasizing how it is the *community of Israel itself* that is to be universalized. Its singularity is maintained, but its boundaries are expanded. Israel's

---

60. Lest this paragraph be taken to espouse some sort of donatism, I am not arguing that the church completely ceases to be the church where and when there is sin. God's action in Christ and the Holy Spirit preserve the church even in spite of itself, ensuring that at least somewhere, there is always part of the church that remains faithful, and that the parts that are not may always avail themselves of repentance, forgiveness, and restoration. However, I am claiming here that where there is sin, the church is not merely the church behaving badly, but rather the church is less than fully church. This is a matter of sanctification, which I am arguing here is tied to identity.

61. Harink, *1 & 2 Peter*, 72.

62. This is O'Donovan's fundamental premise in *Desire of the Nations*, throughout which he explicitly seeks to abstract and generalize from Israel's experience for the sake of a renewal of Western politics.

theopolitics cannot be abstracted and applied elsewhere without fundamentally altering them; rather, a people can only be engrafted onto Israel, and biblically, this occurs with the church through Jesus Christ. Consequently, what is extended to the church is a singular endeavor of constituting and sustaining a visible communal sign of salvation to the world, an embodiment of the kingdom of God on earth. Significantly for Christian nationalism, which has historically and in its many forms sought to make the present nation the direct or indirect continuation of Israel, the church cannot be supplanted from this role without fundamentally altering the salvation narrative it proclaims. Insofar as nationalists claim for their nation the mantle of the definitive community witnessing to God's salvation and prefiguring the kingdom of God on earth, they distort the Christian gospel and make their nation a simulacrum or parody of the church.

Finally, as a manifestation of God's power of initiation, everything necessary for the church to be the church has been accomplished in Jesus Christ. Indeed, in Christ, as indicated in 1 Peter 2:10, a new people has been established via God's own free action in Christ and engrafted onto the people of whom Jesus is the perfect embodiment. Thus, the ecclesia does not attempt to secure itself using the means of the powers, nor does it even define "security" in the same way. It does not require anything taken from the powers, nor does it require the powers to secure for it space in which to operate.[63] Politically, or theopolitically, this means that the identity and mission of the church—as engrafted onto Israel—stems from God's very being, to which the church must become conformed in both the definition and ordering of its life together and its relations with other human communities. In the messianic age, in view of the church's source and sustenance in Christ,

> the Christian community endures, even embraces its precarious, vulnerable, and dispossessive messianic existence as a sojourner and exile in an ungodly society, because it is confident

---

63. On this point, O'Donovan asserts that "if the mission of the church needs a certain social space for men and women of every nation to be drawn into the governed community of God's Kingdom, then secular authority is authorized to provide and ensure that space." Yet this contradicts his earlier principle that "the power which God gave to Israel did not have to be taken from Egypt . . . first. The gift of power was not a zero-sum operation. God could generate new power by doing new things in Israel's midst" (*Desire of the Nations*, 95). It is not clear why the state is necessary to secure such space if God is fully capable of doing so.

that its cause is ultimately secured by God's justice in the cross and resurrection and not by its ability either to secure and control its own place and safety in the wider world or to have its civil rights granted, acknowledged, and protected by the wider world.[64]

As to this last point, the prophetic witnesses examined in these two chapters carry more specific implications. Nationalism and power politics are inherently problematic as practiced within and by the church, whether it is by institutions within the church over against other institutions (inter- or extra-ecclesial), or whether it is by segments of the church acting in the name or interests of various world powers. This has direct relevance for this study, for as I explained in chapter 1, nationalism operates as a twofold project. First, it works to cultivate or enhance or reinforce a particular national identity among a given people, which gives purpose to that people's existence and that binds the people together in a more cohesive manner. Second, it attempts to acquire for that same people a certain measure of political power—usually in the form of an independent state apparatus—that will secure that people's interests (or at least the interests of the nationalist elites). Typically, these two aspects are bound up with one another such that, on the one hand, political power will be sought as a means to further secure the nation's identity, but on the other, identity itself may be crafted as much as possible by elites to achieve political power for the nation, usually in the form of galvanizing the public.

As we have seen from the prophetic witnesses of Hosea and Jeremiah, such activities are deeply problematic to election and covenant. The fact that Yahweh calls Israel—and then the church under Jesus Christ—to be a counter-model to the surrounding polities means that the people of God cannot define itself in the same way or with the same means as those polities. Thus, when a nation or state appropriates elements of the stories of Israel and the church for its own purposes—"projecting its national ego into the world of the divine"—and especially when such a nationalist move emanates from within the church itself, ecclesial identity and mission is clearly corrupted. The church in that context ceases to be the church, and becomes something decidedly other.

---

64. Harink, *1 & 2 Peter*, 58.

Conclusion

In this chapter, I have attempted to construct a theological criterion for the assessment of nationalist discourse, primarily in the form of a theopolitics derived from Scripture. I have therefore examined the nature of Israel's election by Yahweh and the covenant born of that election, looking specifically at the political community being formed therein and the expectations for its practices internally and in relation to the world. Examining Israel's own story, from covenant to state centralization to prophetic critique, I have argued that Israel's attempts to identify itself with more conventional political communities and their practices constituted an abandonment of its singular covenant, and a de-actualization of its election.

With the incarnation, ministry, death, resurrection, and exaltation of Jesus Christ, however, Israel's election is re-actualized and fulfilled. A new community in the form of the ecclesia is established and engrafted onto Israel to continue the mission of embodying God's reign on earth, now definitely and salvifically demonstrated in Christ. The calling upon Israel is applied to the church as well, such that all the essential elements of a new theopolitics and a new social order pertaining to Israel at Sinai are appropriated for the church. The ecclesia is that people charged with embodying the alternative politics of God amidst the powers and before the watching world.

Having established a biblical politics as criterion for evaluation, this study now proceeds into an examination of nationalist discourse within the church in the United States. Chapter 6 looks at nationalism propagated in national narratives by various members of the Christian Right, while chapter 7 looks at the more sophisticated political theologies of Stephen H. Webb and Richard John Neuhaus for the same. In both chapters, particular attention is paid to the ways in which the authors are seeking to authenticate, in Anthony Smith's sense of determining the true essence, America's national story. Inevitably, this requires an interweaving of salvation narratives—the biblical with the national—in a way that inevitably leads to alterations of the former for the sake of the latter.

CHAPTER 6

Nationalism in the American Christian Right

INTRODUCTION

Having put forth in preceding chapters both an understanding of nationalism and its theological content and implications, as well as a theological criterion for its assessment in the form of a biblical theopolitics, this chapter and the next look more closely at Christian nationalism within the American context. The present chapter considers narratives that propagate the explicit conception of America as a Christian nation, even God's New Israel, a conception espoused most fervently by the American Christian Right. It examines conceptions of American national identity as evident in the discourse of major Christian Right organizations, and especially in the literature of figures central to the movement. To this end, I perform a content analysis of this discourse in order to determine to what extent said discourse is, in fact, nationalist in nature, and to evaluate that discourse in light of the biblical theopolitics offered in chapters 4 and 5.

To accomplish the first task—the determination of the nature of the discourse, particularly in the leading figures' written literature—I rely upon Andrew Murphy's notion of the "American jeremiad," in conjunction with Anthony Smith's "sacred foundations" rubric: chosen/exceptional community, territory, golden age and decline, and shared sacrifice and glorious destiny. While these four categories often overlap or are blurred in the discourse itself, I will identify as specifically as possible those claims and assertions that correspond most clearly to these aspects of national identity. As to the second task, since the nationalist narrative taken up here is inherently theopolitical, I provide an evaluation of nationalist claims in light of the biblical theopolitics of Israel and the church. I argue that this nationalist discourse, which emanates from within the church itself, constitutes a syncretistic salvation narrative, distorted from the Christian faith, entailing a theopolitics that supplants the church with the American nation as the extension of a misappropriated biblical Israel.

With both this chapter and the next, it is worth recalling two elements of the understanding of nationalism provided in chapters 1 and 2. The first is the notion of cultural or national renewal, in which the nationalist process is focused on retrieving and embodying a particular ideal vision of the nation that reigned in the past but from which the nation has subsequently declined. The decline is located in acquiescence to various internal and external threats to this ideal national identity that must be resisted if the nation is to survive. Key to this equation is the awareness that more often than not, such a vision is being propagated over and against competing visions of national identity. This is what Brass refers to as "symbol competition" amongst nationalist elites of different stripes.

The second key element is the notion of nationalist *authentication* as the pursuit of national holiness. In both of the remaining chapters, the figures presented seek to recover, articulate, and propagate a particular vision of America's "true self," and insofar as that identity is bound with divine direction, blessing, and judgment, maintaining proper national identity becomes a matter of Christian holiness, faithfulness to the God who has chosen America for a singular purpose in the world. As such, the following are theopolitical accounts, and as I will show, they ultimately challenge the theopolitical account of reality proclaimed in the ecclesia.

Andrew R. Murphy and the American Jeremiad

Andrew Murphy provides a helpful framework for understanding, yet distinguishing between, the nationalism of Christian Right narratives in this chapter and academic political theologies in the next. In both cases, the nationalist message relies heavily on what Murphy considers to be a distinctive form of political discourse: the American jeremiad. Jeremiads (named, obviously, for the Old Testament speeches of the prophet Jeremiah in Judah and Babylon), provide both an explanation of current misfortune or suffering by the community as well as the hope and way of forgiveness and restoration. The jeremiad first specifies the problems that demonstrate a decline in the community as compared to a previous, more ideal life. It identifies those turning points where and when the nation went wrong; it calls for repentance and then renewal, with whatever reform is necessary to accomplish it. Although the historical context varies—from colonial New England, to the Civil War, to the twenty-first century—"the jeremiad seeks to use political power to intervene on one side of a divisive cultural or political issue." The jeremiad cannot be reduced to a set of policy initiatives, but rather constitutes "a vindication of the American past and the virtues of previous generations."[1] It hearkens back to a golden age, an "idealized portrait of a community's founding" that makes certain claims about that community's attributes while simultaneously pointing to contested claims in the present.[2] What makes the jeremiad distinctive and so significant is its "connection to a larger, sacred story tied intimately to the particularities of the nation's origins and development." For this reason, the decline of the nation is significant not only for that people, but for the world at large, since the present nation is so integral to the universal sacred narrative, or in Murphy's terms, "world-historical." Thus, "the American jeremiad is not just a historical or political argument but a theological, even cosmological, one."[3] Notice already the salvation narrative character to the jeremiad.

Story is central, both in terms of its form and in terms of its selective formulation. Narratives are moral stories about how the past has led into the present; for this reason, "jeremiahs" must ignore those elements that do not further their plots, which must come across as both natural and coherent in order to be persuasive. This fact begs questions about

1. Murphy, *Prodigal Nation*, 6–10. One should note here the correspondence of the jeremiad as Murphy describes it with the two main processes of nationalism: the formation of national identity and the pursuit of power to actualize it in political community. While this study concerns itself primarily with the former, Murphy's description here is helpful in demonstrating to what degree the processes can be intertwined.

2. Ibid., 134.

3. Ibid., 10.

how they craft their narratives to be as widely appealing as possible, how they use narratives to accomplish their political goals.⁴ In discussing the past, nationalists must skillfully arrange historical and mythical elements in certain ways so as to galvanize the populace behind their agenda. When such narratives emanate from multiple sources and compete for dominance, it is often not the facts themselves under dispute; rather, claims about the meaning and significance of those facts are at issue, particularly as a larger story is appropriated to situate and interpret the significance of those facts.⁵ The reader should immediately note, therefore, that the jeremiad as a form of political discourse contains both constructive and constraining elements: a deliberate tie is being made by the nationalist to a preexisting, more expansive narrative toward which the people already find themselves compelled. Put differently, recalling Anthony Smith, the jeremiad is part and parcel of *authentication*, that process by which the nationalist determines and propagates the "true" vision of the nation in question.

While the jeremiad exists because of a decline from an earlier or founding ideal, it should not be seen as inherently negative or pessimistic. Rather, it is a discourse of theopolitical hope insofar as it provides within itself direction for national restoration and renewal. In the American case, decline and judgment matter insofar as the nation plays a key part in preparing the world for God's reign. The power of the jeremiad therefore lies in bringing forth "a dynamic tension between despair and hope," combining a lament of decline with celebration of chosenness "into a powerful narrative of imperiled national promise and a yearning for national renewal." America's decline is significant not only for America itself, but because it is key to a "larger, transcendent purpose." Its rise to power is the result of divine blessing upon its earliest settlers and founders, whose legacy must therefore shape the politics of the present.⁶

Murphy distinguishes between two types of jeremiads most prevalent in American political discourse. While both types present the nation's past—as the nationalists frame it—as the standard for evaluating the present and the basis for future hope, they differ in how they appropriate their narratives. *Traditionalist* jeremiads emphasize "concrete

---

4. Ibid., 120.
5. Ibid., 128.
6. Ibid., 11–13.

social practices, institutions, and traditions," lamenting the nation's departure from those elements. Renewal requires a recovery of those elements, largely in their original form. This is why, for example, one would find in traditionalist jeremiads an argument for a strict constructionist interpretation of the Constitution. *Progressive* jeremiads, while providing similar laments of the current situation of decline from a past ideal, focus rather on the "fundamental principles lying at the heart of American nationhood." In this view, the realization of these principles has been thwarted time and time again and must be pursued more fully.[7] So while these jeremiad types differ somewhat in manner and emphasis, both emphasize the recovery of a national ideal as necessary to meet present crises, which are in turn determined according to that ideal as formulated in the process of authentication.

American Christian Right Nationalism

In the spring of 2010, the Texas Board of Education undertook its once-per-decade review of public school history and social-studies curricula.[8] This event held significance beyond Texas, since by virtue of sheer volume, Texas textbook sales often determine the dominance of particular textbooks over others across the entire country. The fifteen-member board, consisting of ten Republicans and five Democrats and led by dentist Don McLeroy, created considerable controversy when it sought to make changes in the curricula reflecting a decidedly conservative approach to American history, with emphases on the definitive contributions of political figures such as Ronald Reagan and organizations such as the Heritage Foundation, the Moral Majority, and the National Rifle Association, to the relative neglect of other figures and organizations usually associated with the American political Left. Particularly evident in the discussions was the pronounced desire to underscore the influence of Christianity on America, and the identity of America as a Christian nation.

As part of the curriculum review process, the board called for a panel of six experts to aid the largely teacher-comprised writing teams

---

7. Ibid., 109.

8. Shorto, "How Christian?"; McKinley, "Texas Conservatives Seek"; McKinley, "Texas Conservatives Win"; Bimbaum, "Historians Speak Out"; Tanenhaus, "Texas Curriculum Fight."

in their revisions. Among the six were two figures of importance for the present study. The first, David Barton, is nationally known as the founder and leader of WallBuilders, an organization "dedicated to presenting America's forgotten history and heroes," and particularly, as one of Barton's books is titled, "America's Godly Heritage." WallBuilders develops educational materials that, contrary to many contemporary histories, emphasize "the periods in our country's history when its laws and policies were firmly rooted in Biblical principles,"[9] and attempt to dispel what the organization considers to be the myth of separation of church and state.[10] The organization emphasizes biographical approaches to national history, particularly the religious faith of American political figures, an approach it considers to be more "inclusive" than typical contemporary historiographical approaches wherein "economic causes are the primary and almost singular emphasis of study." It concentrates on its library of "rare . . . first-edition works of our Founding Fathers" in which it conducts its primary research, and from which "we are able to document the rich religious and moral history of America as well as to establish the original intent undergirding the various clauses of our Constitution."[11] Barton, who is described on the WallBuilders website as a textbook consultant, is a Texas resident, former vice chair of the Texas Republican Party, and a Republican National Convention political consultant.[12]

The other expert worthy of note is the Reverend Peter Marshall, whose organization, Peter Marshall Ministries, is dedicated to "helping to restore America to its Bible-based foundations through preaching, teaching and writing on America's Christian heritage and on Christian discipleship and renewal."[13] Marshall told a reporter for *The New York Times* that the Texas standards "'were seriously deficient in bringing out the role of the Christian faith in the founding of America.'" In response, he urged the writing teams to include in their revisions considerations about the theology of the Founding Fathers and the biblical roots of that theology.[14] Marshall's 1977 book, *The Light and the Glory*, which

9. Barton, "God: Missing."
10. Barton, "Separation."
11. WallBuilders, "Overview."
12. Caldwell, "Barton & the 'Myth.'"
13. "Peter Marshall Ministries."
14. Shorto, "How Christian?"

is a prime example of American Christian nationalism, has informed Christian Right discourse for decades and will be discussed below in detail.

The Christian Right and American National Identity

The Texas textbook controversy illustrates the ongoing influence of the American Christian Right in formulating, propagating, and seeking the institutionalization of a particular understanding of American national identity. Various other organizations are involved in this broad endeavor, acting on a range of public policy issues, including everything from abortion and homosexuality, to school vouchers and prayer in school, to foreign policy and the war on terrorism. In many cases, these issues are cast in terms of America's identity as a Christian nation. American Values, led by former conservative presidential candidate Gary Bauer, sees the America envisioned by its founders as a "shining city upon a hill"[15] and "a nation with a calling," a calling that necessitates a foreign policy promoting freedom and democracy. Such a policy should protect "our homeland and interests abroad" as well as "advance the values necessary to assist other nations and peoples in their struggles for freedom."[16] American culture was founded upon "Biblical truth," according to the American Family Association, and the Bible's usefulness is "evidenced by the vision of our forefathers as set forth in the Declaration of Independence."[17] The Family Research Council sees America's national culture and political system as founded "primarily by Christians," and maintains that "the Judeo-Christian worldview has provided a sound basis for the flourishing of our national culture and our political system."[18] FRC Action, the lobbying arm of the Family Research Council, likewise cites "Judeo-Christian standards of morality" as appealed to in the Declaration of Independence.[19]

Typically for these organizations, national identity is part and parcel of a broader conservative Christian theology, American exceptionalism contextualized within fundamental "biblical" convictions about

15. "Culture and Religion."
16. "National Security and International Affairs."
17. "About AFA."
18. "Religion and Culture."
19. "About FRC Action."

the world. One group that is rather explicit about this is the Christian Worldview Network, directed by Brannon Howse.[20] This group brings together a number of conservative clergy and public figures in a nationally touring seminar called the "Christian Worldview Weekend," which discusses everything from evangelism to the necessity of a six-day biblical creation account, to the virtues of representative democracy and free market economics. As a follow-up to the seminars and as part of a broader educational program, the organization provides a "Worldview Test" containing around eighty-five statements to which the respondent indicates her level of agreement, including the following examples: "The Bible and a biblical worldview played an instrumental role in building our American civilization, original laws and form of government," or "Jesus was crucified on the cross but was NOT physically raised from the dead," or "When you study the Bible as a whole, it becomes clear that God is very supportive of an economic system that is based on private property, the work ethic, and personal responsibility." Based on the test-taker's level of agreement, she is rated according to one of five categories: "strong biblical worldview thinker," "moderate biblical worldview thinker," "secular humanist worldview thinker," "socialist worldview thinker," or "communist / Marxist / socialist / secular humanist worldview thinker."

A telling pointer to the group's interweaving of patriotism and more traditional fundamental theology is a story on their website about a 2003 Worldview Weekend at Immanuel Baptist Church in Wichita, Kansas. At that seminar, speakers "taught a unified theme concerning witnessing, faith and true conversion." Topics at the seminar included "Hell's Best-Kept Secrets," "True and False Conversion," and "The Incredible Faith of Atheism." While evangelism and unbelief are frequent concerns of conservative evangelical theology, what is interesting is the photo of Howse leading congregational singing. In the picture, a massive American flag provides the backdrop for the stage, another flag stands at stage left, and the lyrics projected on the screen for congregational singing are those of "America the Beautiful." Also displayed is the seminar's logo at the time, a modified Great Seal of the United States with the name of the seminar imprinted upon it.[21]

20. "Christian Worldview Network."
21. See http://www.worldviewweekend.com/photos1906.shtml.

What these organizations pay special attention to, since it constitutes their *raison d'être*, is America's *decline* from an earlier period properly embodying its Christian identity. For example, Bauer's American Values asserts that the nation is experiencing a "virtue deficit" where right and wrong have become increasingly ambiguous, a situation that has given rise to "hostility towards organized religion, sexual exploitation, the homosexual agenda, the demise of the family and the culture of death." One of the root causes of this state of affairs is the alleged secularization of the country, involving a "substantial effort by secularist forces to prevent people of faith from continuing to acknowledge religion in the public square." Rather, "Americans need to be reminded of our nation's moral roots and the virtues that spring from those roots." Such would help restore the nation to a place where standards of morality are clear-cut, "where virtue isn't seen as something old-fashioned but as something to treasure and pass on from one generation to another."[22]

Concerned Women for America asserts that Western civilization has traded the Judeo-Christian worldview, once its "bedrock," for "an irrational secularism based on an unthinking and cruel relativism." This "foolish exchange" is worked out in numerous and unjust public policies that strike at Judeo-Christian principles such as the sanctity of life, religious freedom, family integrity, parentally controlled education, and national sovereignty.[23] The American Family Association cites the "ungodliness and depravity assaulting our nation."[24] The Family Research Council criticizes the notion of a "'wall of separation' between all expressions of faith in God and all aspects of public life" and the consequent "bigotry against people of faith, especially Christians (who are the most frequent target)."[25] Vision America laments that "our nation is abandoning the bedrock moral values, which are our heritage from God, and the very foundation of our liberty." This is due in no small part to "those in America . . . who openly ridicule and belittle people of faith," "whose goal is nothing less than the transformation of our country in their own image" and who "seek to silence our witness and to banish Christianity from the public square."[26]

22. "Culture and Religion."
23. "Biblical Support."
24. "About AFA."
25. "Religion and Culture."
26. "About Us."

In short, what these organizations point to, if not provide explicitly, is a narrative of America interwoven with traditional Christian theological themes. America is the covenant nation, founded on "Judeo-Christian principles" in such a way that is unique in world history up to its inception but is not ultimately exclusive to America, since the mission of the nation is to spread those principles of national life around the globe. Yet, America has strayed from its calling, which requires urgent and direct action by Christians in order to be faithful. As such, nationalism—defined as the recovery, propagation, and institutionalization of a particular national identity—is a theological virtue, since it recalls the nation's divine mission, whose enactment constitutes Christian faithfulness.

The Christian Right as Nationalist Movement

Unfortunately, this fundamental impetus behind such Christian Right discourse is not adequately treated by existing secondary literature. Scholarship does helpfully describes the movement's activist history, its organizational makeup and funding, its public leaders, and its direct political involvement in state and national politics in the United States.[27] It also discusses the various ways in which Christian Right leaders were courted by existing conservative figures into overt political activity, participating—and eventually even leading—in a fusion of militarism, moral traditionalism, and free market economics.[28] However, there is a marked paucity of social-scientific treatments of the Christian Right as a nationalist movement. Most of the literature tends to focus on organizational development and activities. These are rarely if ever put into terms of nationalism, and while one could classify them under the second nationalist process of the pursuit of power and institutionalization of a particular national identity, there has been little attention to the Christian Right regarding the *formulation* of national identity in the first place. Other works label the Christian Right as a nationalist move-

---

27. Green et al., *Religion and Culture Wars*; Green et al., *Christian Right in American Politics*. It should be noted that the Christian Right is not treated extensively in most of the theopolitical literature, either. The scholars surveyed in chapter 1, for whatever reason, do not take on the Christian Right in their work. Again, this points to the need for more sustained engagement, given the Christian Right's influence upon Christian nationalism in the United States.

28. Diamond, *Roads to Dominion*.

ment, but they tend not to connect to nationalism scholarship at large or to properly nuance the Christian Right itself.[29]

That said, the literature does provide a useful framework for understanding the basic outlines of the movement. The Christian Right is defined as a "political alliance of evangelical Protestants and politically like-minded Catholics who share their social, political, and moral concerns."[30] Its emergence and growth as a movement is "rooted in the sociopolitical restructuring of the 1960s," with the goal of restoring the Christian character of American culture and providing Christian-based policy solutions to American social problems.[31] Evangelical clergy like Jerry Falwell were wooed by conservative activists such as Paul Weyrich (the Catholic founder of the Heritage Foundation who is widely viewed as the father of the Christian Right) and Richard Viguerie (the inventor of direct-mail campaigns) into becoming leading spokespersons for the movement, not least because of their positions within major American churches and the attendant ability to galvanize large numbers of Christians to the cause.[32] Along the way, the Christian Right became allied with American neoconservatism in a relationship that revolves around "a critique of domestic culture and a foreign policy conducted as a beneficent empire." What unifies these often theologically disparate movements is a combination of cultural issues such as "the quality and content of public education, moral relativism . . . and liberalizing sexual politics, including access to legal abortions and same-sex marriage," and foreign policy concerns about the position of the United States in the world both economically and militarily.[33]

The Christian Right is therefore best characterized by "a collection of overlapping agendas," including a particular take on American civil

29. For example, Goldberg, *Kingdom Coming*.

30. Murphy, *Prodigal Nation*, 87.

31. Hopson and Smith, "Changing Fortunes," 1–2. Sara Diamond points out that surveys done in the 1950s showed American clergy occupied by foreign policy concerns, anticommunism chief among them, but that emphasis shifted after the 1960s to concerns about the traditional nuclear family and the ability of evangelical activists to participate in the American political process (Diamond, *Roads to Dominion*, 100, 161).

32. Diamond, *Roads to Dominion*, esp. 29, 110–11, 161–78. Shortly thereafter, Weyrich and Falwell cofounded the Moral Majority, whose first board of directors included such well-known conservative Christian leaders as D. James Kennedy, Charles Stanley, and Tim LaHaye (174).

33. Kline, "Culture War Gone Global," 457.

religion wherein America is a Christian nation particularly favored by God, "chosen by God to fulfill his will,"[34] and where "Christian Right leaders may be likened to the prophets of the Old Testament, who repeatedly called on Israel to repent." Of course, in the Old Testament narratives, these warnings to Israel are ignored, resulting in various divine punishments. Thus, "many activists see their role as that of 'redeeming America,' calling it to repent for many sins and directing it to the path of salvation." They perceive themselves as "reluctant political warriors who feel the need to protect America from policies that might result in a loss of God's favor." They therefore see the movement as defensive, seeking to safeguard America's Christian heritage from secular Americans who are waging a culture ware against it (and them), attempting to undermine traditional beliefs and practices.[35]

In this light, I believe that the Christian Right is best defined as a nationalist movement because it is, in Donald Heinz's words, predominantly "engaged in a contest over the meaning of America's story," that is, "how Americans choose to understand and interpret their beginnings, their historical experience, their cultural and spiritual meaning and identity, and their calling and destiny." Heinz argues that Christian Right members see "status elites" in American society—government, mass media, education—as opposed to their values and story. These elites by and large control the national socialization process, primarily through "control of public symbol production." The Christian Right therefore seeks to exert its own control over symbol production in order to project a symbolic portrayal of America—a "countermythology"—that is in accord with their understanding of its history and heritage.[36]

Movement leaders have written prolifically, typically viewing America as a chosen nation; they connect the nation directly to the Old Testament covenants, in some of the more pronounced instances "sounding like seventeenth-century Protestants in their description of the special relationship that existed between God and New World Israel." In others, the notions of election covenant are central, presenting the United States as "the chosen power of the contemporary world, the

---

34. Wilcox and Larson, *Onward Christian Soldiers?*, 15, 19. The authors rightly note that civil religion is not the exclusive domain of the Christian Right, and that often, the content of civil religion is contested (15–20).

35. Ibid., 21, 24.

36. Heinz, "Clashing Symbols," 155–56.

strongest and most righteous of recent states." In either case, America is God's chosen people, inheriting its particular theopolitical status as transferred over time and around the world.[37]

According to Andrew Murphy, this is part of the American jeremiad. American traditionalist jeremiads, most prevalent in the discourse of the Christian Right, see the past as a concrete model. The Christian Right emphasizes the concrete practices of society in an earlier period as normative. This includes religious and moral beliefs, discourse, and sociopolitical practices from the past that are still considered binding today. For the Christian Right, the past—particularly the golden age of America's founding era—sets parameters for national life, specific guidelines for contemporary political agendas.[38] Within this conception, "a Judeo-Christian consensus structured public life, and men of great character embarked upon the American experiment in self-government without attempting to separate religion from politics." This golden age embodies "sexual restraint, public religiosity, a commitment to the common good, and deference to traditional sources of authority," with the public role of Judeo-Christian principles acting as the definitive mark of community.[39] It is this model that the traditionalist jeremiad of the American Christian Right holds as normative for American national identity and contemporary political practice.

The Nationalist Narrative in Christian Right Literature

At the root of the wide-ranging endeavors of the American Christian Right is a particular narrative of American national identity. This narrative portrays the American nation as exceptional for its divine calling, as evidenced by the power and prestige it currently enjoys in the world. The nation was born in a covenant context, and was blessed for most of its history for abiding by that covenant. Yet it has been for several decades a wayward vassal, a nation in the midst of a tumultuous identity crisis. This crisis requires direct and immediate resolution in the form of a return to the nation's founding religious and political principles and practices, or the nation will face sure and imminent destruction.

37. Lienesch, *Redeeming America*, 141.
38. Murphy, *Prodigal Nation*, 111.
39. Ibid., 134.

This narrative of American Christian nationalism, which by its very nature constitutes a theopolitical project, is portrayed explicitly in the discourse crafted by certain key Christian Right authors. This section examines such discourse using Anthony Smith's rubric of "sacred foundations": (1) community: rooted in a particular sacred narrative, the nation as divinely chosen and called to a particular mission, requiring a particular holiness; (2) territory: the nation's sacred space; (3) glorious past: the nation's golden age and subsequent decline; and (4) the nation's shared sacrifice and sacred destiny. For the purposes of this study, I have reconfigured the third and fourth foundations to an extent: the third is the golden age narrative, highlighting the contributions of key figures, while the fourth includes a combination of decline and renewal, including some emphasis on the necessity of sacrifice for the latter. With this reconfiguration in mind, this section examines in particular the nationalist narrative in the writings of two of its key instigators—Peter Marshall and David Manuel—as well as three major Christian Right leaders: D. James Kennedy, Jerry Falwell, and Pat Robertson. As the secondary literature attests, the latter three have had an enduring influence on Christian Right formulations of national identity and pursuit of policy objectives over the past three decades. Yet, the existing literature does not adequately discuss the content of their message—that is, the substance of their nationalist narrative—particularly along theological lines.

Community

To properly understand American chosenness within the Christian Right nationalist narrative, one must first address Peter Marshall and David Manuel's 1977 book, *The Light and the Glory*.[40] Historian John Fea cites sales of *The Light and the Glory* at almost one million copies between 1977 and 2008, but points out, as witnessed in the Texas textbook debate, that what is even more significant is "its impact on hun-

---

40. Marshall and Manuel, *Light and Glory*. This book was revised and expanded as the first in the trilogy titled, "God's Plan for America." The trilogy is available as well in children's versions, and *The Light and the Glory* still holds a prominent place in various homeschooling curricula. The final book in the trilogy carries endorsements from Bill Bright, Christian Right activist and founder of Campus Crusade for Christ, and conservative syndicated columnist Cal Thomas, as well as former US Senator Sam Brownback (now governor of Kansas) and former US Attorney General John Ashcroft.

dreds of thousands of Christians, including students in home schools and private Christian academies, in promoting a 'Christian view' of American history. It was not the first (or the last) book to declare that the United States was founded as a 'Christian nation,' but it has certainly been the most influential."[41] The book is explicitly theopolitical, steadfastly portraying America as the modern extension of Israel. Marshall and Manuel begin by arguing that Israel's "corporate covenant relationship" with God was not a singular event, but rather the first and exemplary instance of God's ongoing practice of relating to the nations. Most recently, God elected America to be a "'light to lighten the Gentiles'... a demonstration to the world of how God intended His children to live together under the Lordship of Christ." The earliest settlers saw themselves as a people called to continue Israel's covenant relationship with God,[42] and this self-perception is normative today, for "God was making His most significant attempt since ancient Israel to create a new Israel of people living in obedience to the laws of God, through faith in Jesus Christ."[43] Israel's "Covenant Way" was extolled by the Puritan settlers, who along with the Pilgrims "had known that they were separated unto God and called out for a special purpose."[44] God used "servant-leaders" such as William Bradford, John Winthrop, and George Washington, who were "living out the example of Jesus Christ," to "show the way in the building of His new Promised Land,"[45] which is "a new Jerusalem, a model of the Kingdom of Christ upon earth." Thus, "we Americans were intended to be living proof to the rest of the world that it *was* possible to live a life together which reflected the Two Great Commandments and put God and others ahead of self."[46] As "God's New Israel," America is the ultimate communal advancement to date of the Christian salvation narrative, as well as the salvation of Western civilization. As Marshall and Manuel later posit, "God knew what the twentieth century would hold in store. He also knew the totalitarian darknesses that would arise out of Europe and Asia, and knew that England alone would never have

---

41. Fea, "Thirty Years," 27.
42. Marshall and Manuel, *Light and Glory*, 19.
43. Ibid., 22–23.
44. Ibid., 256.
45. Ibid., 26.
46. Ibid., 23.

the spiritual power to stop them. And so He planted the seeds of light that would make the difference, early in the seventeenth century."[47]

This covenantal understanding of America is picked up quite clearly in the work of D. James Kennedy, Presbyterian minister and major figure of Christian Right theopolitics. For Kennedy, America is "the most blessed nation that has ever existed on the face of the earth," as marked by its "freedom and abundance." The reason for this abundance is "its adherence to faith in Jesus Christ and the Bible,"[48] for "America was a nation founded upon Christ and His Word,"[49] a nation given birth by the "Puritan and evangelical form of Christianity."[50] The early Pilgrim and Puritan settlers came to the New World "to advance the gospel and the kingdom of our Lord, Jesus Christ,"[51] forming a nation Kennedy calls the "last best hope of people on earth."[52] Their settlement and survival were directly aided by God: "the founders of this country had multiple reasons to believe that God was scattering their enemies." Therefore, "we would do well to remember the greatest hero who ever fought for the freedom of America, that One who has fought to establish this Christian land."[53] America, "a nation unique in the history of the world,"[54] is thus the direct product of God's own devoted effort:

> God loves America. When you consider what He went through to bring our forebears to this magnificent land, and when you realize what He accomplished in bringing forth a new nation on this continent—a government founded on Christian principles and dedicated to life, liberty, and the pursuit of happi-

---

47. Ibid., 154.

48. Kennedy and Newcombe, *What If America?*, 133–34. This description occurs in a section on the importance of a "balanced emphasis on patriotism" as part of appropriate Christian education. Until his death in 2007, Kennedy was pastor of Coral Ridge Presbyterian Church in Fort Lauderdale, Florida. From there, he directed numerous initiatives in conjunction with Christian organizations dedicated to propagating a particularly Christian, covenantal understanding of American heritage. These included Coral Ridge Ministries and the Center for Reclaiming America for Christ, the latter of which closed down following his death.

49. Ibid., 4.

50. Ibid., 18.

51. Ibid., 7.

52. Kennedy, *Character and Destiny*, 52.

53. Kennedy and Newcombe, *What If America?*, 6–7.

54. Ibid., 10.

ness—you have to realize that He had a dramatic vision and purpose for this nation.[55]

Jerry Falwell is largely in agreement with Kennedy's description of the nation. In his view, "God promoted America to a greatness no other nation has ever enjoyed because her heritage is one of a republic governed by laws predicated on the Bible."[56] Despite her numerous failures, "it is right living that has made America . . . without question the greatest nation on the face of God's earth."[57] According to Falwell, "God has blessed this nation because in its early days she sought to honor God and the Bible, the inerrant Word of the living God." America was to be a Christian nation, for while the Founding Fathers were not all Christians, "they developed a nation predicated on Holy Writ. The religious foundations of America find their roots in the Bible,"[58] roots which are essential to liberty. For this reason, "we have enjoyed a unique relationship toward God."[59]

Pat Robertson echoes these authors but more explicitly relates the biblical narrative to the American constitutional system. As a divinely elect and ordered nation, America is without precedent, save one, namely that "established thousands of years before by the tribes of Israel in their covenant with God and with each other."[60] According to Robertson's study of the documents and testimony of the founders, it is the "Old Testament stories of God at work with His people, Israel, and the New

---

55. Kennedy, *Character and Destiny*, 18.

56. Falwell, *Listen, America!*, 16. Before his death in 2007, Jerry Falwell was a Baptist minister and televangelist, who became a major Christian Right leader in the 1980s in association with Paul Weyrich, when with Weyrich he founded the Moral Majority. Earlier, in 1971, he founded what would become Liberty University, a major conservative evangelical college in Lynchburg, Virginia, boasting in 2009 a residential enrollment of about twelve thousand students, and an online enrollment of more than thirty-six thousand ("About Liberty").

57. Ibid., 20. As he states later on, "America has been great because her people have been good. We are certainly far from being a perfect society, but our heritage is one of genuine concern for all mankind" (243).

58. Ibid., 29.

59. Ibid., 252.

60. Robertson, *America's Dates*, 90. Marion Gordon (Pat) Robertson is a televangelist and the founder of numerous Christian Right organizations, including the Christian Coalition, as well as the still operating television network CBN and its flagship show, *The 700 Club*, and the American Center for Law and Justice. In 1988, he campaigned for the Republican nomination for President of the United States.

Testament stories of the Christian church" that most influenced the development of the US Constitution. Reading the Constitution within the framework of the Declaration of Independence (which one must do since the former does not directly reference God), one finds God as (1) the source of liberty: "God is the Lawgiver, a biblical precedent for the legislative branch of government"; (2) "the nation's ultimate protector": "God is the Chief Executive, the Commander-in-Chief, a biblical precedent for the executive branch of government"; and (3) "the nation's judge": "God is the Chief Justice of the universe, a biblical precedent for the judicial branch of government." In light of this direct divine connection, "the Constitution could not survive a people who did not believe in God or his laws."[61]

Quoting several founders on the necessity of religion for sustaining the country, Robertson also asserts that "without a people governed individually by God's laws, the nation would self-destruct." Free society depends on individual self-restraint, which is rooted in the biblical conviction that each person will be rewarded or punished according to the divine standard. In the New Testament, the desire to live righteously is "reinforced by the presence of the Holy Spirit and by the comfort and discipline of the church." The grace of God in Jesus, while promising forgiveness, nonetheless motivates obedience. In this way, the "law of the heart" orients one's response to the nation and its laws.[62] In short, as the lone theopolitical reflection of Israel, America's political order is established by God and modeled directly on God's own exercise of authority. Christianity thus supports the nation and its political institutions by ensuring the individuals proper disposition, through God, to the nation and its political order.

Territory

The sacredness of land is not a primary theme in Christian Right nationalist discourse as a whole, but neither is it entirely absent. The territory of America-as-New-Israel, while taking a backseat to the people's chosenness, is viewed within the context of God's covenant for global salvation. This is apparent in at least two ways. First, the New World is a specially and divinely reserved land. Notwithstanding the indigenous

61. Ibid., 91–93.
62. Ibid., 93–94.

peoples already present, the land is described as the "virgin wilderness of America."[63] The discovery and settlement of the Americas by European Christendom was central to God's "grand design for the New World." As Marshall and Manuel explain, "He had withheld it from man's knowledge this long, in almost virginal purity. He had stocked it with an abundance of game and fertile soil, natural resources and beauty—all that a people would ever need—as a fitting abode for the followers of His Son."[64] Kennedy echoes Marshall and Manuel's claim, stating that "God in His infinite wisdom and providence reserved this nation, separated by two oceans from the civilized world of that day, until such a time as this. I believe He set this land and these people apart as the last best hope of people on earth."[65] Quite in the tradition of Israel, then, the explorers and settlers who were led to the New World were brought providentially into a land of abundance—one might say, "flowing with milk and honey"—as the site of their theopolitical mission. The territory in North America thus becomes sacred, a divinely designated instrument—in conjunction with the people—of God's salvation of the world.

The second way in which territory plays a role for Christian Right nationalism is as the cosmic battleground between God and Satan. As Marshall and Manuel portray the situation, the Americas of the fifteenth century constitute the final unchallenged earthly domain of the devil. In reference to explorers such as Columbus, they write that "Satan had failed to keep the Light of Christ from establishing a beachhead in practically the only part of the world in which he still reigned unchallenged."[66] Satan is implicated in the sinking of the *Pinta*, in fact, because he is "unable to thwart the Christ-bearer's mission or keep him [Columbus] from invading his [Satan's] domain."[67] So not only is the New World the "Promised Land" for the nation America as the "model

---

63. Marshall and Manuel, *Light and Glory*, 22.

64. Ibid., 46. These quotations illustrate a tension in the book between the so-called virgin wilderness of the Americas and the role of the native peoples there, with whom Marshall and Manuel elsewhere demonstrate a certain sympathy.

65. Kennedy, *Character and Destiny*, 52.

66. Marshall and Manuel, *Light and Glory*, 42.

67. Ibid., 46. Incidentally, they conclude that while Satan was likely behind the actual sinking, God allowed it possibly as a way to humble Columbus and reorient the Christ-bearer back to his proper mission (46–47). This is another example of the theologically framed speculation that fleshes out documented fact throughout their work.

of the Kingdom of Christ," but it must be wrested from the hands of its current overlord, the ultimate enemy himself. This fits very well within the context of covenant, not only as a general though mistaken echoing of Israel's conquest and settlement period, but also in terms of a particular land as the unique and definitive geographic locus for God's salvation of the world.

Golden Age/Heroes

The third sacred foundation is the nation's "glorious past," which is prevalent throughout much of the Christian Right's nationalist discourse. While some narratives begin or end earlier or later than others, there is universal acknowledgement of the importance of the early settlers, particularly the Puritans, as well as the major figures of the founding period of the United States. As Anthony Smith and Andrew Murphy both point out, these golden age narratives are exemplary: they are both the primary criterion for interpreting the present national condition, delineating its areas of present deterioration, as well as the *telos* toward which the nation must strive for salvation. Often within the literature, golden ages will be presented in both a general sense—broad statements about the way things used to be—and more specifically, in the form of particular stories and figures.

The notion of "golden age" is reflected specifically in the various biographical sketches and particular stories found throughout these works. One example is Marshall and Manuel's depiction of Christopher Columbus, whose first name, meaning "Christ-bearer," becomes the authors' theme for America's discovery. Columbus, whose story comprises the first two chapters of the book, had become convinced of a divinely given, "almost mystical mission: to carry the Light of Christ into the darkness of undiscovered heathen lands, and to bring the inhabitants of those lands to the holy faith of Christianity."[68] Unfortunately, over time, Columbus's pride and greed get the better of him, and his mission

---

68. Ibid., 31. The authors rely for this claim on excerpts from a translation of Columbus's journal, in which he cites the Holy Spirit as giving him the inspiration to sail to the Indies (17) and appropriates for himself biblical prophecies regarding conveying a "light to the nations" (31). Interestingly, Columbus's "mystical" experience occurs, according to the authors, in a "half-waking dream" while he was "sick with a fever and in the depths of despair" (21). Yet the credibility of Columbus's claim in such a context goes unquestioned in their account.

of discovery descends into one of conquest.[69] Marshall and Manuel are frank when it comes to acknowledging certain instances of European exploitation, and some of the greatest villains of their narrative are figures such as Cortez, Pizarro, and the Conquistadors. Conversely, their heroes of the period are the humbler figures of the Franciscan and Dominican friars who sought a relative level of protection for the indigenous population. As they put it, "the Columbus era soon deteriorated into such a debacle of rape, murder, and plunder throughout Central America, that we could not conceive what possible connection it might have with any divine plan for the establishment of a new Christian commonwealth." This development is viewed by the authors not as a disconfirmation of their claims of American election, but rather as a divergence from that election.[70]

In a later era, it is the Puritans who are the heroes of the story, for they "more than any other, made possible America's foundation as a Christian nation." It is the Puritan conviction that "the Kingdom of God really *could* be built on earth, in their lifetimes" that provides the very foundation of New England, and therefore the nation. Persecuted in England, the Puritans undertake an "exodus" to America in order to build "a Biblical Commonwealth in New England." With their "Moses," John Winthrop, they executed "an essential maneuver in the drama of Christendom" against its own corruptions. As such, "these Puritans did not flee to America; they went in order to work out that complete reformation which was not yet accomplished in England and Europe."[71] While Kennedy describes their move as essentially a "church-relocation

69. Ibid., 47.

70. Ibid, 67. In places, the authors demonstrate a candor and judgment rather uncharacteristic of the Christian Right on these issues, and particularly for a book published in 1977. At one point they state, "In Mexico, where silver was abundant, the Indian farmers were forcibly taken from their fields and set to mining, with no thought for the crops on which the population was entirely dependent. Widespread famine was the result, and that, plus their total lack of immunity to the white men's diseases, amounted to genocide of mind-numbing proportions" (ibid., 68). And in contrasting the two types of Spanish newcomers, they write, "The Conquistadors had brought monks with them, possibly to salve their consciences, or to boost the morale of the men who were so far from home. But these Franciscan and Dominican friars were not straw men; they loved God—deeply and totally. They were as committed to serving Him, as their military masters were to serving themselves" (69). They specifically cite with approval the efforts of Bartolomé de las Casas to redress injustices done to the native population and to protect them from further exploitation (71ff.).

71. Ibid., 146–57.

project,"[72] Falwell writes, "The heritage of the Puritan Pilgrims is one not of a church, but of a nation; these were men and women who were not only the progenitors of a state, but also the ancestors of a nation." They provided the religious foundation for the liberty that Christians enjoy today.[73]

Winthrop was central to this as, in Cotton Mather's words, the *Nehemias Americanus*;[74] under his leadership, in covenant, the Puritan settlers demonstrated a commitment that is normative for Americans today and that is "more demanding than most of us are willing to make."[75] This twofold commitment—"vertical" between the nation and "Christ as Lord and Master, as well as Savior," and "horizontal," from neighbor to neighbor "and ultimately to that specific body of Christian neighbors of whom God calls one to be a part"—is the foundational contribution of the Puritans to America as a Christian nation. God raised them up deliberately as "foundation stones, not merely of American democracy, but of the Kingdom of God in America."[76]

A third major golden age event in these narratives is the Great Awakening, during which Americans, by way of Christian conversion, came to see themselves as a cohesive nation defined by the "Covenant Way." As part of a succession of clergy who would spiritually prepare the colonies for later resistance to Britain, Jonathan Edwards and George Whitefield helped revive the Puritan covenant identity through an intensive emphasis on Christ's forgiveness and freedom from sin. It was through revival meetings that "the Body of Christ was forming in America" and "Americans were rediscovering God's plan to join them together by His Spirit in the common cause of advancing His Kingdom."[77] As Robertson explains, "people were also tired of dull, ineffectual religion, forced upon them" by either colonial forefathers or by representatives of the Crown. Spiritual awakening prompted "new commitment to personal and political freedom."[78] In continuity with Israel, this awakening "was actually a *reawakening* of a deep national desire

---

72. Kennedy and Newcombe, *What If America?*, 20.
73. Falwell, *Listen, America!*, 30.
74. Marshall and Manuel, *Light and Glory*, 160.
75. Ibid., 146.
76. Ibid., 168–69.
77. Ibid., 251.
78. Robertson, *America's Dates*, 59.

for the Covenant Way of life."[79] Note here the significance for American identity: in the Great Awakening,

> we began to become aware of ourselves as a *nation*, a body of believers which had a national identity as a people chosen by God for a specific purpose: to be not just 'a city upon a hill,' but a veritable citadel of Light in a darkened world . . . Now, through the shared experience of coming together in large groups to hear the Gospel of Jesus Christ, Americans were rediscovering God's plan to join them together by His Spirit in the common cause of advancing His Kingdom.[80]

In revival, then, the nation is becoming self-aware. There, the gospel of Christ is seen as solidifying American national identity, for it is America that is to be the definitive theopolitical embodiment of Christ on earth.

Kennedy cites the Great Awakening as the impetus for the American independence movement. As Americans were much more likely than the British to be active in their churches, the Declaration of Independence was not only a secular act, but a religious one as well.[81] This is the fourth golden age period to be considered here: the American Revolution and early constitutional deliberation. As Marshall and Manuel explain, the colonies had already practiced democratic government for a century before the British began making increasingly stringent demands on them in the form of taxation without representation[82] and especially with renewed Anglican worship and church control.[83] The founders, Robertson explains, had been raised to understand politics within the context of a fallen world dominated by sin. For this reason, "civil government was instituted by God to protect people's rights."[84]

But the biblical narrative itself is suspicious of kingship, specifying for Israel's kings the specific scope of their authority.[85] According

79. Marshall and Manuel, *Light and Glory*, 240.

80. Ibid., 251.

81. Kennedy and Newcombe, *What If America?*, 31.

82. Marshall and Manuel, *Light and Glory*, 263.

83. "It was now clear to even the most undiscerning Puritan that passive, docile submission to English rule would mean the reimposition of the oppressive authority of the Church of England from which God had delivered their forefathers. The struggle *was* spiritual" (Marshall and Manuel, *Light and Glory*, 260).

84. Robertson, *America's Dates*, 68.

85. For Robertson, this suspicion is not part of a general disapproval of state cen-

to Robertson, the covenant between God, the king, and the people required the king to protect the people's "unalienable rights"; if he failed to do so, he would be removed from office. Thus, George III would only retain his office if he did the same; but "King George had broken the compact."[86] Even then, though, the founders' behavior is exemplary: they "listed their grievances carefully, proclaimed their liberty, declared their separate and equal status, defended their honor, and defeated their kin ... By their example we learn that it is our right and duty as citizens to judge the laws and the lawmakers of this nation by the laws of God in the created order and in God's Word, and then to act."[87] Because George III had violated the proper, God-ordained exercise of earthly authority in demanding total submission to himself—constituting "tyranny and oppression"—American colonists were forced to react and seek their independence, an understanding strongly reinforced by colonial clergy at the time. The authors mention in particular the 1773 Declaration of Marlborough (Massachusetts): "Death ... is more eligible than slavery. A free-born people are not required by the religion of Jesus Christ to submit to tyranny, but may make use of such power as God has given them to recover and support their laws and liberties ... [we] implore the Ruler above the skies, that He would make bare His arm in defense of His Church and people, and let Israel go."[88] Thus, "the American church became the cradle of a revolution,"[89] and here was born the cry, "No king but King Jesus!" As these authors understand it, resistance and revolution were a return to gospel theopolitics.[90]

Marshall and Manuel gauge God's approval of the American Revolution by its success, for "if there is one thing that the Bible teach-

---

tralization and *realpolitik* as portrayed in chapter 4 of the present study. Rather, it exists in his argument as a way to justify democracy, ultimately via violent means.

86. Robertson, *America's Dates*, 71. Unfortunately, Robertson does not make clear how the notion of God's direct removal of an Israelite king is equivalent to armed rebellion by the people.

87. Ibid., 72.

88. Marshall and Manuel, *Light and Glory*, 267.

89. Robertson, *America's Dates*, 59.

90. Marshall and Manuel, *Light and Glory*, 267. As they quote Samuel Adams upon voting for independence, "'We have this day restored the Sovereign, to Whom alone men ought to be obedient. He reigns in heaven and ... from the rising to the setting sun, may His Kingdom come'" (309).

es, it is that God honors obedience with His blessing."[91] Central to this success is the role of George Washington, whom the authors present as an iconic figure of Christian devotion and humility. They describe Washington, alluding to his many prayers, as "a man under authority—God's and Country's."[92] Robertson, too, is enamored with Washington, whom he admires for consistently allowing personal faith to interact with politics: "Not once during his distinguished service to this nation did he minimize or shelve his deeply felt commitment to God, to the Bible, or to his Lord and Savior, Jesus Christ . . . he established for all time how Christian people can live by their own convictions and at the same time govern all the people fairly and wisely."[93] As Washington consistently "heeded his inspired intuition," the colonial army was able to tactically trump the moves of the numerically superior British regulars.[94] Marshall and Manuel go into some detail on the events of the Revolutionary War, including simultaneous colonial attempts at reconciliation with Britain, which they repeatedly compare to Israel yearning to return to Egypt.[95] In the end, the colonial victory demonstrated that "God was with them all the time," God's grace favoring them to succeed, such that "Americans had the unseen aid of their strongest Ally."[96] In this event, "we had seen how miraculously God would intervene to preserve and protect his covenanted people . . . God made certain that those same covenant promises which He made to our forefathers when He brought them here, would always be a viable possibility in the United States of America."[97]

91. Ibid., 270.
92. Ibid., 288. The authors find these prayers in Johnson, *George Washington*.
93. Robertson, *America's Dates*, 107.
94. Marshall and Manuel, *Light and Glory*, 298.
95. Ibid., 301–3. They write regarding deliberations in the Continental Congress considering reconciliation with Britain, "The situation was reminiscent of the Israelites in the wilderness, convincing one another that they had been better off in Egypt, and daily growing more and more certain that the only thing to do was to go back. For out in the wilderness they were forced to face the unknown and put their entire trust in God" (302). Yet "realists" like John Adams prevailed, arguing that British rule would be even worse, to which the authors add, "Nine plagues in a row had failed to soften Pharaoh's heart, and the comparison between him and George III was now being made in more sermons than ever" (303).
96. Ibid., 313, 317.
97. Ibid., 336.

Much of the same is claimed for consitutional deliberations. For Kennedy, the signers of the Constitution "were definitely Christian for the most part. At least 90 to 95 percent of them were practicing, Trinitarian Christians." Even the 5 percent who were not orthodox were "pro-Bible and had somewhat of a Christian worldview."[98] Thomas Jefferson is a key figure, particularly as Kennedy considers the debate over separation of church and state central to the question of national identity. Jefferson, as the deist portrayed in typical histories, is a "fictional character . . . the creation of the secular elite, our secular educational system, the media, and of liberal judges."[99] Rather, Kennedy portrays Jefferson as a consistently churchgoing Anglican who suffered a crisis of faith under certain family circumstances. The so-called Jefferson Bible was simply intended as a book on ethics and morals, not an indictment of Christianity. Jefferson's own personal religiosity was unmistakable,[100] and his letter to the Danbury Baptist Society, from which the explicit claim of separation of church and state originates, was never meant to preclude Christianity from the public arena. Of course, "I don't think that we could say that Jefferson was a genuine Christian in the sense of one who had been transformed by the regenerating power of the Holy Spirit, one who trusts in the death of Jesus Christ for his salvation." He saw Christianity as little more than a code of ethics. But even as a "nominal Christian," Jefferson's beliefs and actions were "totally antithetical" to what the American people have been told.[101]

Decline and Renewal

In all of the accounts discussed here, there is a sense that what was going in a more or less straight trajectory with regard to America's maturing in its covenant identity—and particularly its rise to global power by the mid-twentieth century, which is seen as indisputable proof that America is blessed by God for its faithfulness—was radically derailed in the 1960s. Not only do the political, economic, and cultural developments arising from that decade constitute decline from the nation's

---

98. Kennedy and Newcombe, *What If America?*, 206, 216. Kennedy relies for these numbers on the work of David Barton, discussed above.
99. Ibid., 42.
100. Ibid., 49ff.
101. Kennedy and Newcombe, *What If America?*, 52–53.

identity as forged in its founding golden age, but they act collectively as the impetus for these works of nationalism. In response, the nation must recover the political, cultural, and religious practices that once defined it, according to the Christian Right narratives. Only then can it be saved from judgment. Yet even past or prospective judgment acts not to falsify the nationalist accounts, but are read within them as part and parcel of covenant: God's peculiar people are punished for violating covenant, but the blessings of covenant can be regained with proper repentance and obedience.

For Marshall and Manuel, America had been up to the 1960s a paragon of nationhood in the world; optimism reigned, and "the American Dream was about to come true." Yet, "with a suddenness that is still bewildering, everything went out of balance." The United States began to suffer military defeats in Vietnam; its president was assassinated; America's youth began rebelling against authority in all forms; emerging nations that had benefitted from American generosity turned "unanimous in their hatred of us"; and US foreign policy lost its proactive assertiveness. The economy declined, educational scores waned, and psychiatric disorders erupted. "Most mystifying" was the "loss of moral soundness"; there had always been isolated breakdowns, but now the problem was widespread. Above all, the scandal of Watergate defied expectations for the presidency, which up to that point "was a symbol of all that was right and decent in America." Tearing down such an "idol of our 'civil religion' . . . was such a shattering experience for so many." This decline, they assert, is due to forgetting the nation's Christian heritage, rejecting a national life wherein people would live in obedience—as a nation—to Jesus Christ, so as "truly to be *one nation under God*."[102]

Kennedy's earlier work places America's decline firmly within the context of covenant and national chosenness. Even though God went to great pains to bring America about, "God is also our loving parent, and His heart is broken by the way we have neglected Him . . . He will not allow us to continue in rebellion forever."[103] Great nations fall, he explains,

102. Marshall and Manuel, *Light and Glory*, 13–16.

103. Kennedy, *Character and Destiny*, 18. It is interesting to note that Kennedy's earlier book is considerably more strident in tone than the later one, which could have something to do with the political climate at the time. *Character and Destiny* was published during the Clinton Administration, which is specifically cited therein as contributing to America's precarious position (23), while *What If America?* was published during the administration of George W. Bush, and contains a strong, if in-

usually because of internal moral deterioration, their "compromise of their own foundational beliefs, loss of faith in the values that made them great..."[104] Such compromise has been foisted upon America by secular humanists, "liberal educators," and socialists in American universities. In response, "the Christian church is being forced to defend itself against the blatant, premeditated, willful, and malicious attack of those determined to overthrow the freedom and spiritual values of this nation." Christians face "a radical and totalitarian agenda to seize control of the media" in order to control the flow of ideas and subject Christians to scorn.[105] As victims of this assault, Christians are simply trying to preserve "what is our own: a nation discovered, tamed, founded, defended, and nurtured from infancy to greatness by men and women of faith ... We did not start the culture war, but we have a profound commitment to this nation and its values, and we *will* stand up for them."[106]

Kennedy laments that the nation has turned its collective back on the God of the founding fathers, choosing to exclude religious principles from culture and politics.[107] The culture wars are largely to blame: the priority of tolerance and the loss of "absolutes," the deterioration of the nuclear family, the loss of the sanctity of life for the unborn, sex education,[108] and liberal jurisprudence caused by activist courts and organizations such as the American Civil Liberties Union.[109] He is particularly concerned with secular humanists in public education, "amoral and anti-Christian" educators who are exposing students "to a deadly virus that will eat away their souls."[110] The "liberal establishment" has incrementally revised history in order to "take Jesus Christ out of the picture." This bodes ill for America: "When we freely confessed that this is a Christian nation, in days gone by, we prospered. We were the 'shin-

---

direct, defense of aggressive Bush Administration policy toward terrorism following September 1, 2001, which, true to form for American exceptionalism, he calls "the day that changed the world" (173ff.).

104. Kennedy, *Character and Destiny*, 47.
105. Ibid., 77.
106. Ibid., 71.
107. Kennedy and Newcombe, *What If America?*, 41.
108. Ibid., chapters 6–9.
109. Ibid., 220. See also pp. 202ff., which discuss the First Amendment and the question of separation between church and state.
110. Kennedy, *Character and Destiny*, 47.

ing city on a hill.' Alas, we are no more."[111] Kennedy writes that until the mid-nineteenth century, the Bible was the "chief textbook" in a fairly explicitly Christian public education system.[112] However, he now sees anti-Christian prejudice in educational curricula, not to mention general ignorance about the founding fathers: "If the educational elites get their way, not only will schoolchildren not know about the Christianity of the founders of this country, they won't even learn about our founders. Period."[113] The problem most recently includes "antipatriotism" in post-9/11 curricula criticizing US foreign policy.[114] Left unchecked, Kennedy concludes, the consequence of these developments will be that "your children and grandchildren are going to live in a godless society where life will be but one tragedy after another. In that day no life will be worth living."[115]

Pat Robertson is quite specific about sources of American decline, discussing such things as the humanism of Charles Darwin, Karl Marx, Friedrich Nietzsche, Sigmund Freud, and John Dewey; biblical higher criticism; the similarities between the social gospel of Walter Rauschenbusch and the "The Humanist Manifesto" of 1933, and their alleged rejection of both supernaturalism and capitalism.[116] He also specifically cites the American Civil Liberties Union as complicit in "the loss of majority rights," especially the right to practice faith in the public square. This is manifested in evolution versus creationism cases as well as "the undermining of the nation's spiritual heritage" by defending the removal of prayer and Bible reading from public schools.[117] Added to this is judicial activism and its results, such as *Roe v. Wade* and the legalization of abortion, not to mention Vietnam and the "loss of honor and the will to win."[118] At the end of it all, writes Robertson, one sees America in very much the same condition as biblical Israel:

> At the time Isaiah wrote, the people of Israel, like the citizens of America, had departed from their spiritual roots. They were in

---

111. Ibid., 247.
112. Kennedy and Newcombe, *What If America?*, 134.
113. Ibid., 124.
114. Ibid., 132–33.
115. Kennedy, *Character and Destiny*, 248.
116. Robertson, *America's Dates*, 175–81.
117. Ibid., 192–95.
118. Ibid., chapters 19 and 20.

deep trouble. They had forsaken the ways of God and were living in immorality and corruption. Their treasury was bankrupt. Their military might had ebbed away, and they found themselves surrounded by a powerful enemy. The end was in sight for their once proud and prosperous nation.[119]

Falwell is even more centrally concerned with both the economic and military aspects of America's decline: "she has, both economically and militarily, lost her prominence among the nations of the world."[120] Near the very beginning of his book, written at the end of the Carter Administration, he laments that "the United States is for the first time, in my lifetime, and probably in the lifetime of my parents and grandparents, no longer the military might of the world."[121] By disarming to any degree, the country surrenders its sovereignty, and consequently, its liberty.[122] Falwell makes an adamant, if brief, biblical case for strong militarization, rooted in Romans 13:1–6, and states plainly that "nowhere in the Bible is there a rebuke for the bearing of armaments."[123]

While the country is far too weak in projecting power abroad, it is far too strong in projecting power domestically: "Today government has become all-powerful as we have exchanged freedom for security." Speaking economically as he is, redistribution of wealth is tantamount to tyranny, and is therefore "alien to the Founding Fathers of our country." Rather, a biblical economic approach would emphasize the priority of free enterprise, as espoused by such figures as Milton Friedman.[124]

119. Ibid., 274.
120. Falwell, *Listen, America!*, 97.
121. Ibid., 9. This book was written around the time that Falwell joined with Weyrich and Viguerie in galvanizing the nascent New Christian Right. While the context certainly dates his argument, it does not *outdate* it, for the concern expressed animates Falwell's discourse throughout his career, to no less a degree than it did the direction of the Moral Majority at that time.
122. Ibid., 97. As he laments, "Ten years ago we could have destroyed much of the population of the Soviet Union had we desired to fire our missiles. The sad fact is that today the Soviet Union would kill 135 million to 160 million Americans, and the United States would kill only 3 to 5 per cent of the Soviets because of their antiballistic missiles and their civil defense" (98).
123. Ibid., 98.
124. Ibid., 12–13. On this count, he writes, "The free-enterprise system is clearly outlined in the Book of Proverbs in the Bible. Jesus Christ made it clear that the work ethic was a part of His plan for man. Ownership of property is biblical. Competition in business is biblical. Ambitious and successful business management is clearly outlined as a part of God's plan for His people."

Free enterprise is consistent with individual political freedom, and "no nation has survived long when its citizens were denied the free market and individual initiative."[125]

Yet, for Falwell, "there is a bond among personal freedom, political freedom, and economic freedom that is an indissoluble one," which means that "at the root of America's problems today is the decay of our individual and national morals."[126] This is due in large part to the state of education, which since World War II has seen "a continuing infiltration of socialism onto the campus of our major colleges and universities." Bible and prayer were replaced with "courses reflecting the philosophy of humanism." At the primary and secondary levels, "basic values such as morality, individualism, respect for our nation's heritage, and the benefits of the free-enterprise system have, for the most part, been censored from today's public-classroom textbooks." The result is increasing moral chaos, marked by greater sexual promiscuity and violence in schools.[127] All of these problems—military, economic, cultural—are rooted in America's "spiritual condition," which is "desperately in need of a divine healing."[128] As Falwell puts it in a section titled, "The Need for National Repentance," "We are literally approaching the brink of national disaster. Indeed, 'if God does not judge America soon, He will have to apologize to Sodom and Gomorrah.'"[129]

Falwell may have had something like this in mind when on September 13, 2001, he commented to Pat Robertson on *The 700 Club* that all those who have attempted to secularize America—pagans, gays, abortionists, feminists, and the ACLU among them—were culpable for the attacks on the World Trade Center and the Pentagon two days earlier. Falwell was excoriated in the press for his comments, but his explanation and apology the next day were even more revealing of his nationalism. In a phone interview with CNN, he referred directly to Scripture and particularly to Proverbs 14:23, which for him points to

---

125. Ibid., 73.

126. Ibid., 56.

127. Ibid., 205–6. Along with his concentration on the military inadequacy of the late 1970s, his fear of socialism or even communism may seem antiquated to the reader. However, in the same way these themes continued unabated throughout Falwell's career, they continue to this day in the discourse of some of the Christian Right organizations discussed above.

128. Ibid., 243.

129. Ibid., 248.

the necessity of Christian principles undergirding national identity and public policy.[130] He explains that those who have pursued secularization in America "have removed our nation from its relationship with Christ on which it was founded." This in turn "created an environment which possibly has caused God to lift the veil of protection which has allowed no one to attack America on our soil since 1812."

If America's recent decline is due to a rejection of its founding covenant identity, then the way forward must be a recovery of that identity. Second Chronicles 7:14, a ubiquitous reference in these works, is interpreted as promising that if Christians humble themselves and pray, God will heal the entire nation.[131] As exemplified by America's forefathers, say Marshall and Manuel, renewal of the vertical and horizontal aspects of the Covenant Way is both necessary and possible.[132] For Kennedy, to achieve a "new birth of freedom," America will need to rediscover its Christian roots, its "genuine history" marked by more or less explicit Christian faith at both the popular and elite levels.[133] Moreover, "a new birth of freedom will not take place until there are multiplied new births in the hearts of Americans," namely, that rebirth made possible in Christ, and "liberty under law" attendant to that.[134] Evangelism and conversion are therefore central to American national renewal,[135] integral to the "cultural mandate" for Christians to influence society and exercise proper dominion as instructed as early as Genesis 1:28. Therefore, the political and cultural institutions that "have been taken over by unbelievers who have produced monstrosities that give glory not to God but to Satan," must be recaptured (through the system) and redirected.[136] "The time has come, and is long overdue," Kennedy

---

130. If the transcript is accurate, Falwell quotes Proverbs 14:23 to say, "'living by God's principles promotes a nation to greatness, violating those principles brings a nation to shame'" ("Falwell Apologizes"). This is a misquotation, or at best a loose paraphrase; the verse actually states, "In all toil there is profit, but mere talk leads only to poverty."

131. Second Chronicles 7: 14 reads, "if my people who are called by my name humble themselves, pray, seek my face, and turn from their wicked ways, then I will hear from heaven, and will forgive their sin and heal their land."

132. Marshall and Manuel, *Light and Glory*, 358.

133. Kennedy and Newcombe, *What If America?*, 168.

134. Ibid., 69. See also p. 191.

135. Ibid., 200.

136. Kennedy, *Character and Destiny*, 58–59. Kennedy explains at this point that he does not subscribe to the dominion theology most commonly associated with

declares, "when Christians and conservatives and all men and women who believe in the birthright of freedom must rise up and reclaim America for Jesus Christ." This heritage is "what is ours by right," so "we must be just as persistent and as unbearable to our adversaries as the Israelites were to Pharaoh."[137]

For Robertson, the importance of and potential for renewal is exemplified in the events described in the final part of his book, titled "Finding Our Way Again." Here, the 1980 "Spiritual March on Washington," and the 1981 inauguration of Ronald Reagan exemplify what renewal requires, and the imminent 1988 election provides renewal's next significant opportunity. The 1980 march exemplified the centrality of prayer and of solidarity. Robertson reflects that as he sat on the platform at the event watching a variety of men and women pray, he marveled at their ethnic, economic, and denominational diversity; yet, "they were one, and their prayer for the nation was one prayer."[138] Reagan's inaugural is noteworthy for its encapsulation of core commitments of the Christian Right in covenant America: the priority of the nuclear family, opposition to abortion, the importance of school prayer—"Ronald Reagan was committed to the renewal of the spiritual life of the nation from the beginning of his first term"—the fight against crime, and supply-side economics.[139] Reagan's reelection confirmed the rightness of his commitments,[140] and the upcoming presidential election between George H. W. Bush and Michael Dukakis would be their next major test, the next national opportunity to definitively return the nation to its foundation and proper identity.

Rousas John Rushdoony and Gary North, which calls for direct Christian control of the country with a legal system forcibly remade in the likeness of Old Testament Israel. As Kennedy maintains, "I think that teaching gives the impression that Christians believe they are to lord it over unbelievers, and I believe that only isolates us even further . . . We are not simply to hold on to our faith and rule the world, but we are to share our faith and love with all mankind and, together, we are to live in peace until Christ returns" (60).

137. Ibid., 80–81.

138. Robertson, *America's Dates*, 281.

139. Ibid., 285ff.

140. Reflecting on Reagan's reelection in 1984, Robertson writes, "The president had kept his inaugural promise to begin an era of renewal for the nation and her people. As President Reagan stood to speak, millions were thanking God for hearing and answering their prayers" (ibid., 291).

For Falwell, national renewal requires "godly leadership" in the family, church, and nation, which alone can put America "back on a divine course." Divine healing will come when people pray and obey God, "but we must have leadership in America to deliver God's message."[141] Godly leadership is tied to good citizenship, such that "the pastors, the priests, and the rabbis of America have a responsibility, not just the right, to see to it that the moral climate and conscience of America is such that this nation can be healed inwardly." Inward healing will bring outward healing.[142] This hope of healing lies squarely with the "Christian public in America,"[143] and only "if God's people will humble themselves, pray, seek His face, and turn from their wicked ways."[144] The situation is urgent: "We must turn America around or prepare for inevitable destruction . . . God has no reason to spare us if we continue to reject Him."[145] Like Kennedy, and Robertson less explicitly, Falwell calls for a spiritual rebirth rooted in the individual citizen, a "regeneration in Christ Jesus" that will return the nation "to God and to the Bible as never before in the history of America."[146] As he writes, "We need a revival of righteous living based on a proper confession of sin and repentance of heart if we are to remain the land of the free and the home of the brave!"[147]

True renewal, however, will inevitably involve sacrifice. This is the point where these narratives most closely connect to Smith's fourth sacred foundation of sacrifice and destiny. "How few people today are willing to sacrifice for the salvation of the Western world," laments Kennedy. Too many are concerned more with their own personal interests and pleasures. Commitment to God must be paramount for freedom to reign; anything short of that leads to national destruction.[148] Is it not possible, asks Kennedy, that we may have to suffer for national renewal?

---

141. Falwell, *Listen, America!*, 17.

142. Ibid., 19.

143. Ibid., 20. This is as opposed to "the liberals," who here are lumped together with "the pornographers, the smut peddlers, and those who are corrupting our youth."

144. Ibid., 243.

145. Ibid., 22.

146. Ibid., 243, 263.

147. Ibid., 266.

148. Kennedy and Newcombe, *What If America?*, 64–66.

America, a Christian nation, demands an equal sacrifice from each of us. Did you ever consider the fact that birth itself involves great sacrifice? . . . Even when President Abraham Lincoln uttered the phrase 'a new birth of freedom,' the ground surrounding him was saturated with blood, and tears were flowing throughout the land. There was a new birth of sorts after the Civil War. The Union was safe, and slowly the nation healed.[149]

Christians are losing the culture war because they are too comfortable and lackadaisical in the face of very active opposition. God will raise others up if today's Christians do not step forward, but "if we don't get involved, we will suffer loss."[150] For that reason, "it is absolutely essential that we be victorious." Indeed, it is not merely the earthly state of the nation at stake; the success of the cultural mandate is tied directly to the eternal fate of the believer. Kennedy states, "Unless we are overcomers who claim victory over tyranny in this world, then we shall not be with Christ in heaven . . . Heaven is for victors. It is not the resting place of losers and defeatists who simply gave up and let the secular liberal elite dictate policy and pervert the world."[151] National renewal via the cultural mandate, then, is of ultimate, eschatological importance to faithful Christians.

As a final point with regard to these narratives of decline, it is worth noting Andrew Murphy's discussion of nostalgia in Christian Right jeremiads. Nostalgia "returns individuals to times and places of real significance in their lives," which for many senior Christian Right leaders is the 1950s. Nostalgia often tends toward an overestimate of both the virtue of the past (as reconstructed) and the decline of the present. These leaders' emphasis on the decline beginning in the 1960s is part and parcel of the effort to connect the experience of their audience with the reconstructed past. Yet, it is not simply the 1950s that they long for; rather, "they believe the 1960s destroyed traditions that had existed, virtually unchanged, since the founding."[152] This nostalgic turn is evident in the literature considered here. Marshall and Manuel's introduction alludes to it, portraying the breakdown of the 1960s just

---

149. Ibid., 234.
150. Ibid., 237.
151. Kennedy, *Character and Destiny*, 263.
152. Murphy, 131–33.

as "the American Dream was about to come true," presumably in the preceding decade. Kennedy, for his part, equates the "authentic history of America" with "the history that I learned as a child."[153] And Falwell laments that "the United States is for the first time, in my lifetime, and probably in the lifetime of my parents and grandparents, no longer the military might of the world."[154] Moreover, "I remember a time when it was positive to be patriotic, and as far as I am concerned, it still is. I remember as a boy, when the flag was raised, everyone stood proudly and put his hand upon his heart and pledged allegiance with gratitude."[155] The point here is not that these authors are merely universalizing their own experience, but rather that they see their own personal narratives taken up in the national narrative they are attempting to empower. Their own histories have in certain ways bound them to particular understandings of American nationhood over against others. Their personal identities are therefore part and parcel of the national identity that they espouse, whose decline they lament, and whose renewal they pursue with vigor. In this sense, nostalgia acts as a constraint on their nationalist endeavors, their own upbringing acting to limit the possibilities of available materials for their nationalist message. Yet it also acts to interpret or reinterpret elements that transcend their heritage, such as the biblical narrative, which are then reinterpreted in light of their nostalgia to authenticate a particular national identity.

Evaluation

One notices within these texts the overwhelming concern with the meaning of American national identity. These authors are, indeed, in Heinz's words, "engaged in a contest over the meaning of America's story," and go to great lengths in fashioning an alternative story—comprised of historical and theological claims alike—that will effectively resist the secular "status elites" and their "control of public symbol production," or one might say, public *narrative* production. They advocate what they consider to be the nation's cultural core over against those whom they perceive as propagating changes to that core or alternative cores altogether. To this end, they attempt to inculcate in their readers

---

153. Kennedy, *Character and Destiny*, 71.
154. Falwell, *Listen, America!*, 9.
155. Ibid., 18.

a particular vision of the American nation that entails an interweaving of elements of the Christian theological tradition, especially the biblical narrative, with national history and myth. This is their project of authentication, by which they seek to champion America's "true self" over against opposing understandings of American national identity. As Smith's theory indicates, it is also a sort of pursuit of holiness, in which faithfulness to the proper conception of America is faithfulness to the God of Jesus Christ. Thus, in the end, they are advocating a syncretized theopolitics.

In *The Light and the Glory*, Marshall and Manuel regale the reader with a mixture of historical fact and narrative speculation,[156] typically within an explicitly theological framework rooted in a particular interpretation of the biblical narrative. However, upon examining their appropriation of both the historical and biblical narratives, one finds that the authors have read them somewhat carelessly and certainly selectively, conforming those texts to a preexisting nationalist understanding or agenda. This is evident in several ways throughout the book. First, they provide little explanation of their own historiographical method, and where they mention it, it prompts more questions than it answers. For instance, daunted by the fact that the historical documents might take them at least a year to read through, Marshall's church congregation pitches in as "research assistants." Mentioning no requirements or training for the task, the authors relate how these parishioners "were pressed into service . . . responsible for reading through each book, article, sermon, and letter, and making a preliminary assessment of its potential usefulness." "Usefulness" is never defined, and no standard or method of content analysis is cited for this process; the authors are simply thankful to end up with "a distillation which could be assimilated in a few months."[157] Elsewhere, they refer to Marshall's "steadfastly maintained professional skepticism" in carefully sifting through "the new ore samples, looking for the occasional nugget."[158] While the reject pile regularly dwarfed the "keepers" pile, no explanation is given as to the criteria involved in source selection, which means the reader is left with

156. Their regular practice is to flesh out the facts they find with imaginative narrative sequences, usually qualified with "we can almost hear" or "one can imagine what transpired." It becomes difficult at points to distinguish between the documented and the imagined.

157. Marshall and Manuel, *Light and Glory*, 21.

158. Ibid., 67.

no ability to know if documents rejected would have contradicted the authors' claims. Whether by accident or by design, their authentication of the true American story is inherently selective.

Second, there is the appropriation of the biblical covenant model for America. Contrary to the biblical theopolitics explained in chapter 4 of the present work, Marshall and Manuel assume that a covenant relationship between a nation and God is not unique to biblical Israel, but can be established even now.[159] Of course, this is not a common occurrence, or the case of America would not be so unique and special as they claim it to be. Rather, it must be that America is singularly elected for this modern covenant. However, they do not provide a theological or exegetical justification for this claim, generally or in the American context. Rather, they base it on the historical discourse of the early American settlers and figures of the founding era. At every turn, they provide evidence after evidence to demonstrate that these historical persons perceived God as acting directly in their circumstances to form a new nation defined by post-Reformation separatism. While their historical case is intriguing and somewhat persuasive, they have not established that America *was* actually elected to covenant, but merely that its early settlers and founders *thought* it was. At one point they write, "Whenever we began to wonder if we might not be 'shoehorning' history to fit our presuppositions, we had the recorded beliefs of the settlers themselves as a guide."[160] Yet they miss the fact that those recorded beliefs do nothing to prove their theological covenant hypothesis, but merely demonstrate that the hypothesis itself is recurrent in American history. What *The Light and the Glory* offers, then, is little more than a historical account of American self-perception.

Third, covenant, as a presupposed given, then becomes the lens through which they filter the setbacks of colonial America; what might from the outside seem to falsify claims to covenant are rather rationalized as part of the covenant context. So even Columbus's pride and greed are not a repudiation of his claimed calling, but only a divergence from it. The Spanish friars, not the conquistadors, are the proper locus of the continuing narrative of American settlement. And when it comes to the later New England colonists, the authors read the historical evidence to indicate a consistent approach on the part of the colonists of

159. Ibid., 18–19.
160. Ibid., 25.

repentance in response to calamity, which fits well within a covenant context of blessings and curses for obedience and disobedience, respectively. Blessings would continue to the colonists for generations, "as God continued to honor the obedience of their fathers and grandfathers (Deuteronomy 7:9). But inevitably, because He loved them (and because even God's patience has an end), he would be forced to lift the grace which lay upon their land, just enough to cause them to turn back to Him." Then the "wisest among them" would call the people back to repentance, and blessing would be restored.[161] Because the covenant argument has become tautological, with no possibility of falsification, all included evidence is read as affirming of their hypothesis. On top of this, they argue that their approach actually militates against nationalism:

> And incidentally, from *this* position, it is impossible to enter into nationalistic pride. Inherent in God's call upon our forefathers to found a Christian nation was the necessity to live in a state of constant need and dependency upon His grace and forgiveness. Anyone tempted today to take an elitist attitude regarding our nation's call need only look at how badly we have failed—and continue to fail—to live up to God's expectations for us.[162]

What the authors have failed to grasp, or at least to admit, is that they have defined even America's failures as extraordinary, because these failures occur within the unique covenant context of "God's New Israel." Therefore, even their emphasis on America's failings is still a form of exceptionalism, and especially as it is tied to renewal according to the nation's unique covenant identity.

Perhaps most seriously, there is their problematic appropriation of Scripture. Besides the unjustified abstraction and appropriation of biblical Israel's covenant, which pervades the work as a whole, Marshall and Manuel distort the contexts and traditional meanings of various biblical pericopes to support their argument. Again, their hypothesis is not open to falsification. For example, while they claim that submission to civil authority is taught clearly in Scripture, Marshall and Manuel argue that "America was a new event in the history of man," in which a "body of Christians" was placed in a new land with no existing civil authority; they were to establish their own. Relying on Galatians 5:1—"For

---

161. Ibid., 25.
162. Ibid., 26.

freedom, Christ has set us free; stand fast therefore, and do not submit to a yoke of slavery"—the authors justify violent rebellion by American subjects of "King Jesus" against the British. This one, proof-texted verse, divorced from its original context concerning the requirements of Gentiles for Christian conversion and discipleship, "proved to be the key to all that followed." From this, they argue that had the colonists submitted to the increasingly stringent demands of the British Crown in the eighteenth century, "it would be like the Israelites—after all God had done for them to bring them out of Egypt—turning around and inviting Pharaoh to bring his troops to Canaan and put them back under servitude."[163] Since submission to the Crown would be tantamount to "a repudiation of all that God had been building in America, ever since He had first called them to His new Canaan," violent rebellion—necessitating the killing of Christians by other Christians—is not only justified, but is the only responsible and "realistic" course of action. That this might in fact contradict other major portions of Scripture, such as Jesus' Sermon on the Mount, does not come up in their narrative.

What is particularly fascinating about *The Light and the Glory* as nationalist discourse is that it is not only a narrative of God's activity in the formation of the American nation, but it is also a story about the *recovery* of that narrative, which Marshall and Manuel are at pains to portray as no less divinely directed, if on a smaller scale. From the compilation of historical data to the process of writing, the authors claim "providential" guidance.[164] Whenever they found the going difficult—often in relation to especially problematic findings—"we spelled out our doubts to the Lord in prayer. If we were going to navigate through the rocks and shoals that lay ahead, He would have to put His hand on the helm, and fast."[165] Apparently in response, key sources appeared "with a timing only God Himself could have directed."[166] And on one hazy morning, as Manuel objected to Marshall's claims regarding Puritan convictions about the possibility of building the kingdom of God on earth, "suddenly a breeze came out of nowhere and scattered several chapters' worth of manuscript across the patio. As we gathered up the pages, it occurred to David [Manuel] that this was the only breeze to

163. Ibid., 254, 257.
164. Ibid., 21.
165. Ibid., 67.
166. Ibid., 80.

stir a paper in the last three days." Apparently associating this with the breath of the Holy Spirit, Manuel dropped his objections and listened again to Marshall's argument. And then, "for the next hour and a half, the Holy Spirit gave us insight after insight . . ."[167] The Holy Spirit is thus seen by the authors as directly involved in formulating their claims and confirming the trajectory of their argument. In short, not only is America providentially brought into being, but Marshall and Manuel's *authentication* of that narrative, that is, of America's covenant identity, is likewise divinely directed. Yet it is interesting to note the degree to which such confirmation of their research takes the form of appeals first to spiritual experience rather than to Scripture or theological tradition, a move typically associated with Protestant liberalism rather than the evangelical biblicism in which context *The Light and the Glory* is usually received. It is this experience, filtered through their presuppositions, that then governs their reading of the sources, historical and biblical alike.

Several concerns arise as well when evaluating the arguments of D. James Kennedy. Like Marshall and Manuel, he unjustifiably abstracts and misappropriates biblical Israel for use in the American context. America's unprecedented freedom and abundance are credited to its genuine Christian faith, a relationship that only makes sense biblically within a covenant context of stipulations, blessings, and curses. He indicates this specifically when he discusses the significance of 2 Chronicles 14 for the American situation:

> Certainly the Israelites needed to repent and turn to God. But that is not what the verse says. It says *we* need to repent. It says *we* need to turn from our wicked ways, and then God will heal our land. God indicates His proprietary interest in His own. We are His own peculiar people who belong to Him ("who are called by My name"). These words are a great command from God to repent. There is no doubt that the United States needs to repent of its wickedness. We are overrun with pornography and blasphemy and ungodliness and immorality—perversion of every sort. We are called by the name of the second person of the Triune Godhead, Jesus Christ. We are Christians—a name first applied to us as a word that was meant to be an insult. Yet we consider it a noble title to be called after the name of Him who loved us even unto death. We are His people. We are the

---

167. Ibid., 145–46.

ones who are commanded to repent, to turn from our wicked ways. Then and only then will God heal our land. Judgment begins at the house of God.[168]

Not only do we see here how easily this discourse can slide from identifying the "we" as either the church or the nation—after all, the comment occurs within a discussion of *American* renewal[169]—but it relies on an all-too-common deliberate redirection of a particular covenant promise. As discussed in chapter 4, upon dedicating the temple, Solomon is told by Yahweh in 2 Chronicles 7:13–14, "When I shut up the heavens so that there is no rain, or command the locust to devour the land, or send pestilence among my people, if my people who are called by my name humble themselves, pray, seek my face, and turn from their wicked ways, then I will hear from heaven, and will forgive their sin and heal their land." The promise occurs within a specific context of covenant blessings and curses, hypothesizing God's judgment on the physical land—Israel's source of sustenance—if and when they are disobedient, and allowing for the possibility of renewal as God's covenant people. In widespread Christian Right discourse, however, verse 14, beginning with "if my people," is appropriated alone, thus abstracting it and making it applicable to societal rather than natural and agricultural problems, to the "land" as the nation and/or state and not the tilled earth. Thus, the promise is misappropriated for the sake of national renewal, which by implication reinforces American national identity as formulated within divine covenant.

Second, in his more recent work, Kennedy explains in an endnote that he is relying for his historiography on the works of two nineteenth-century historians, Sir Edward Shepherd Creasy (1812–1878) and George Bancroft (1800–1891), the latter of whose history "was the standard for at least half a century," but is no longer widely read "because he is politically incorrect."[170] That the academic study of history

---

168. Kennedy and Newcombe, *What If America?*, 224.

169. Just the page before, Kennedy states, "If America is truly to be renewed, it will not be through the political process, as important as that is. I believe we need a renewed vision, for 'where there is no vision, the people perish.' God can do the impossible, so we can experience a renewal in this land. And a genuine revival is what we need most if there is to be a new birth of freedom in America" (ibid., 223).

170. Ibid., 235n3. Considering coauthor Jerry Newcombe's undergraduate degree in history, it is inexplicable that no more recent historiography was consulted, save that of conservative activist David Barton and Paul Johnson, a British journalist to

might have developed and advanced since the early-to-mid-twentieth century (Kennedy's childhood), much less the nineteenth, or that new sources may have been uncovered that reinterpret earlier sources and methodological approaches does not seem to matter. Rather, the same hermeneutical lens used by those historians is used a century later, with no justification given for its continued adequacy.

One must also question his clearly functional take on the faith of Thomas Jefferson, which seems to get at some underlying assumptions in Kennedy's work. While admitting explicitly that Jefferson was not a Christian in an orthodox sense, Kennedy goes into considerable detail on Jefferson's religiosity in order to counter claims that Jefferson advocated a two-way separation of church and state. In this sense, Jefferson's religiosity is exemplary, as it functions to uphold Kennedy's conception of American identity and principles. That Jefferson was not committed to "real Christianity," as Kennedy puts it, appears to be beside the point. In other words, for Kennedy, the question of the theological truthfulness of Jefferson's convictions takes second place to their usefulness to the American project, a point that puts into some question Kennedy's later exhortations to Christian evangelism. If Jefferson's religiosity was so useful to the founding of the country, then why conclude that Christian conversion is necessary for renewal, *in addition to* the rediscovery and acknowledgment of the country's religious heritage?

This sort of functionalist approach to Christianity comes out in Robertson's writing as well. Faith—centering on a conviction of divine reward and punishment—breeds individual self-restraint and responsibility, which is integral to sustaining the nation and its republican political order. This order, meanwhile, is predicated—even directly modeled—on reading key founding documents as direct embodiments of specific biblical characteristics of God and God's dealings with Israel. With no theological justification to speak of, Robertson simply equates America's situation with Israel's, drawing direct parallels, for instance between the American colonial situation under George III and Israel's trouble with human kings. This allows him to equate Yahweh's judgment of Israel's kingship with colonial armed rebellion against the British Crown.

Such a move is quite blatant in Falwell's writing, although for Falwell it is even more problematic given his unqualified advocacy of

---

whom the authors refer as an "eminent historian" (43).

militarism and unbridled capitalism. *Listen America!*, appearing early in his political advocacy career, emphasizes again and again the necessity of a strong American military as essential to its identity. He laments America's declining military strength—which may be interpreted as an inability to kill enough of its enemies—and equates it directly with the dissolution of the country. There is little indication that he changed his mind later, given his statement during the 2004 election season exhorting followers to "'Vote Christian. This means pro-life, pro-family, and pro-national defense. These are second nature to God's people...'"[171] Yet, when one considers the prophetic critiques of Israel's militarism, state centralization, and *realpolitik*, it would seem that not only has Falwell inappropriately abstracted biblical Israel as a model for the American nation, he has also misunderstood the Old Testament covenants altogether, and is attempting to conform America to the very *distorted* theopolitics for which Israel was later condemned. As Cavanaugh points out, for Old Testament Israel, "one of the concrete signs of God's favor is a *lack of military strength and preparation*. Indeed, the emphasis is often on the military weakness of Israel."[172] Since, as chapter 4 explained, Israel is indicted specifically for its institutionalization of power politics, continuing to advocate them as "second nature to God's people" constitutes the perpetuation of grievous theopolitical error that, in the very narrative to which Falwell appeals, results in divine condemnation.[173]

Secondly, following Milton Friedman's lead, he ties economic autonomy directly to individual freedom. This, of course, raises questions about Falwell's definition of freedom, but that is of less concern to this project than his use of Scripture to justify it. He writes that "the free-enterprise system is clearly outlined in the Book of Proverbs," but how can a collection of individual proverbial observations "outline" anything, much less a "system" in any genuine sense of the word? Falwell seems to be reaching for any semblance of a biblical rationale that he can lay his hands on, no matter how loose. Moreover, to make his argument, he must ignore the prophetic critique of Amos, which implicates mili-

---

171. Wilcox and Larson, *Onward Christian Soldiers?*, 9.

172. Cavanaugh, "Empire," 17.

173. This is also why, given the forms of divine judgment in the prophetic literature—i.e., typically as logical extensions of the sins themselves—it is interesting that 9/11 was perceived by Falwell and Robertson as a judgment on homosexuality and secularism rather than the militarism and capitalism epitomized by the institutions attacked, institutions embodying the very ideologies Falwell advocates.

tarization in the ongoing problems of domestic poverty and economic injustice. This puts Falwell's militarism/free-enterprise schema into considerable doubt, as it does his stated commitment to the inerrancy of Scripture.

For this project, however, the most significant problem manifested in these works is that by misappropriating biblical Israel as they do, that is, by making the nation America the extension of Israel as central to God's plans for global salvation, these authors supplant the church, and by implication, Jesus Christ as Lord. The burden of chapter 5 was to demonstrate the ways in which it is the church, not any particular earthly nation, that is engrafted onto Israel as God's people and that constitutes the embodiment of Jesus Christ's fulfillment of Israel's covenant. It is the church, as a theopolitical community and alone of all political communities in the world, that acts as the embodiment of the Christian gospel and carries forth in community the mission of global salvation. Yet for Marshall and Manuel, it is America, not the church, that brings "light to the Gentiles" as the direct continuation of Israel's covenant relationship with God, and in the form of a people living through faith in Jesus Christ. For Kennedy, it is America, not the church, that is the new and unprecedented nation called to model liberty to the world. It is America, not the church's Lord, that constitutes the "last best hope of people on earth." For Robertson, it is America, not the church, that is the unique polity established according to God's own character and attributes, the unprecedented theopolitical extension of Israel. For Falwell, it is America, not the church, that is the society predicated on the Scriptures, in unique relation to God. For these authors, the saga of America is the definitive salvation history today, the most formative story that shapes American Christian identity and that points us to God's salvation of the world. The church—supposedly transcending all earthly barriers and separations—can thus be divided for the sake of the American project, its members enlisted to fight for the realization of its national identity over against Christians claimed by other national identities.

Finally, I argued in chapter 2 that Adrian Hastings is mistaken to claim that nationalism, particularly exceptionalism appropriating biblical Israel, tends to flourish among the "theologically untrained laity," the common people, who do not know better than to substitute their own nation for the church. I argued that by his own historical account, the role of educated clergy in fostering national identity amongst the populace could only mean that nationalism arose not in the absence, but fully in the presence—and even in consequence—of certain hermeneutical and theological frameworks. I believe the present account of the literature of prominent Christian Right leaders substantiates my argument. Marshall, Kennedy, Falwell, and Robertson are all clergy, and it is largely by virtue of their pastoral teaching, both spoken and written, that their nationalist narrative is propagated.

Note that, true to nationalist form, these authors have had to be highly selective in what aspects of the American narrative they choose to highlight or even to repackage in order to portray the nation as exceptional, as unprecedented (except by Israel), and as founded and living within a unique covenant relationship with God.[174] This is true for the biblical narrative as well. Not only is their own nation placed in the role of the church as the extension of biblical Israel, but the authors *misappropriate* Israel's own narrative in the process, interpreting Israel as more of a supernation—a kingdom operating with divine favor according to the politics of the world—than as an *alternative to* the nations. There is no acknowledgment of Israel as a counter to empire, to the ways of the nations in their continual turmoil and strife. Rather, Israel is to these authors a model of a nation that acts as the locus of God's salvific activity on earth, and simultaneously as a uniquely rich and powerful country. This is an aberration of genuine biblical theopolitics; yet their congregants, listeners, and readers would not know it from their teachings.

It is this clergy-propagated theopolitical aberration that constitutes an alternative and competing salvation narrative to that of orthodox Christianity and the biblical texts. Here, salvation is viewed in distinctly national terms, rather than either the *de*nationalized language of certain New Testament texts (e.g., Gal 3:28) or the *re*nationalized language of the ecclesia in others (e.g., 1 Pet 2:9–10). Salvation, in the form of national renewal, entails the exaltation of American national identity, rather than its relativization. This salvation narrative requires the distortion of the biblical text in order to reconceive the present nation in *revised* covenant terms, terms that are divorced from the genuine bibli-

---

174. For example, there is a remarkable absence of any substantive treatment of the slavocracy in the American South, except to point to Lincoln and emancipation as heroic and consistent with America's divine calling. That slavery was inextricably bound with earlier heroic figures and political developments goes virtually unaddressed.

cal conceptions of either Israel or the church. This results in distorted teaching and the propagation of an altered and syncretized theopolitical identity; it also gives rise to rationales for the pursuit of power, both to institutionalize or reinstitutionalize America's covenant identity, and to justify the use of violence against any entities perceived as threats, from the British Crown during the American Revolution to twenty-first-century international terrorism. Hence, Christian Right nationalism, emanating from within the church itself, acts as a countercurrent to orthodox theopolitics.

Conclusion

In this chapter, I have examined Christian Right discourse as a case study in American Christian nationalism, using Anthony Smith's rubric of "sacred foundations." I argued that such Christian Right discourse constitutes a form of nationalism, in which America is portrayed as uniquely and divinely chosen for a sacred mission, which it has subsequently rejected and to which it must return, lest it face judgment. It does this by selectively interweaving elements of American history and myth with elements of the biblical narrative. I then evaluated the discourse as to its own internal coherence as well as its coherence to the biblical theopolitics outlined in chapters 4 and 5, finding that—as a nationalist narrative highly selective and distortive in its use of national and biblical elements—not only is the discourse marked by numerous internal inconsistencies that effectively undermine many of its claims, but it improperly appropriates the biblical text to which it claims allegiance in a way that is theologically problematic. In effect, America replaces the church as the definitive theopolitical community engrafted onto biblical Israel.

I believe this case study supports my argument in the first chapter regarding what I perceive as inadequacies in current theopolitical critiques of nationalism. These treatments tend either to neglect nationalism as a problem distinct, though rarely separate, from the activities of state and market, or to present nationalism—in conjunction with certain problematic scholarship—as the exclusive purview of the state, entailing an utterly fabricated narrative by elites free from internal or external constraint, and relying upon a transnational, transcultural understanding of religion. Rather, as I have attempted to demonstrate, the nationalism of the Christian Right is a nationalism formulated and propagated within segments of the church itself, often in resistance to certain moves by state elites. It deliberately interweaves national history and myth with elements of the biblical narrative—a very particular source and tradition—certain interpretations of which have formed nationalist elites and their audiences alike prior to the nationalist movement in question. Yet it distorts that biblical narrative, a problem that can only be discerned and neutralized with a robust recovery of biblical Israel's theopolitics—particularly in conjunction with the presentation of ecclesial theopolitics in the New Testament. This will be true as well for the next and final chapter, in which I take up the nationalism found within the political theologies of Stephen H. Webb and Richard John Neuhaus.

CHAPTER 7

Nationalism in American Political Theology

INTRODUCTION

The previous chapter examined the nationalist narratives of major figures in the American Christian Right. I argued there that these narratives, understood through Anthony Smith's rubric of "sacred foundations," constitute nationalist discourse in that they aim to authenticate a particular vision of American national identity in the face of perceived threats. They do this by selectively interweaving reinterpreted elements of the biblical narrative with American history and myth, producing a syncretized salvation narrative that makes America central and indispensible to the divine project of global redemption. This narrative identifies the nation as especially chosen and established by God, as attested to in accounts of its earliest years, its so-called golden age, in which the nation's Christian character was ostensibly beyond question. The nation subsequently declined from that identity, necessitating the Christian Right's current efforts at national renewal, central to which is a "recovery" of this narrative, and particularly of the beliefs and practices of America's golden ages, the periods of the nation's early settlers and founding fathers. As I explained, Andrew Murphy calls this type of narrative a "traditionalist jeremiad," named for its prescribed recovery of specific sociopolitical practices and institutions.

The other type of jeremiad Murphy cites is the "progressive jeremiad," a narrative that focuses not so much on specific *practices* as fundamental *principles* of American nationhood. It looks to the ideals of the past, especially America's founding period, and laments how those principles have been "co-opted and frustrated by the apathy or, worse yet, the active collusion of elites eager to maintain their own positions of power."[1] While the progressive jeremiad pays less attention to the specific practices and institutions of prior periods, it no less than the traditionalist jeremiad selectively reads, appropriates, and reconstructs a narrative of American national identity that is in line with its particular vision.

This final chapter discusses two examples of the progressive jeremiad, as found in the work of theologians Stephen H. Webb and Richard John Neuhaus. In both cases, fundamental principles of American national identity are under threat and require immediate recovery and safeguarding. As opposed to the more straightforward narratives found in Christian Right discussion, Webb and Neuhaus articulate these American principles or ideas via more systematic political theologies. For Webb, it is the notion of providence, which he reads as a particularly American theological orientation. For Neuhaus, it is the idea of democratic freedom, rooted in a dialectic of social contract and transcendent covenant. Both theologians see America's (Judeo-) Christian identity at stake, portraying that identity and threats to it in theological terms, and both pursue theopolitical projects aimed at recovering earlier theological understandings. I take up these two scholars for several reasons. First, it is important to point out that nationalism exists not just in popular narrative accounts by well-known clergy, but also in more sophisticated academic theologies. Second, their accounts are both "contemporary" and salient to political theology in the early twenty-first century. Third, they have both engaged and been engaged by some of the thinkers surveyed in the first chapter of this study. Neuhaus and Hauerwas have engaged each other directly for years, and Neuhaus has been engaged by Hauerwas's students at various points. As well, Webb has engaged Hauerwas in each of his works of political theology, and Webb and William Cavanaugh have held a public exchange over one of Cavanaugh's articles. Thus, both theologians, Neuhaus's death in 2009 notwithstanding, remain direct interlocutors in theopolitical scholar-

---

1. Murphy, *Prodigal Nation*, 114.

ship, and I discuss them here in part to argue how that scholarship ought better to evaluate them.

This chapter examines Webb and Neuhaus in turn, looking at the ways in which each of their projects constitutes not only a jeremiad, in Murphy's terms,[2] but like more popular Christian right discourse, a nationalist project of authentication: selectively recovering, reinterpreting, and propagating a particular vision of American national identity—America's "true self"—seen to be in continuity with biblical Israel and the Christian salvation history, and under threat from contemporary forces. Again, this entails both the notion that they are defending a particular national identity against perceived threats, as well as the idea that authentic national identity, as tied to particular theological moves, is tantamount to a form of political holiness.

These authors are more theologically sophisticated than the figures discussed in the previous chapter, and as such, their arguments are not as easily fitted to Smith's four sacred foundations of community, territory, glorious past and decline, and sacrifice and destiny. However, I believe that some of these important elements can be found throughout their schemas, and I will highlight where they are most pronounced when appropriate. My primary aim, however, is to examine the form and content of their arguments to discern the ways in which the biblical narrative, and often other elements of the Christian theological tradition, are distorted in order to reach their theopolitical conclusions. These distortions are rooted in an *a priori* American exceptionalism, which guides both authors throughout their discussions, fomenting a selective and sometimes self-contradictory reading of both the American and biblical narratives, and determining in advance political theologies that in both their form and content amount to nationalist narratives.

---

2. Admittedly, Murphy may not see Webb and Neuhaus as examples of the progressive jeremiad (indeed, he fits Neuhaus within the traditionalist camp), since he would not view their jeremiads as resulting in religious pluralism, one of the hallmarks of his progressive depiction. However, as he explains it, the form (traditionalist or progressive) is determined more by its content than its effects, and in terms of accounts of particular practices and institutions versus fundamental principles and ideas, Webb and Neuhaus clearly articulate the latter. It should also be noted that the jeremiad is not distinctively conservative, in American political terms. Murphy discusses at length various manifestations on the political Left, such as discourse by Robert F. Kennedy, Martin Luther King Jr., and especially Bill Moyers.

Stephen H. Webb: American Providence

Having written on theologies of rhetoric and sound, compassion for animals, vegetarianism, and the role of theology in secular education, Stephen H. Webb can be considered a theologian of eclectic interests.[3] Perhaps his best-known and most controversial theological treatment, though, concerns his political theology of providence. His work on the subject, and especially his book *American Providence: A Nation with a Mission*, is an argument for a recovery of the Christian doctrine of providence as a source for Christian influence in the political arena. He seeks to demonstrate that political theology dealing with nationalism, globalism, and ecclesiology requires a robust theory of providence, and that America cannot be understood apart from that theory. In particular, Webb is concerned about America's place in political theology in recent years—and especially since 9/11—when so much of political and theological discourse has disparaged American hegemony and international dominance. Webb sees American global leadership, which he and his critics alike refer to as "empire," as both necessary and divinely directed—in a word, providential. America mediates democracy and capitalism to the world, which for Webb facilitates the mediation of American-style Christianity to the world, as a distinctive prefiguring of the kingdom of God. He therefore undertakes the recovery of providential theology as a "reasonable theological assessment of the role that America, along with its particular brand of Christianity, plays on the world stage."[4] As I will demonstrate, however, Webb's is less an objective assessment of either the theology of providence or of US foreign policy than an active rationale for American empire via an account of America's exceptional calling and mission. It is, in short, a nationalist narrative articulated via a political theology of providence

A Political Theology of Providence

Webb makes a number of assertions about providence, both in terms of the content of the Christian doctrine as well as the doctrine's role in

---

3. Stephen H. Webb is Professor of Religion and Philosophy at Wabash College, a liberal arts college for men in Crawfordsville, Indiana. Some of his works on these subjects include *Blessed Excess*, *Taking Religion to School*, *Good Eating*, and *Divine Voice*.

4. Webb, *American Providence*, 2.

American history and identity. In terms of content, providence assumes that the biblical account of what God is doing in history is trustworthy, an accurate revelation of God's nature. The doctrine of providence is the attempt to discern history according to its end, with particular attention to "the continuities that connect the Bible's vision of the end to the vicissitudes of the moment."[5] A robust providential theology revolves around belief in a personal God. It entails not just *general* providence, that is, "God's uniform and regular guidance of natural and human affairs," but rather an account of God's *special* providence, that is, "God's miraculous interventions into nature and history." Webb eschews the immanentism of the general, which perceives God as a "hidden cause" behind historical events, rather than history's "driving agent." Rather, "all of God's action in the world is special in the sense that it is based on the biblical history of Israel and the Father's care for the Son. All of God's action in the world is also personal in that a triune God, and not a distant superpower in the sky, guides history and nature alike."[6] Providence is the foreseeing God's direct, ongoing, personal involvement in human affairs.

While recognizing God's *creatio ex nihilo*, special providence constitutes *creatio continua*, a "continuing creation" that is always bringing new things into being rather than simply preserving the past.[7] Theopolitically, God continually creates the world by bringing new social forms into being over time. These social forms—political and economic—are "parables" of the coming of the kingdom of God.[8] As such, "how God acts in history cannot be unrelated to the ways in which humans organize themselves to achieve their own ends." More specifically, the doctrine of providence stipulates that God demands of a given nation particular duties in proportion to its divine blessings—including certain political institutions and practices—which means that "providence asks Christians to get off the sidelines and into the game of history."[9]

Hence the centrality of the nation-state in Webb's theology of providence. While history progresses toward the kingdom of God, that should

5. Webb, "Eschatology and Politics," 509.
6. Webb, *American Providence*, 13, 89, 103.
7. Ibid., 7.
8. Webb, "Eschatology and Politics," 509–10.
9. Webb, *American Providence*, 6–7.

not suggest that God is sidestepping earthly kingdoms in the process: "the very notion of a divine kingdom suggests some kind of heavenly realm that transforms and thus is in fundamental continuity with the all-too-human political organizations of this world." As demonstrated biblically in God's election of Israel, God works through nation-states to carry history to its conclusion. Webb therefore does not subscribe to claims of Israel's theopolitical singularity, a model in the midst of the world of the alternative politics of the kingdom of God. Rather, Israel as the foremost of nation-states is the "template" for understanding how God uses nation-states to accomplish the divine plan.[10] While Israel is central to providential theology, "God also chooses other nations in order to accomplish the task God gave to Israel," working through these nations to implement the divine agenda.[11] Simply put, "God rules the world through the work of the nations,"[12] and any theology that does not give the nation-state its providential due in this regard risks being "romantic and abstract" in its eschatology.[13] Redemption within history requires national identity.

As I argued in chapter 4, however, this is a profound misreading of Israel's identity and mission. Called to be a communal sign of God's reign and salvation in the midst of the world, Israel was, as God's "treasured possession," an utterly unique endeavor, quite in contrast to the "nation-states" of its time. An alternative to the power politics of the surrounding kingdoms and empires, Israel was to embody the social order of Torah. As it gradually accommodated to and adopted the political practices of the surrounding nations, it diverged from Torah, from its divinely appointed "task." As Torah was fulfilled in Christ—whose role is all but absent in Webb's political theology—the *church*, not the nations, was engrafted onto Israel's covenant (1 Pet 2:9–10). As such—and contra Oliver O'Donovan, upon whom Webb in part relies—Israel was never meant to be a "template" for earthly nation-states, except indirectly, insofar as they surrender their pretentions and give way to their inherent temporality in light of the reign of Yahweh. Biblically, their role in the "divine plan" has always been peripheral at best, so to ground an entire political theology in that role—especially a theology that posi-

---

10. Webb, *American Providence*, 7, 23; "Eschatology and Politics," 510.
11. Webb, *American Providence*, 10, 20.
12. Ibid., 72.
13. Webb, "Eschatology and Politics," 510.

tions the church and the Christian tradition—is to profoundly mistake the locus of God's salvific activity in the world. Nevertheless, Webb locates God's redemptive activity today squarely in the identity, mission, and contemporary power of the United States.

Chosen Community: America as Providence Embodied

To appropriate again Anthony Smith's nationalism rubric of "sacred foundations," what Webb articulates in part is a narrative of America as God's chosen community in the contemporary world for prefiguring and helping to establish the kingdom of God on earth. America is "an idea, something like a hypothesis, or a laboratory for the strongest mixture of faith and freedom," and the key to American national identity is the theological notion of providence. Providence is a sort of "grammar" that enables a discussion of the meaning of America, and it acts in lieu of traditional cultural features of nations: "We are not a particular people, in terms of a shared set of rituals and beliefs, which makes us a people set apart from other nations, whether we like that status or not." America's very lack of shared cultural traits distinguishes it from other nations, but then one must ask, "What (or who) has set us apart, and for what purpose?"[14]

In short, the God of the Christian Scriptures has set America apart for the purpose of prefiguring the kingdom of God on earth. America does this by spreading "American-style Protestantism" via the vehicle of globalism, with America acting as mediator between the two, projecting forth the "universal impulse" of Christianity.[15] America and divine providence are inseparable in that "so much of the American dream comes from and continues to overlap with the Christian dream of the kingdom of God." Webb calls American providence "prophetic, which means that it has a universal message. Providence is not for the benefit of America alone."[16] In this sense, America carries forth biblical Israel's own task of covenant, a mission on behalf of the world.

For Webb, providentially mediating globalism as the facilitator of Christian evangelism requires America to be the chief agent and guardian of democratic capitalism. He maintains throughout his work that

14. Webb, *American Providence*, 29–30.
15. Webb, "On the True Globalism," 125–26; Webb, *American Providence*, 5.
16. Webb, *American Providence*, 10, 39.

democracy is a theological good, located squarely in Christian principles.[17] American democracy is so amenable to Christianity because it is "a universal political form that not only springs from the great Christian theme of freedom but also facilitates the global growth of the church."[18] The expansion of democracy and the expansion of Christianity—particularly Protestantism—are tied together because proclamation of the gospel constitutes a "powerful speech act" that challenges societies without freedom of speech. Such a "theology of free speech" is able to evaluate and safeguard the proper conditions for evangelism. In this manner, Protestantism functions like the American Constitution, "guaranteeing the conditions that make proclamation possible." And America must continue that twofold commitment to exporting Christianity and democracy—its "holy task." Christian support for America's ability to "reshape the world in its own democratic image" is crucial, for "freedom is not a neutral value, and its export abroad cannot be separate from the work of the Christian church."[19] While Protestantism is rooted in the priesthood of all believers, America is the political outworking of that priesthood. Such immediacy to God has a "democratizing effect" on the church, and this is nowhere better demonstrated than in the global explosion of American-style Pentecostalism. Pentecostalism "reinforces the virtues necessary for democracy" by emphasizing indigenous leadership as well as the good of material prosperity. This is true to form, for Americans "prefer to use democracy, human rights, and open markets—rather than colonies and conquest—to achieve our ends."[20]

Hence the central importance of capitalist globalization: "Capitalism, Christianity, and democracy are sufficiently intertwined that pulling one out of the equation might leave all three undone, to

---

17. Ibid., 114.

18. Ibid., 117.

19. Ibid., 139–50. Unfortunately, Webb never defines "freedom" as he understands it.

20. Ibid., 123. This points to another of the many tensions in Webb's work, for shortly thereafter he writes, "Pentecostalism . . . also represents a potential dead-end for Protestantism as a whole . . . the Roman Catholic Church alone of all churches gives shelter to a theologically coherent and historically consistent principle of religious universality. Because Christian unity is integral to the gospel, the reunification of all Christian churches with Rome must be articulated as one of the primary goals of all evangelization" (ibid., 125). This concern for Christian unity, incidentally, is exclusively a spiritual concept for Webb that has no political outworking in his writing.

everyone's detriment."[21] Webb suggests that there are two globalisms at work, one economic and one religious. While there is tension between them, he argues that they are actually complementary. On the one hand, the expansion of markets has enabled America to export its own Christian traditions, while on the other, that expansion of the faith has allowed Christians to challenge and shape global capitalism where necessary.[22] For this reason, Webb does not think there is much for Christians to be worried about. He justifies this biblically by arguing that rather than being a movement of the poor, Christianity was spread in apostolic times "by merchants and artisans, not beggars and outcasts." Jesus preached the liberation of the poor and was often critical of the wealthy, but "'poor' and 'rich' were deeply metaphorical terms in his teachings." For Jesus, poverty "was a teaching tool, not an ideology."[23]

Christian traditions like Pentecostalism can restrain globalism's excesses, since by locating discipline in biblical principles, "Pentecostalism fights against global capitalism by shifting the ground on which prosperity rests,"[24] presumably locating its source in God. Of course, considering globalism's unqualified providential role, it is unclear why Webb thinks Christianity should resist in the first place. Indeed, Webb argues that "traditional societies" should embrace Christianity not only for their salvation "but also as a prelude to their entry into world markets." Christianity is functional for their economic welfare. Conversely, Webb asserts that the success of Western missions can be explained similarly to that of American globalism: "Just as capitalism works not by selling what it thinks people should buy but by exploring and expanding their needs, Christianity works not by telling people what to believe but by cultivating, as well as questioning, their religious needs."[25] It is the inculcation of religious sensibilities, not the content of the Christian witness, that is the church's contribution to globalism.

This is Webb's tale of two globalisms, one economic and tied to American interests, the other religious and shaped by American strands of Protestantism. The former is a "necessary prerequisite" of the latter. American commerce serves the advancement of the gospel today in the

21. Ibid., 57.
22. Ibid., 125.
23. Ibid., 58.
24. Ibid., 123.
25. Ibid., 142.

same way the Roman Empire facilitated early evangelism: "America, as the defender of free markets and democracy, represents the best hope for the triumph of political forms congenial to Christianity and therefore indicative of the kingdom to come. Capitalism and democracy are paving the way for global Christianity today just as the Roman roads enabled the spread of the church in the ancient world."[26]

This treatment of American globalization confirms the nationalist nature of Webb's account, which reads the theological doctrine of providence through the lens of contemporary American power. Webb construes this power as both the result and confirmation of America's divinely directed mission in the world. Indeed, it is safe to say that Webb's account of providence is really a theological rationale for American exceptionalism: "America is a nation whose very being is providential. The American experiment, because of its fragile nature, requires a providential reading of history."[27] It is the nature of America that thus determines theological reflection. While Webb ostensibly undertakes a treatment of providence using America as a case study, he actually never provides any systematically theological account of the doctrine itself. He makes frequent assertions about providence as a doctrine, and he alludes to the biblical text at points, but never actually constructs a theological case. Rather, his starting point is America's economic and military dominance in the world, which he chooses to reflect on only after presuming that it is good. Webb's chief concern is America, and his work has the effect of asking what America has to teach us about providence, rather than determining whether or how America is providentially empowered. As Tim Beach-Verhey nicely puts it, "Webb argues that American religious, economic, and political institutions and values are dominating the world, which could not happen apart from God's will, which means it must be in accord with God's good and benevolent intentions for the world."[28]

As a result, Webb's political theology requires not only an account of the doctrine of providence, but a providential reading of history

---

26. Webb, "Eschatology and Politics," 508. In *American Providence*, Webb makes this exact analogy between American globalization and the road system of the Roman Empire (145), even though there he states in criticism of Stanley Hauerwas and John Milbank that comparisons between America and Rome are nonsensical and "obnoxious" (124).

27. Webb, *American Providence*, 13.

28. Beach-Verhey, Review of *American Providence*, 377.

that "must account for America's miraculous rise to world power" and provide "an interpretation of God's blessings for America as well as America's responsibilities for those blessings."[29] He writes that "America is so determined . . . by the conviction that we have a special destiny in world history that only a careful account of the doctrine of providence can shine a clear light on the course that lies ahead." This "course" is not that of a theological evaluation of the conviction of special destiny, but rather the outworking of that conviction in US foreign policy. The conviction itself remains unquestioned throughout Webb's work. As he continues, America's dominance in the world is "the Great Fact of our day," rendering "pernicious" any attempt to deny providential import to "America's shaping of the globe."[30] Note that America's dominance as personally actualized by God is presupposed in this discourse, governing all subsequent considerations of providence. Note also America's power as "miraculous," a descriptor tying the nation's status directly to Webb's understanding of special providence, "God's miraculous interventions." While Webb denies that America is uniquely providential, the fact that "America is doing more than any other nation to spread the kind of political structures that can best prepare the globe for God's ultimate work of establishing the final kingdom is not theologically insignificant." Many countries view themselves as providential, "but America's providential theology came together at a propitious time."[31] Not only is America providential, but the very narrative of American providence is itself providentially formulated and propagated.

As Webb portrays it, the doctrine of providence recognizes that all theology is socially located in space and time, requiring responsible contemporary theologians to read providence through American history, given its prominent status. Neither political theology nor ecclesiology can afford to do otherwise, given that any discussion of the church's destiny requires reflection on "how God is using the most powerful nation in the world."[32] Christianity has been central to America's role in the world, precluding for Webb any sharp distinction between America's global agenda and the Puritan notion of "a nation conceived as the ve-

---

29. Webb, *American Providence*, 9.
30. Ibid., 2.
31. Ibid., 6–7, 30.
32. Ibid., 5, 9.

hicle of God's will."[33] The Puritans borrowed the theology of covenant from John Calvin, seeing themselves as the instrument of God's will in the world, in line with Israel. For this reason, "America cannot be analyzed apart from the way providential theology has shaped its understanding of foreign affairs . . ."[34] The doctrine of providence lies at the heart of American history and the discernment of America's role in the world: "the further back you go in history, the clearer it becomes just how habitual and ordinary are claims about an American providence."[35]

Of course, Webb is correct to note the prevalence and role of various theologies of providence in American history, but like the work of Marshall and Manuel (which Webb affirms for its "meticulous" research and thought-provoking findings[36]), Webb conflates the historical appropriation of the doctrine with that of *actual* providence in American history, as though the prevalence of the belief makes real its content. For instance, he writes that "a providential view of America is dependent on the covenantal theology of the Puritans."[37] No doubt his claim is correct in strict terms of the genealogy of the idea, but it remains unclear why the historical fact of the belief justifies theological commitment, that is, why the Puritan theology should be taken for granted as *true*, then or now. Webb makes no clear distinction between the historical occurrences of doctrine on the one hand, and its theological truth on the other, and he vacillates between them throughout this work.

Decline: The Eclipse of Realism

Webb's account of decline illuminates the nationalism within his political theology even more than his account of America as chosen community. This is one of the more intriguing aspects of his argument, for the primary decline he cites is only indirectly that of the national culture. Post-9/11, he laments church conflict over US foreign policy, which is "particularly disheartening for American Christians who want the church to take a stand on issues of national importance."[38] He roots the

33. Ibid., 2.
34. Ibid., 2.
35. Ibid., 20.
36. Ibid., 47.
37. Ibid., 84.
38. Ibid., 2.

conflict, beginning in the 1960s, in a decline in "providential rhetoric," particularly within academic theology. The main agents responsible for this decline are "professional theologians and other intellectual elites," whom Webb calls "anti-providentialists."[39] In Webb's nationalist discourse, these theologians fill the role of "status elites," akin to those secular elites in Christian Right discourse who control "public symbol production" in government, the media, and education.[40] Here, the symbol at issue is American providence, and the problem is that these theological elites are creating doubt among Christians as to the nation's divinely ordained role in the world. Against these elites, Webb pits his own, self-described populist theology: "I have come to my own understanding of providence only by trusting in the basic wisdom that has guided most Americans on this subject. Most Americans believe that God acts in history, and they believe that one of those acts is the choosing of their nation for a special mission in the world." This claim by "ordinary American Christians" seems like "common sense" to Webb.[41] Hence his approval of Marshall and Manuel, whose work he describes as "grassroots history . . . with a populist edge."[42] Whereas some elites may eschew the doctrine of providence for its disputable notion of divine favoritism, "popular Christianity in America has been unmoved by such metaphysical constraints. American Christians know better than to think that the inscrutable ways of providence can be reduced to the idea of fairness."[43] Thus, Webb champions the theology of the common people against the efforts of the theological academy to relativize America's place in the narrative of global salvation.

His chief "elite" target of critique is Stanley Hauerwas, whose ostensible dismissal of providential theology goes hand-in-hand with his "anti-Americanism."[44] Indeed, insofar as America is essentially providential in Webb's conception, to reject providence is to reject America itself. For Hauerwas, America represents "the opposite of everything Christianity must defend." But as such, Hauerwas addresses America

---

39. Ibid., 11.
40. Heinz, "Clashing Symbols," 156.
41. Webb, *American Providence*, 11.
42. Ibid., 47.
43. Ibid., 55.
44. Webb, "Very American Stanley Hauerwas," 15.

as a mere idea, rather than "anything concrete and real."[45] Indeed, what Hauerwas and like-minded scholars are guilty of is a decidedly *unrealistic* politics. Hauerwas's advocacy of pacifism "is powerful rhetoric rather than clear-eyed politics (or theology). Only if Christians have no investment in any secular order can Christians embrace an absolute pacifism."[46] Webb is concerned that a Christian status as aliens precludes contribution to foreign and domestic policy discussions.[47] Contra Hauerwas's idealistic pacifism, providence teaches that God works through human endeavors, including war, to accomplish the divine intent.[48] While the theology of American providence requires that "America's wars abroad should be for the sake of spreading freedom, not spreading the faith," Webb posits that "political freedom is both an appropriate expression of Christian faith as well as a mighty means of enabling Christians to spread their faith." It would seem then that for Webb, aggressive military policy is useful for spreading Christianity after all, quite in line with his providential understanding of the nation; Hauerwas's pacifism is therefore anti-providential. Consequently, since American hegemony is so tied to providence, Christians cannot be resident aliens in America but must be "residential advisors," ensuring the nation stays true to its providential course.[49]

According to Webb, the central problem of Hauerwas's theology is that "he does not believe in politics." He is unable to imagine a "constructive political correlate to his ecclesiology."[50] This claim is helpful for getting closer to the core of Webb's thought. Rather than acknowledging, even if to challenge, Hauerwas's notion of the alternative politics of the church-as-*polis*—that is, ecclesiology *as* political theology, *as* constructive politics—Webb must dismiss Hauerwas and like theologians as being apolitical. Scripture must be rendered apolitical as well—"the New Testament does not address its audience in terms of a nation or a polis"—despite 1 Peter 2:9–10's appropriation of Exodus 19:5–6, calling the church a "nation" and a "kingdom" in a certain continuity with Israel, or the language of "citizenship" or "commonwealth" in Philippians 3:20.

45. Webb, *American Providence*, 71.
46. Webb, "On the True Globalism," 120.
47. Webb, *American Providence*, 10.
48. Ibid., 21.
49. Ibid., 74–76.
50. Ibid., 70, 74.

Webb makes these moves because he has tied politics exclusively to the nation-state, and to the extent that the kingdom of God is a political notion, only the nation-state, not the church, can prefigure it. Indeed, "without a reading of the constructive role that nations play in global history, the kingdom of God becomes an oppositional force, the arrival of which will destroy the powers of this world." Webb resists this understanding, because it means that "God is not using nation-states to further the divine plan. Instead, God is exercising patience with the nations, while planning for their complete removal."[51] Note the tautology here, a function of his aforementioned logic of special providence, wherein God moves in the world directly through human sociopolitical orders to achieve the divine aims and to rule the world. For this reason, eschewing the nation-state is unfaithful, for "to be alienated from political authority is to be alienated from ourselves and God."[52]

However, this is also because Webb views the nation-state as the main agent of "significant historical change" in the world. God moves in the world primarily through nation-states, and "God moves nations by working through history, not against it," that is, not in contention with national politics. His critique of liberation theology is illustrative. Here, Webb asserts that "by definition, the poor are not effective agents of significant historical change," presumably because, unlike states, they are not carriers of historical power. "The poor *are* agents of God's grace," however, "as opposed to being agents of significant historical change."[53] This point is key, for here Webb clearly suggests that God's grace is not an agent of significant historical change. This directly repudiates the notion discussed in chapter 5 (referencing Douglas Harink) that grace is a form of divine power in which the church participates. According to that principle, it is not in the actions of the earthly nation-state but in the suffering and glorification of Jesus Christ that "God's way of making history" is revealed.[54] Thus for Webb, no political theology governed by orthodox Christology, by the cross of Christ as pivotal for human community and destiny, or by the church as the Body of Christ can be tenable, for none of these can produce effective, concrete change in the world order. As Cavanaugh succinctly puts it, for Webb, "Jesus' nonvio-

---

51. Webb, "Eschatology and Politics," 511.
52. Webb, *American Providence*, 105.
53. Ibid., 62.
54. Harink, *1 & 2 Peter*, 50–51.

lence and death on a cross are peripheral to a providential reading of history."[55] Rather, if the promise of the kingdom of God is to have present significance, "Christians must try to discern the movement of the Holy Spirit . . . in the political orders within which they find themselves."[56]

America as Global Sovereign: Carl Schmitt and the Politics of Exception

Webb does not leave his nationalist narrative at the point of decline, but specifies what is required for renewal. Here, the reader arrives at another, even more definitive strand of thought at work in Webb's account of politics, providence, and America's national narrative: the political theory of Carl Schmitt. By Webb's own admission, Schmitt is the theorist "who has most shaped my thinking about the nature, limits, and future of democracy."[57] Given that American democracy and its propagation constitute the center of Webb's account of America's providential mission (and thus of providence itself), and given Webb's approving overview of Schmitt's thought with only minor qualifications, it is reasonable to assume that Schmitt's theory constitutes the center of Webb's political theology of providence. It is ironic that this "rather curious chapter," as Jean Bethke Elshtain calls it in her approving review,[58] falls at the end of Webb's book. Elshtain even notes that "Webb might have done better to save this discussion of Schmitt for another day." In fact, as I will show, its inclusion is not curious at all, nor could Webb put it off, since it underlies his entire schema. What is peculiar is its placement at the end of the argument. Considering Webb's expertise in rhetoric, the reader wonders to what degree this was a conscious move by Webb, and if so, why Webb would choose to relegate such a critical discussion to an almost appendix-like status. Given that Webb thinks of providence as a "grammar" to read the meaning of the American nation, Schmitt's theory is crucial to understanding Webb's account as nationalist discourse.

Two major aspects of Schmitt's political theory are relevant here. First, only the nation-state is properly political:

---

55. Cavanaugh, "Messianic Nation," 271.
56. Webb, "Eschatology and Politics," 509.
57. Webb, *American Providence*, 153.
58. Elshtain, Review of *American Providence*, 40.

> The political has to do with a basic distinction between friends and enemies. Only the state can determine who is the enemy, and only the state can decide to fight the enemy. Outside of the political sphere, there is no way to justify whether an enemy is actually a threat to a nation's way of life. The friend-enemy distinction is what gives meaning to national politics.[59]

For Webb, this points to the central issue in the decline of theological treatments of providence, for "nearly the whole of political theology today is in denial of the friend-enemy distinction as Schmitt understands it."[60] That central issue is political authority, and the current problem with certain political theologies is that therein, "the church wants to displace the political sphere with its legitimate determination of who is to count as the enemy."[61] Authority, not ethics, is the central determinant of justice for Webb,[62] and while Christians are taught to forgive their enemies (a manifestation of grace), the church has also historically recognized the need for political authority in the pursuit of justice. Since God works through history, God defeats those who would thwart the movement of providence in history. "God's enemies are not necessarily our own," Webb continues, "but to be a friend of God is to seek out God's purposes in history, and those purposes are not unrelated to the struggle for freedom, a struggle that involves the tragic necessity of war."[63] Contra the theological elites against whom Webb pits himself, only a theopolitics operating free from the constraints of grace and grounded in the proper authority of the nation-state to determine its friends and enemies, and perhaps God's as well, is a true politics, a producer of significant historical change, and thus, properly providential.

The other crucial element Webb appropriates from Schmitt is the notion of the "exception." While the normal proceduralism of a democratic political order is usually sufficient for governance, from time to time threats arise to that order's integrity and authority. These "exceptions" are emergency situations wherein "democracies need an external

---

59. Webb, *American Providence*, 156.

60. This is why Webb rejects Hauerwas's account of martyrdom as a political act: "Martyrdom . . . is not a political decision. It exists outside of the friend-enemy distinction" (ibid., 159).

61. Ibid., 156.

62. Ibid., 65.

63. Ibid., 156.

principle of authority that can bring public debate to an end."[64] This principle is that of the "sovereign," which Schmitt defines as the entity or person who decides on the exception.[65] As Webb puts it, "the consequence of the exception is the need for someone to take charge." Notice the circularity thus far: the exception—the emergency situation—results in the need for a sovereign, but the sovereign is the one who determines the exception in the first place. Webb goes further: "Legal systems can operate only under normal conditions, but the obligation of the sovereign is to determine what those normal conditions are by deciding how to deal with the exception." The logical converse of Schmitt's definition, here the exception is the standard, according to which the sovereign determines what counts as unexceptional. Authority, which again is the ground of justice for Webb, "by definition is a transcendent and not immanent phenomenon." When nation-states make life-and-death decisions, including war, sovereign authority is required, something liberalism cannot acknowledge.[66] Of course, one question begged by this theory is how to account for situations where the sovereign, who alone has authority to distinguish the ordinary from the extraordinary in sociopolitical affairs, actually contributes to or even produces situations of crisis to maximize that sovereign's opportunities to project power. Webb does not address this question, an ironic oversight considering Schmitt's well-known, albeit temporary, involvement in 1930s German Nazism.[67]

Schmitt's theory of political authority is correlated with providence in Webb's account. Webb argues that providence is best conceived as "always special and particular, not regular and general."[68] What marks providence as Webb understands it is the transcendent and miraculous involvement of God in human affairs; any notion of immanentism is rejected. Likewise, the sovereign in Webb's appropriation of Schmitt acts from outside the normal procedural system; it, too, is transcendent. Like God, it alone determines those situations in which it must directly exercise its authority. In short, the sovereign is providential, even perhaps the personification of God's action in history.

64. Ibid., 153.
65. Hollerich, "Carl Schmitt," 110.
66. Webb, *American Providence*, 154, 158.
67. Hollerich, "Carl Schmitt," 108–9.
68. Webb, *American Providence*, 89.

What has all this to do with nationalism? Webb's account is nationalist because he is authenticating over and against theologies marked by "anti-Americanism" a self-understanding of America as divinely ordained for hegemony. Recall his description of providence as a "grammar" for discerning the meaning of the American nation. For Webb, Schmitt's theory of politics and the exception constitutes that much-needed "providential reading of world history" that provides a hermeneutics for American power and responsibility.[69] America has been chosen to fill the role of sovereign in the world today, as evidenced by its hegemony. America propagates its system of democratic capitalism, hand in hand with its own version of Christianity, throughout the world, setting the stage for the coming kingdom of God. Yet, if Webb's account is nationalist, and Christian nationalism inevitably requires the selective—and thus distortive—appropriation of the biblical narrative, then Webb's account of providence becomes theologically suspect.

Lest American dominance be construed as traditional empire, Webb relies on the irony of Reinhold Niebuhr to point out the inherent safeguards of American integrity. The great irony of the contemporary situation is that the good America does for the world is due, in Niebuhr's terms, to American ignorance.[70] Americans are inherently naïve, so we are unaware of the dangers of empire: "Our innocence, in fact, keeps us from naming our ambition as a species of imperialism. Yet that very same innocence allows us to avoid many of the faults of empires of the past. We actually believe we can do good in the world." American individualism saves the empire from doing more damage than it does, given that it prevents the formation of a socially coherent imperial vision. "Our very respect for freedom," he continues, "both fuels our overseas

---

69. Ibid., 9.

70. Unfortunately, Webb provides no specific references for Niebuhr at this point. He describes Niebuhr here as "the great theologian of irony, perhaps because Niebuhr had an appreciation for both the strengths and the limits of American providence." As a theologian of rhetoric, Webb explains that irony requires a great deal of sophistication, and is fitting for the providential discourse due to its "almost godlike view of events," which "sees the inevitable outcomes of which historical actors are unaware" (ibid., 84). This is as opposed to hyperbole, which he attributes to Hauerwas, and which he characterizes as "a seductive trope" that is "so excessive that you think you have done what it demands just by speaking it" ("Very American Stanley Hauerwas," 15). Niebuhr is thus providential, while Hauerwas is anti-providential.

endeavors and inhibits us from developing the kind of ideology that could result in global domination."[71]

Yet a chief irony of Webb's account is that America avoids the imperial pitfall only by acting as global sovereign. Within a globalized world order, there are threats to the system's integrity. As such, "America cannot always act democratically on the world stage, even as it acts to increase the number of democracies in the world. Globalization requires management, and without some kind of world religion, global management will have to work through the imposition of power rather than the quest for consensus."[72] Thus, in today's world, "the United States will have to make the difficult decisions in times of crisis, as with the question of how to handle terrorist states." Rather than patient international deliberation, the exigencies of the moment demand immediate action by the United States, the only power that can effectively deal with them. Of course, as that sovereign power, America alone determines what constitutes an emergency and what thereby necessitates its unilateral imposition of power. America has been set apart providentially as the instrument for prefiguring the kingdom of God, for establishing the political structures that herald that kingdom,[73] and for dealing with any obstacles that might arise in the process of its establishment. America's sovereignty, not merely as one member of an anarchic international system but actually *over* that system as empire, is for Webb the clearest case since biblical Israel of God using a nation-state to rule the world. Hence, for Beach-Verhey, Webb's clear implication that "anything which stands in the way of American dominance, therefore, must be counter to God's will and, by definition, evil."[74] American *exceptionalism*, now with significant added meaning, simply *is* providence. And as such, remarks William Cavanaugh, "America itself becomes the criterion for locating God's activity in the world."[75]

However, the exception-providence relationship brings up a potentially significant contradiction underlying Webb's argument, as

71. Webb, *American Providence*, 85. Webb's is precisely the type of argument Cavanaugh seeks to repudiate in "Empire," referenced in chapter 1. See the interchange between Cavanaugh and Webb on this subject in Webb, "Response to William T. Cavanaugh" and Cavanaugh, "Reply to Stephen H. Webb."

72. Webb, *American Providence*, 114.

73. Ibid., 7–8.

74. Beach-Verhey, review of *American Providence*, 377.

75. Cavanaugh, "Messianic Nation," 270.

demonstrated by two competing premises. First, providence, by definition, requires foreknowledge. Special providence as Webb advocates it—God's personal and direct involvement in human affairs, including the use of the nation-state—logically requires foresight into human behavior and the consequences of God's own miraculous intervention in order for God not to undermine God's own plan. While Webb does not address foreknowledge directly, he arguably holds to it as evidenced by his rejection of open theism, and because it is central to the American Christian understanding of providence, to whose "basic wisdom" he commits himself. However, second, Webb correlates special providence with political authority, making the sovereign analogous to God in transcending the system and acting upon it from the outside. This is precisely for Webb how America is providential. As Webb appropriates Schmitt, sovereignty is constituted by a determination of the exception, that "emergency" or "crisis"[76] in which standard rules can be suspended and direct, transcendent authority be exercised. Sovereignty, in its essence, requires the existence of the unforeseen and unexpected. And the emergency must be unforeseen, or the sovereign is nothing more than a tyrant, engineering artificial crises for its own aggrandizement, which would invalidate Webb's claims. But herein lies the contradiction: How can a theology of foreseeing providence be rooted in an account of sovereignty that requires the unexpected in order to be actualized?

Leaving such contradictions aside, how does the church fit under America's global sovereignty? Clearly, the church is not political, since it possesses "its own authority, distinct from the political realm." The church, as apolitical, has nothing to say regarding the friend-enemy distinction. In times of war, it is not the place of the church "to vilify the enemy or to rationalize the conflict." Of course, "neither is it the role of the church to pretend that it can be the site of a politics that—this side of the coming kingdom—transcends the political altogether."[77] A politics alternative to that of the nation-state is impossible by definition. Thus, the church is not political, nor is it not allowed to render a judgment either way on the legitimacy of any particular nationalist pursuit or state projection of power. Paradoxically, as Webb appropriates George

---

76. Webb uses this term multiple times in his work in justifying exceptional American authority over the international realm. See "Very American Stanley Hauerwas," 15; *American Providence*, 19, 78, 114, 168.

77. Webb, *American Providence*, 159.

Weigel, "the very fact that the church is *not* a political institution is its greatest contribution to the realm of politics," for it limits the state by demanding of it "space to practice the ministry of word and sacrament."[78] The church as sacrament "symbolizes the future unity of humankind"; however, the *actual* unity of humankind "must be achieved on a political basis."[79] Note here the connection with the earlier discussion of "significant historical change": the divine grace manifested in sacrament is insufficient to accomplish genuine human unity; such unity can only be fully achieved by the politics of the nation-state.

Instead of a site of alternative politics, the church is "resident advisor" to the state. This is particularly true in America with its Christian history and the inherent overlap of the American dream with the kingdom of God.[80] As Webb puts it, "Christians can reside comfortably in America because their faith provided the foundation for the success and the shape of the new nation"; yet Christians must remember that they are obligated to keep the nation on its providential course.[81] However, this conception of the church limits the scope of ecclesial theopolitics according to the dictates of the state. The very fact that the church must "demand" space from the state to practice its ministries suggests that rather than limiting the state's power, the church is subjected to the state, particularly if—following the theory of the exception—the state is a providential entity authorized to determine the scope of its power and the occasion of its exercise. More specifically, as Cavanaugh points out, the problem here is that "the political presence of the biblical God is mediated through the official discourse of America, and not through a distinctively Christian body that stands under the explicit authority of Jesus Christ."[82] The church's political significance is only derivative of the nation-state's, and only insofar as it supports the nation-state's providential role. To participate in any politics, the church *in* America must be the church *of* and *for* America.

With regard to globalism, "only the church can play the role of globalism's *other*, precisely because the church is both inside and outside of Western capitalism." Like a parent and child, "Christianity is the source

78. Webb, "Eschatology and Politics," 507.
79. Webb, *American Providence*, 169.
80. Ibid., 10. As he states later, "the church dreams of America" (74).
81. Ibid., 74.
82. Cavanaugh, "Messianic Nation," 275.

of much of globalism's success, so only Christianity can be sufficiently inside this economic process in order to divert it away from its own most destructive tendencies."[83] Yet, this is no better an arrangement than that with the nation-state. For note how the church, to the degree that it is "inside" the process of globalization, becomes immanentized to that process, that is, the church becomes decidedly *unprovidential*, in Webb's terms, which is to say, removed from effecting significant historical change. The church becomes a facet of ordinary human history, while the nation-state alone transcends that history and is able to determine whether that history is moving forward properly. It is unclear how the church can act as a check on any emergency produced by globalism's excesses. Again, only the nation-state can provide the necessary correction.

Webb's political theology of providence is thus a thoroughgoing nationalist account of America. In his process of authenticating the nation via his theology as "grammar," Webb must rely on political theory that is quite antithetical to biblical theopolitics, in the process distorting the biblical narrative itself and relegating central tenets of the Christian theological tradition to a secondary status at best. What results is a salvation narrative in which a wholly domesticated (and thus unbiblical) church exists to support the nation-state in its purportedly divinely ordained endeavors—in this case, America as global sovereign.

Richard John Neuhaus: Democratic Freedom and the Kingdom of God

Like Webb's account, the theopolitics articulated by Richard John Neuhaus entails what can be considered, in Murphy's terms, a progressive, rather than traditionalist, jeremiad. While Neuhaus is erroneously characterized by Murphy and others as a member of the Catholic wing of the Christian Right,[84] and is therefore categorized by Murphy in the traditionalist camp, he is more accurately understood as a quasi-neoconservative public theologian. His jeremiad is progressive because it concentrates on recovering a fundamental idea of America, rather than certain historical practices and institutions. Indeed, he rejects a theology of "return," a "renewal through regression or through the recapitu-

---

83. Webb, *American Providence*, 112.
84. See Murphy, *Prodigal Nation*, 88.

lation of a past and presumably better time" in favor of a future-oriented approach concentrating on America's destiny. As he puts it, "home is still ahead of us."[85]

This section discusses Neuhaus's nationalist discourse via an examination of his political theology, one that is undergirded by a theology of American historical particularity. The discussion references several of Neuhaus's key works on the subject that are taken to be representative of his understanding over his entire career. While Neuhaus's work certainly shifts over time in nuance and emphasis—changes that will be addressed where pertinent—his generally realist political theology remains constant. The following discussion is therefore not intended to flatten out the development of his thought over time, but rather considers his understanding as largely continuous with respect to his fundamental theopolitical claims. As I will demonstrate, these claims constitute a nationalist narrative, an attempt to authenticate American national identity via a political theology of democratic freedom rooted in a dialectic of social contract and transcendent covenant. The covenant aspect is particularly problematic in Neuhaus, since his use of it requires a distortion of the biblical narrative. This distorted narrative is then interwoven with an American national narrative such that a syncretized identity is produced, one for which Neuhaus claims theological legitimacy. In examining Neuhaus's discourse, I hope to show that once again, nationalism arises as a crucial problem for ecclesial identity in a way that requires a robust biblical theopolitics to counter.

A Political Theology of Historical Particularity and Transcendent Hope

The nationalist narrative Neuhaus espouses is subtle and restrained compared to the preceding cases in this study, a product of a political theology carefully developed and reflected upon over time.[86] It is there-

---

85. Neuhaus, *Time Toward Home*, 22. Neuhaus (1936–2009) was a Lutheran pastor turned Catholic priest, a political theologian and prolific writer, and the founder of, among other organizations, the journal *First Things*.

86. An exception to this characterization would be Neuhaus's post-9/11 editorial in *First Things*, helpfully examined and evaluated by Michael Baxter (Baxter, "God Is Not American"). Baxter's chapter is a trenchant critique of Neuhaus's post-9/11 rhetoric, and contains, among other insightful elements, a section titled "The Story of 'Christian America'" (64–67), where Neuhaus is read to present an authenticating narrative of American national identity quite similar in configuration to those discussed in chapter 6.

fore necessary first to deal with the general outlines of that theology in order to discern America's place within it. In his early work, Neuhaus unabashedly declares his belief in the "sovereignty of politics in the making of history." Politics is obviously conditioned by other forces, but it is the political—those deliberations and uses of power that determine how people order their lives together—that constitutes the Christian's primary venue of action.[87] Politics is about "making the arguments and showing the ways in which interests can compete, overlap, and sometimes converge in serving the common good."[88] The power entailed in politics is not self-legitimating, but "requires a moral rationale."[89] This moral rationale comes from religion, which lies at the heart of culture, of which politics is a function. Culture is the "motor force of history," which "proposes or excludes the possibilities which are the subject of political decision."[90] It is also something that is both formed by and a shaper of religion. Religion, on the other hand, is the "ground or depth-level" of culture, the heart of culture even as culture is the "form of religion," religion's tangible embodiment.[91]

Particularly in democratic politics, religion provides a "transcendent point of reference" that both mandates a moral rationale for the exercise of politics and holds a nation accountable to that rationale.[92] Public values, so necessary for democracy, emerge from religious traditions, the latter providing for most "the primary definition of what the world is all about."[93] For this reason, "the religious phenomenon" must be defined in substantivist, rather than functionalist, terms; it must reference the content or truth claims of a tradition rather than being reduced to categories that are applicable to assorted other phenomena. Yet, it cannot be so "substantivist" as someone like Karl Barth, "who would remove Christianity from the category of religion altogether."[94] In the Augustinian sense of *religare*—binding obligation—religion is what "holds the promise of binding together . . . a nation in a way that

87. Neuahus, *Time Toward Home*, vii.
88. Neuhaus, *American Babylon*, 186.
89. Neuhaus, *Time Toward Home*, 45.
90. Ibid., vii, 49–51, 206.
91. Neuhaus, *Naked Public Square*, 132.
92. Ibid., 76, 120.
93. Neuhaus, *Time Toward Home*, 154.
94. Ibid., 191–92.

may more nearly approximate *civitas*."[95] Religion keeps the state under transcendent judgment and affirms the rights of all persons in society. It is thus a "limiting challenge to the imperiousness of the political," and it points to a "sacred canopy that brings all institutions and belief systems, and most particularly religion, under judgment."[96]

Most importantly, religion provides ethical direction in the midst of a history that "has not yet got itself together."[97] Existence in that history, for the Christian, is marked by the incompleteness of the kingdom of God. Such an existence entails "dialectics and contradictions" that render untenable any claims to the presence of the kingdom in the world today. Yet, history is still God's project, the whole of reality that has ever been and will ever be, and God has promised to bring that project to completion. God is, in Neuhaus's words, the world's "Absolute Future," in whom history is realized. History is therefore the "unfolding story of God's purposes, culminating in the vindication that is the kingdom of God."[98] This historical fulfillment is God's plan of salvation, but it is neither here nor now. It is yet to come.[99]

The future kingdom of God cannot be perceived apart from our own existence, so "God's promise invites us to analogize from our experience." While God's kingdom is radically different from anything we know in this world, it must also be in continuity to some degree with that known experience. In the incarnation, God "has made himself, so to speak, accountable to history," an accountability in which he calls us to join. God therefore has personal concern in our own historical experience, including our political communities: "Thus it is that God has something at stake in the American experience." And God must, for if he did not, "then we who seek our life's purpose in doing his will have no stake in the American experience."[100] Note already the presupposed

---

95. Neuhaus, *Naked Public Square*, 60. In this book, by contrast with *Time Toward Home*, Neuhaus's understanding of religion takes on a more functionalist tone: "With greater and lesser degrees of reflection, we thus bind ourselves in friendship, in marriage, in vocation, and a host of other decisions. The obligation that we affirm most deeply, most daringly, and perhaps most desperately, that is our religion" (250).

96. Ibid., 117-23.
97. Neuhaus, *Time Toward Home*, 25.
98. Neuhaus, *Naked Public Square*, 61.
99. Neuhaus, *Time Toward Home*, 52.
100. Ibid., 57-58.

and unquestioned priority of Christians participating in American politics and culture.

All history is therefore one history, that history of redemption that does not distinguish between sacred and secular histories or between narratives of salvation and nation, a history to which God has committed himself. For Neuhaus, this has direct implications for identity: "When I meet God, then, I expect to meet him as an American." While Neuhaus admits his humanity and Christian identity are prior to American national identity, "I am not quite sure what the assertion means since I am inescapably an American human being and an American Christian." As he elaborates, "I look for the vindication of myself in my historical particularity, and of the American experience of which I am a part." The American experience is vindicated because it is such a large part of this history, "or at least it is a large part of our limited moment in history."[101] Indeed, "for those of us who are Americans, we are *as Americans* part of the story that is the story of the world." America *as a nation* is part of that story, that is, the story of God's redemption of the world.[102] The alternative to those mistaken theologies that see America as a direct type of Babylon—an already divinely condemned center of illegitimate power in the world—is to "meet the judgment of the future in the full particularity of our historical identity" as Americans, discerning "a promise and hope within the American experience that are deserving of our devotion."[103]

American Covenant and Public Piety

Neuhaus's account of America is a form of Christian nationalism, a narrative conceiving of American national identity as a signal or prolepsis of the kingdom of God by means of democratic freedom. This narrative is tied directly into his Christian theology of historical particularism. Neuhaus is concerned about reviving the "American experiment," and seeks "models for reconstructing the American reality." As I mentioned

101. Ibid., 56, 64. As he argues earlier, "The American experience is an important part of the history whose fulfillment is promised . . . In a larger sense it is important because America is such a large part of this historical epoch. If the fulfillment of history bypasses the hundreds of millions of people whose lives have, in one way or another, been shaped by the American experience, it is not a very interesting fulfillment" (52).

102. Neuhaus, *American Babylon*, 30.

103. Neuhaus, *Time Toward Home*, 56.

above, Neuhaus sees the most promising course of action for American renewal in the "interplay between explicit biblical religion and the American tradition of public piety."[104] Note immediately the nationalist project of authentication: Neuhaus is concerned, beginning in the aftermath of Vietnam and Watergate but continuing through the 1980s and 1990s and intensifying after 9/11, with formulating and propagating a particular vision of American national identity with the hope of persuading Christians that Christian truth claims "contain the resources by which the American experience can be creatively redefined."[105] This vision involves the deliberate interweaving of biblical and national theopolitical narratives, an endeavor that, as I will demonstrate, ends up distorting the former in favor of the latter.

"Public piety" is Neuhaus's preferred term for civil religion.[106] American public piety and the biblical tradition exist in "symbiotic relationship, each supporting and, to some extent, checking the other."[107] Within public piety, America is considered a radical experiment contingent upon a future promised fulfillment, namely, the kingdom of God.[108] As such, "patriotic piety" cannot sustain itself, but requires a robust moral account of America's purpose and mission, combined with a concerted reassertion by churches of "the gospel of the Kingdom from which America and all human enterprises derive their religious significance."[109]

Neuhaus's account of America's public purpose is located primarily in covenant.[110] Covenant is what provides in the American context the transcendent point of reference to God as Absolute Future, as the one

---

104. Ibid., 18–19.
105. Ibid., 50.
106. Ibid., 190.
107. Ibid., 19.
108. Ibid., 26.

109. Ibid., 196. By "churches," Neuhaus here means more generally "institutions of religion," with preference given to Christian churches and Jewish synagogues (207). However, post-9/11, his references tend to be more sharply directed at institutions of Judaism and Christianity over against those of Islam. See, for example, *American Babylon*, 188–89, as well as "Contract and Covenant." In the latter, he writes, "The Judeo-Christian factor in American identity is reinforced by the challenge of Islam, which believes it has displaced both Judaism and Christianity in the purposes of God, and by a violent jihadist ideology set upon forcing the submission of the world to Allah by any means necessary."

110. Neuhaus, *Time Toward Home*, 130.

who will bring to completion his cosmic covenant with creation.[111] Just as individual moral accountability must be worked out within the social reality of America, American covenant must be seen in light of God's covenant with creation and as a specific manifestation thereof.[112] For Neuhaus, covenant is profoundly meaningful in the contexts of both the biblical narrative and American history. It assumes that human beings and society are disordered, less than what they should be in light of the transcendent reality of Absolute Future. It therefore maintains the proper tie between the present and the future that judges it, as well as the attendant need for repentance and forgiveness.[113] While Neuhaus is convinced that God has made a general covenant with creation and a specific covenant with Israel and the church, the American covenant is less certain, for it is not clear whether God has entered into such a covenant. Yet Neuhaus risks trusting that God has done so, making his theology vulnerable to "repudiation by the future." American covenant is "derivative, to be accepted insofar as it conforms to the 'revealed' intentions of God in history." It is a gamble, but "such a risk should not scare off people who are prepared to bet their lives upon the unlikely proposition that an itinerant rabbi who was executed in the boondocks of history almost two thousand years ago will be revealed as Lord of the universe."[114]

Covenant is inextricably tied to social contract. As Neuhaus portrays it, "covenant makes possible the vision without which the people perish" while "contract keeps this vision always vulnerable to challenge and revision."[115] Covenant and contract therefore help preserve each other, and as such, are part and parcel of American national identity. As a "nation under law by constitutional contract—a contract presupposing covenantal accountability," to say that America is constituted by said contract is to say that it is a nation "under God," that is, under both promise and judgment. It is a nation constituted by "contract tied to covenantal aspiration and covenantal aspiration restrained by contractual agreement."[116] From this dialectical interplay between covenant

111. Ibid., 168.
112. Ibid., 47.
113. Ibid., 19.
114. Ibid., 54.
115. Ibid., 169.
116. Neuhaus, "Contract and Covenant."

and contract emerges "one of the great achievements—maybe the great achievement—of the modern era," the principle of democratic freedom. Democratic freedom performs a prophetic role within the American covenant context, in response to the "biblical and prophetic urgency of protesting idolatry." It enforces a modesty within the social order that is reflective of the gospel, and is therefore essential to keep the state in check. For this reason, sustaining and defending democracy are religious imperatives, as said freedom is the commonweal, the good of the country, and a "good" fostered in relation to Absolute Future.[117]

Neuhaus values democracy because it reflects his theology of historical particularity and contingency: "democracy is the process of keeping options open, of opening ever new options, so the present can be brought under the judgment and healing of the future." Democracy is key to properly orienting human politics—and thus history—to its proper end, and is therefore an "absolute value . . . not unlike 'the Will of God.'" It is not self-contained or self-sustaining, but contingent upon "*the* absolute which is the Power of the Future." For this reason, democracy has theological import as a "necessary expression of humility in which all persons and institutions are held accountable to transcendent purpose imperfectly discerned." Democratic government is premised on acknowledgement of that transcendent truth, and it assumes interaction by people acting out of values grounded in religious belief.[118] Neuhaus admits that some might argue an absolute commitment to democracy is itself a type of idolatry, but that would only be true, he claims, if the commitment was to one particular method or structure of democratic governance; there is no method worthy of such commitment. Christian commitment to democratic freedom can be absolute because "it is implicit in the very gospel of the kingdom." In view of the kingdom, every earthly order is relativized. In light of the covenant-contract dialectic, democratic freedom is such a relativizing instrument, and "the value of the relativizing function itself cannot be relativized. It is absolute. It is revealed."[119] It should be noted here that Neuhaus has conflated function and instrument, such that the mere *tool* of democratic freedom is made indispensible from the standpoint of Christian theology. What is precluded is the possibility that a different sort of community

---

117. Neuhaus, *Time Toward Home*, 170–72.
118. Neuhaus, *Naked Public Square*, 116, 120.
119. Neuhaus, *Time Toward Home*, 171.

altogether, such as the Christian church, might sufficiently perform that relativizing function.

With the principle of democratic freedom, one notices how Neuhaus's discourse slides in and out of American exceptionalism. As he claims, democratic freedom is "a peculiarly American, or at least modern Western" idea.[120] While this requires the principle of "constant judgment," that judgment in no way lessens the idea of democratic freedom as uniquely Western, and primarily American. For Neuhaus, America is the "primary bearer of the democratic ideal today." While it embodies the democratic ideal imperfectly, America nevertheless has a "singular responsibility" in this regard.[121] It is this singular responsibility that makes America such an unprecedented "experiment," a term used throughout Neuhaus's work. But it is also America's unique construction. America has been "fabricated . . . by ideas and beliefs," deliberately constructed under the "sacred canopy" provided by religion. Its democracy was possible only because the "values and virtues that the polity assumed" were already there.[122] America as an ideal is premised on its "promised benefits to all of humankind";[123] as a nation, it is conceived to "signal a new birth of freedom for mankind."[124] Indeed, "the American experience is an inescapable factor in our moment of history's yearning." While God is impartial to nations, this does not mean he never singles out a nation for particular use. Suggesting America as a "sacred instrument of divine purpose" may seem scandalous, but "it is but a small part of the scandal of God's becoming man," wherein God threw his very existence into doubt until it is definitively demonstrated in the coming kingdom of God, "in the creation finally fulfilled."[125] People balk at the notion of "universal mission," but it is not inappropriate if it is understood that any particular social order, no matter how superior, is promising only insofar as it signals "a new and more universal unity" in which that particular is fulfilled.[126]

---

120. Ibid., 169.
121. Neuhaus, "Christianity and Democracy."
122. Neuhaus, *Naked Public Square*, 140–41.
123. Neuhaus, *Time Toward Home*, 41.
124. Ibid., 44.
125. Ibid., 55.
126. Ibid., 165.

Both the notion of "signal" and this particular-universal relationship are integral to Neuhaus's account of America's special role. America is "at its best a signal or prolepsis of future possibilities," which, when fulfilled, will transcend America itself.[127] American democratic freedom, as an outworking of the covenant-contract dialectic, is an "intuition of the ultimate," of the future. It is therefore of "revelatory significance,"[128] indicating America's "revelatory and instrumental role" in the coming of the kingdom.[129] As the church is a "signal community" of how human life can be ordered by grace, America can be seen as a community signaling "the universal future of democratic freedom."[130] America signals a universal future, but only to the extent that it signals "the promise of freedom" in its own life.[131] When it is at its best, America is the trustee of democratic freedom for the whole world, "an ultimate value that proleptically participates in the future confronting the whole of humankind."[132] Again, America's signals are not derived from its own essence, but rather from the religious traditions of its citizens, which provide the content of America's piety: "during most of American history, the churches have been a ready lender of the signals of transcendence."[133] Thus, not only does Neuhaus's nationalist account entail a syncretism of biblical and national narratives, but such a fusion constitutes for him the content of the authentic American national identity. Public piety is inherently and properly syncretistic.

The covenant-contract dialectic is a "distinctly American way of joining the particular and the universal." Neuhaus rejects the claim that America, as the "first universal nation," is constituted not by ethnic or cultural identities but by universal principles, and is therefore open to any person subscribing to those principles. In fact, he argues, America is inextricably tied to the story of "a particular people who joined contract and covenant in constituting this *novus ordo seclorum*," people who identified in different ways and to different degrees with

---

127. Ibid., 168–69.
128. Ibid., 128.
129. Ibid., 214.
130. Neuhaus, *Naked Public Square*, 115.
131. Neuhaus, *Time Toward Home*, 170.
132. Ibid., 175.
133. Ibid., 195.

Judeo-Christianity.[134] This phrase, *novus ordo seclorum*, recurs throughout Neuhaus's work.[135] Appearing in the Great Seal of the United States, it indicates the "new order of the ages" that America was founded to initiate: a bulwark of democratic freedom that, guided by covenant, would reveal universal truths to be realized eventually throughout humanity. America's ethnic heritage or historical particularity do not detract from this universal significance: "while our idea of the universal may not be universal, that does not mean there is nothing of the universal in it." For this reason, Neuhaus declares that "the intuitions that inform democracy and its ideal of freedom are universally valid and of revelatory significance. That is, they are a part of the future that God intends for all people."[136] America's particularity is itself a signal of the universal. America's political institutions and its "political ethos" are both marked by this heritage, "making America still today a derivatively 'sort of' Christian nation."[137] Indeed, where the modern state has typically attempted to subsume spiritual authorities rather than suffer competition, the United States is the exception as evidenced by the First Amendment; this is an "American exceptionalism" that must be "vigorously defended."[138]

Discussion of America and the universal-particular conjunction brings up the question of empire. Throughout his work, Neuhaus harbors little doubt that the United States is a sort of empire.[139] The question is not whether that status in itself is problematic. While it is troubling, it is simply fact, part of the historical condition in which America currently finds itself. The question is how America uses its imperial power, its "imperial ethic," which depends entirely on how the American experience is defined, that is, the nature and condition of American public piety. A proper imperial ethic should aim toward a global network of mutual acknowledgment and accountability among human persons; while this may seem antithetical to empire, "the language of empire is necessary . . . precisely because it underscores both the scandal and the

---

134. Neuhaus, "Contract and Covenant."

135. In addition to "Contract and Covenant," see *Time Toward Home*, 30; *Naked Public Square*, 94–95; and *American Babylon*, 40–44, 107–15.

136. Neuhaus, *Time Toward Home*, 170.

137. Neuhaus, "Contract and Covenant."

138. Neuhaus, *American Babylon*, 35.

139. Neuhaus, *Time Toward Home*, 38–39, 42–44, 184–86.

responsibility implicit in the fact of American *imperium* ... There can be no equation between the historical obligations of the United States and those of Equatorial Guinea."[140]

Of course, it could be that American empire is simply the newest incarnation of Babylon. If so, then Christians must come out of it and "be anti-American for the sake of the kingdom." Yet this is not presently apparent; only the future will tell.[141] It is an irony of Neuhaus's writing that if America is Babylon here and now, it is not particularly Babylon relative to other nation-states, but, like all other nation-states, only in comparison with the coming order of justice in the kingdom of God.[142] This, over against its positive exceptionalism: its greater power and responsibility relative to others and its singular achievement and responsibility for democratic freedom. Even where it is Babylon in the sense of a "foreign country" of exile for those awaiting their final eschatological homeland, "it is not just one foreign country among others."[143] Neuhaus's depiction of America is largely tempered relative to the authors previously examined, but America is nevertheless the best Babylon has to offer, and its public piety must sustain that condition.

The Decline and Renewal of Public Piety, and the Role of the Church

As much as for his realism, Neuhaus is known for his narrative of national decline. His concern throughout most of his work in political theology is a decline in American public piety, specifically in the form of marginalizing religion from discussions of politics and public policy. This marginalization is what he has so famously referred to as the "naked public square." It is the effect of actions by both a secularized elite in academia and culture, as well as the elite of Protestant liberalism. Since at least the 1960s, "Americans have largely lost their story and its place in the story of the world." This includes "religious thinkers" who have been taken in by "the false-consciousness of having transcended the American experience" and now display a marked anti-Americanism. In

---

140. Ibid., 185.
141. Ibid., 53.
142. Neuhaus, *American Babylon*, 2, 26, 37, 55.
143. Ibid., 49.

short, too many Americans are "not sympathetically engaged with the story of their country."[144]

The naked public square strikes at the heart of Neuhaus's notion of transcendent covenant, for within it, no agreed-upon authority exists above the community itself.[145] This is to deny America's proper identity, according to which the American experience is derived from religious belief. The denial is in large part the responsibility of "secular historians and social theorists,"[146] those elites overseeing the "control centers of our cultural self-consciousness,"[147] who are seeking a different source of social cohesion. They reflect a "style of liberalism that, in its 'pure' form, has neither need nor use for religion."[148] They manifest a "secular prejudice against Judeo-Christian truth claims because they are thought to be nonrational or even irrational."[149] Neuhaus, concerned about maintaining a proper dualism between politics and religion that allows religion to act upon society, complains particularly of the "secular monists" who create the naked public square by limiting reasoning to one sphere alone without interference from other authorities. This results in division from the larger populace, who "heedless of the wisdom imparted by their presumed betters," continue to participate in religion in socially significant ways.[150] For so many Americans, the primary definition of reality is derived from and articulated in "explicit religion." Yet, "by their virtual monopoly on intellectually respectable public discourse," these "religiously emancipated" elites preclude the larger American population from including their religion in the political process. As a

---

144. Neuhaus, *American Babylon*, 31. Throughout his work, Neuhaus is respectful of the pacifist positions articulated by thinkers such as Jacques Ellul, John Howard Yoder, and Stanley Hauerwas, among others, even while he sharply disagrees with them. Unlike Webb, he believes that while they are wrong, these thinkers nevertheless "are taking history seriously" and are being "historically responsible" (*Time Toward Home*, 56). As he puts it, "The burden of the argument is not against those who try, as best they can, to come out from among the condemned of the American Babylon. The argument is rather with those who partake fully in the glories or abominations, as the case may be, of the American experience yet accept no religious responsibility for that experience" (54).

145. Neuhaus, *Naked Public Square*, 76.

146. Ibid., 95.

147. Neuhaus, "Ambiguities of 'Christian America,'" 286.

148. Neuhaus, *Naked Public Square*, 137.

149. Neuhaus, *Time Toward Home*, 50.

150. Neuhaus, *Naked Public Square*, 96.

result, "discussion of public policy has been enfeebled by a dishonesty that refuses to be explicit about the religious dimensions that are in fact in play."[151]

Despite their relative power, these elites are not so disturbing to Neuhaus as the Christians, mainly liberal Protestants, who acquiesce to them. These Christians, although concerned about society, have "lost their confidence in the explicit traditions that gave religious pertinence and plausibility to their witness."[152] They support an understanding of liberalism in which "religion can impinge upon, but never really belong in, public space."[153] As a result, since the 1960s, "the churches that had been a primary bearer of the American story have been of little help in restoring a politics of democratic deliberation about how we ought to order our life together."[154] Note here the primacy of the church in propagating the American narrative, a task whose abandonment Neuhaus laments.

In Neuhaus's view, these Protestant churches lost confidence in their doctrine. Eager to accommodate modernity in the early twentieth century, they gradually acquiesced to doubts about the truths they proclaimed in return for maintaining "usefulness to the world, as others defined the world." From this emerged a more leftist, "radicalized" approach to politics, as Protestants found it advantageous to join with the "liberal, progressive, avante-garde." As the Left became more radical, Protestant leadership followed suit. When America failed to change accordingly, they lost confidence in religion. Their reliance on the secular elite "to provide the terms of discourse, to produce the good causes to which the church hopes to be helpful,"[155] has made American Protestantism impotent to address the moral and political crises of the nation, and especially to preserve American public piety. What is required, then, is "an imaginative reappropriation of its own tradition," in conjunction with a recovery of courage and confidence in "the distinctiveness of its own truth claims, a new courage to live in dialectic with a larger culture, an unembarrassed readiness to affirm the scandal of its particularity." As he notes, "Only such a church can 'save its own

---

151. Neuhaus, *Time Toward Home*, 154.
152. Ibid., 20.
153. Neuhaus, *Naked Public Square*, 137.
154. Neuhaus, *American Babylon*, 54.
155. Neuhaus, *Naked Public Square*, 215–17, 222.

soul.' Only such a church can contribute significantly to renewing and reshaping the public piety."[156] After all, the church's mandate is to be a type of "'signal community'—a model of how human life can be ordered by the redeeming grace of God."[157]

In short, the nation needs a reorientation of democracy by means of a renewal of public piety. Public piety, as we have seen for Neuhaus, is in dialectical relationship with "biblical religion." The Christian church is that community of biblical religion that "signals, anticipates, celebrates and supports" the coming kingdom of God. Those within the church concerned about its social witness have an opportunity in public piety, for "there is a meeting point between that hope for the kingdom and America's constituting vision."[158] The church's prominence in cultural formation was created by a faith community grounded in distinctive truth claims; it can only be recovered by such. Neuhaus thus proposes retrieving the model of "the church militant," the church that is "against the world for the world" in which "the church's significant contribution is to significantly challenge." Such challenge means "throwing all positions into question." Such "againstness" is a "yes" to the eschatological hope of the kingdom, and a "no" to "all lesser hopes of influence." Herein lies the church's influence in the here and now. Alluding to H. R. Niebuhr, it is "'Christ transforming culture' by pointing the culture to a transformation that is beyond its own means to attain or even imagine." This is the church's mission: to "proclaim the revolution of the coming kingdom" that will bring all existing institutions "under divine promise and judgment."[159]

Indeed, the churches are indispensible for this endeavor. In his early work, Neuhaus refers to such entities (which here he calls "churches" but means "all religious institutions") as "mediating structures": small groups or associations of kinship or common interest that provide personal contact with people, shaping and supporting personal values. Such mediating structures provide a link between the governing institutions of society and the everyday values and value communities of people.[160] Those values generated are "inseparably related to specific

---

156. Neuhaus, *Time Toward Home*, 209.
157. Neuhaus, *Naked Public Square*, 115.
158. Neuhaus, *Time Toward Home*, 21.
159. Neuhaus, *Naked Public Square*, 225.
160. Kerrine and Neuhaus, "Mediating Structures," 11.

religious traditions."¹⁶¹ Hence religion is the "motor force" of culture, which then drives politics, and thus history. Such a project "should have a major claim on the energies of churches, synagogues and other voluntary associations in the country." While social influence is not those institutions' primary mission, but rather a direct by-product of their witness and service,¹⁶² mediating structures are nevertheless the primary "value-generating and sustaining institutions" in a given society. Since they are the only ones expected to define the religious values so central to culture, they have in the formulating of public piety "a singular role in filling in the whys and wherefores and warrants for what otherwise remains an empty transcendence." And since the judgment of substantive transcendence is the means by which the nation-state is held accountable, these structures offer "heightened vigilance toward the limitations of the state with respect to society and, most importantly, with respect to that part of society that is the church."¹⁶³ This means public policy should utilize them and for purposes determined by those structures' members. While certainly there will be tension between church and state in this regard, such tension is both necessary and constructive for reorienting American politics.¹⁶⁴ Notice the strains of authentication here: this is the church playing its "culture-forming role," a direct role in the shaping of public piety, in the formulation and propagation of the narrative that defines national identity. Covenant is central to this role, since insofar as a theory of covenant can be reinvigorated in Christian theology, it can significantly affect the church's role in "shaping the general consciousness and public piety of America." This is the first step in recovering "an ethic that is serviceable in public discourse." "Particular religion," especially the church, serves to criticize and enrich the American experiment. Public piety, therefore, is "symbiotically related to, and inexplicably apart from, the explicit religious traditions that give it shape and life."¹⁶⁵

Central to the Christian religious tradition are its liturgies. In his earlier work, Neuhaus states that Christians partake in Christ's spiritual

161. Ibid., 15.
162. Neuhaus, *Naked Public Square*, 206.
163. Ibid., 117.
164. Kerrine and Neuhaus, "Mediating Structures," 12–13.
165. Neuhaus, *Time Toward Home*, 130, 155, 188.

prolepsis of the kingdom via sacramental and perhaps other means.[166] However that participation is accomplished, though, the kingdom of God cannot be sought apart from the world. While Christian commitment is to the world to come, it must nonetheless be oriented to the present world, "which is the world that is to be in progress of becoming." While there is a sense in which the world is left behind in pursuit of the kingdom to come, "it is *this* world that is to be transformed." All that is done is for the sake of the present world. So, in liturgy, Christians enact in the present the hoped-for future, symbolically setting "against all present definitions of reality a reality that, we believe, is yet more really real." The liturgy acts as an "eschatological sign" relativizing the present order in light of the kingdom of God, "an acting out in present time the meaning of the future for which we hope." As such, it is a celebration of what is to come: "the triumph of good over evil, the realization of perfect community, the defeat of suffering and death."[167]

In his later work, Neuhaus refers specifically to the Eucharist as "the supreme act of prolepsis" for Christians, "the 'source and summit' of the Church's life." Here, liturgy becomes more directly political than in his earlier formulations. He writes that the Eucharist is "a supremely *political* action in which the heavenly *polis* is made present in time."[168] For this reason, contrary to discourse by American evangelicals, "the Church is not the soul of Christ but the *body* of Christ. It is a distinctive society through time—a society distinct from the societies in which, sometimes for better and sometimes for worse, she is compelled to live through time toward the End Time."[169] Neglect of this truth has led to an "ecclesiological deficit" in American theology, "leading to an ecclesiological substitution of America for the Church through time."[170] Rather, robust Christian liturgy is a foretaste of the promised kingdom

---

166. In *Time Toward Home*, Neuhaus mentions specifically the "aesthetic and the sacramental"—"in worship, in the arts, in music, in mystical experience, in the anguish of love"—as chief means of experiencing the hope of the kingdom to come. In some of his later work, he concentrates much more specifically on Christian liturgy and particularly the Eucharist. See *American Babylon*, 14, 50, 184.

167. Neuhaus, *Time Toward Home*, 163.

168. Neuhaus, *American Babylon*, 14.

169. Ibid., 37.

170. Ibid., 41.

of God, the Feast of the Lamb, and relegates the "American Proposition" to its properly provisional status.[171]

Eschatology, the Church, and Biblical Theopolitics

Liturgy seems in this conception to be an eschatologically conditioned practice, one that could imply a more robust biblical theopolitics for the church. Yet for Neuhaus, this reenactment is a central means by which churches provide religious content to American public piety, enriching culture and social capital while restraining the pretensions of the state. In fact, Christian worship does not seem to escape Neuhaus's understanding of national historical particularity. Such historical embeddedness resists any theology of "realized eschatology," which Neuhaus defines in his early work as "saying that the Kingdom has come if you only believe it has come." This is talk of "salvation history" in which "God has kept all his promises and the plan of salvation is neatly wrapped up." We are to pay no heed, argues this theology, to "ordinary, secular history" in which people suffer here and now. But this theology is contrary to the kingdom described by Jesus: "he knew nothing about a spiritualized Kingdom that drew back from the itching, sweating particularities of historical experience." Believing that God's promises have been fulfilled when, in fact, they have not, does not glorify God.[172] Jesus preached that the kingdom of God had arrived for those who received him, and he spoke often about the social, political, and economic changes that would result. Yet he also said that his kingdom was not of this world. For Neuhaus, "herein lies the notorious 'now' and 'not yet' character of Christian thinking about the rule of God and all its relation to earthly government."[173] Where Jesus declares to his audience that the kingdom of God is in their midst (Luke 17), "he is telling them that *he* is in their midst"; wherever he speaks of the kingdom at hand, writes Neuhaus, "the Kingdom is always future," yet Jesus is declaring himself person-

171. Ibid., 50.
172. Neuhaus, *Time Toward Home*, 52, 63. As Neuhaus analogizes, it is like a friend who has promised to do something and defines himself by that promise. It is unfaithful friendship to tell him he has fulfilled it when he has not: "Far from honoring him, you have patronized him with your patent lack of trust in his purpose. Thus we patronize God when we do not take with ultimate seriousness the covenant that is contingent upon the coming of his promised Kingdom."
173. Neuhaus, *Naked Public Square*, 168.

ally to be a "prolepsis" of that future in the here and now.[174] While the Christian hope is political in the sense that it aims at "the *polis* of the New Jerusalem," the means of experiencing that hope are "not exclusively, nor even primarily, in the realm we call political."[175] By contrast, a theology of realized eschatology would "relieve the tension between the Now and the Not Yet," and as such constitute a "premature synthesis" that is tantamount to idolatry. In fact, "there is no relief short of the Kingdom Come," and it has not come yet.[176]

It seems, therefore, that despite Neuhaus's later eucharistic thought, his political theology is still bound to an understanding of a purely future judgment and resolution of our inescapably dialectical existence. To put this in perspective, Cavanaugh writes that prior to the modern era, the *saeculum*—in contrast to modern notions of the "secular"—was understood as the time between the fall of humanity and the second coming of Christ during which various institutions of power, providentially directed, existed to restrain sin.[177] Here, to be clear, the definitive underlying narrative is that of Christian salvation history, ultimately the reign of God in Christ and Christ's subjugation of the powers through the cross (Col 2). Christian liturgy celebrates and participates in this messianic age, in an outworking of messianic theopolitics. Within this age, the kingdom is not yet consummated, so institutions of authority exist to restrain sin and maintain peace. Institutions that absolutize themselves, such as the nation when it claims elect and salvific warrant or the state when "secular" is turned from contingent temporality into autonomous space, are not reflective of this order of time but are rebelling against its divine arrangement. Here, liturgy reflects the norm, the reality of the situation; the rebellious powers reflect the exception, attempting to overturn that reality.

Neuhaus argues the reverse: "liturgy is time in parenthesis, a blocked out time. We return to the tasks of a world in which the glorious truths we had celebrated in liturgy seem at best ambiguous and partial, at times even preposterous."[178] For Neuhaus, Christian celebration

---

174. Neuhaus, *Time Toward Home*, 66–67.

175. Ibid., 152.

176. Ibid., 59.

177. Cavanaugh, "God Is Not Religious," 104. See also Milbank, *Theology and Social Theory*, 9, as well as Cavanaugh, *Theopolitical Imagination*, 9–52.

178. Neuhaus, *Time Toward Home*, 163.

of the reign of God in Christ is exceptional to time, indicative not of present realities but of future ones, realities that condition the church's current political practice not so much by prior vocation and expectation as by prospect of future judgment. While this understanding is expressed early in his work, it is confirmed in his most recent book, *American Babylon*, in which he employs D. F. Watson's definition of Babylon as "the sphere of idolatry and worldliness under the temporary control of Satan, a worldliness in opposition to the people and the work of God, a worldliness epitomized first by Babylon and then by Rome. Babylon . . . is the antithesis of the Church as the Bride of Christ, the New Jerusalem, and the Kingdom of God."[179] It is a self-absolutizing movement of power, embodied in various institutions, in direct rebellion against the messianic order. The book then takes up the question of to what extent America can be considered Babylon, a discussion to be addressed below. What is important here is to note the key move that Neuhaus makes midway through the book:

> We have no alternative to this moment of time that is Babylon. More accurately, we have no *presently available* alternative. Babylon is for all time short of *the* alternative which is the promised New Jerusalem. Babylon is life in the realm of what Saint Augustine calls *libido dominandi*—the realm of the earthly city ruled by the lust for power and glory. For centuries Christians have prayed, "Thy kingdom come, thy will be done." And it is possible Christians will be praying that prayer for centuries more.[180]

Note here that Babylon is no longer merely a movement or institution in rebellion to the messianic order of time, but rather constitutes *its own order of time*, however "momentary." It is "life" here and now, the inescapable configuration of disordered theopolitics that marks our existence, wherein Christian worship is parenthetical, the exception to the rule, but something less than an actual alternative. As framed by Neuhaus's prior work, this means that Babylon *is* history, to which God has made himself accountable, calling us to do the same. God is invested in the political communities of Babylon-as-history, since he is redeeming the world through it. Thus, for Christians here and now, Babylon is the current form of *salvation* history. There is no alternative

---

179. Neuhaus, *American Babylon*, 10, quoting Watson, "Babylon in the NT."
180. Neuhaus, *American Babylon*, 119.

but to participate in its imperfect systems, even while by their very insufficiency they make us long for the fulfillment of the kingdom. In the end, eschatology for Neuhaus is arguably more about how the *telos* of the kingdom of God points theologically to the incompleteness and inadequacy of our contemporary situation, than how that *telos* disciplines our present participation, much less breaks into it as alternative. While throughout his work he emphasizes the "now"/"not yet" dialectic—"we live 'between the times'"[181]—his political theology overwhelmingly favors the "not yet" over the "now," such that the present age is marked by the incomplete victory of Christ.

I distinguish here between the terms "incomplete" and "unconsummated," which, as I use them, correspond respectively to degree and scope. Christ's victory over the powers is complete, as stated unequivocally in Colossians 2:15. At the same time, God's reign in Christ is not yet consummated in the sense of being globally present in its fullness (as evidenced by the world's conformity to it), nor will it be until Christ's return. That said, while the powers still exist and operate in their disordered state, it is not their rebellion but their rebellion *defeated* that marks the present messianic age. It is worth recalling Harink to the effect that messianic time, characterized by God's decisive reign, is not yet consummated, but it is present here and now in the world. And especially apropos in light of Neuhaus is Harink's statement that "in the face of often seemingly powerful evidence that the powers are victorious ('Be realistic!' as they say), what is called for from the church is an act of hopeful resistance, an act of disciplined 'counterintelligence,' in which the already present and coming messianic age is grasped in thought and action as the all-determining truth of the church's life, and indeed of the life of the world."[182]

The upshot of this is that while one should not expect to see the nation, state, market, university, and other powers of the world (including, all too often, the church itself) cease their rebellion against the messianic order at this point, there does exist the possibility of full-fledged alternative theopolitical communities in the world, which, empowered by the Holy Spirit, embody biblical theopolitics faithfully at different times and places. In the Christian salvation narrative, therefore, Christ's victory is the rule celebrated in Christian worship, to which Babylon is

---

181. Ibid.
182. Harink, *1 & 2 Peter*, 53–54.

the limited and temporary exception. This suggests that the Christian church, by the power of the Holy Spirit and to the degree that it is faithful in proclaiming and practicing its proper narrative, is in fact able to embody a theopolitics of the kingdom alternative to, and in the presence of, the politics of nations and states. Certainly sin abounds, and the church is no exception—far too often, it, too, has acted as a power in this very sense. But an inability to act in its proper theopolitical capacity is not, biblically, a foregone conclusion, as Neuhaus's realism would make it seem. Rather, any failure is, by virtue of the church's calling and empowerment, an exception to the rule of the messianic order. This is the "history" of the theopolitics of Scripture; even as it resides within it, the church is not bound to the history over which disordered politics is, in Neuhaus's understanding, sovereign.

However, given Neuhaus's eschatology, which is key to his "realistic" political theology, the ecclesia-as-alternative is difficult to find in his work. Short of the consummation of the kingdom, that is, in the time that is Babylon, "we live not in true community but in society."[183] There, our submission to the transcendent "is always premised upon the promise that God's will is to vindicate the human struggle of which we are part."[184] And that human struggle that God wills to vindicate is inevitably marked by violence. Neuhaus recognizes and respects the various theologies of pacifism and power critique that question "whether God necessarily works through power, and systems and laws, and even tragedy and violence to achieve his redemptive purposes," but for Neuhaus, this question is really "whether the promised redemption is through history, apart from history, or even against history."[185] Here the reader again recalls his declaration of the sovereignty of politics in historical development. If salvation is going to work through history, as the incarnation requires, then redemption is thereby intertwined with such power and tragedy; it cannot help but be if it is to reflect God's stake in our historical, especially political, experience. As Neuhaus explains, "the political tasks of determining public purpose and policy are part of the reality for which we seek redemption." These can either "welcome or resist the coming of the Kingdom" that is itself beyond politics. A "public ethic" is therefore necessary, consistent with the view of reality

---

183. Neuhaus, *American Babylon*, 184.
184. Neuhaus, *Time Toward Home*, 61.
185. Ibid., 54.

expressed in the faith—that is, Babylon—lest there be an artificial division between private religion and public politics.[186] Such is the "ethics of responsibility," which takes upon itself "the risks of participating in a compromised political order." While Christians of this approach do not compromise on central doctrine or the community that espouses it, they are "realistic" about the larger world, aware that "in the games of power politics they may end up with 'dirty hands.'"[187]

This public ethic—which Neuhaus defines as "the interplay between explicit biblical religion and the American tradition of public piety"—is necessarily a gamble[188]: "All bets are made in the name of him whose power of forgiveness is greater than our errors." Christians in the United States may therefore act with courage in the face of uncertainties. While one may be a pacifist, challenging the false claims of power politics, perhaps condemning the American dream as a false hope, another reluctantly uses force to defend his neighbor, uses politics to aim for the lesser rather than greater evil, and embraces the American dream for its foretaste of the kingdom. Each one, uncertain, decides on faith: "As to who is right, 'Let no man judge before the time' (1 Cor. 4)."

The church's politics, then, is a "politics for the time being," which for Neuhaus's schema means a politics for Babylon. Referring to the second-century *Letter to Diognetus*, as well as recalling Jeremiah, Neuhaus reminds Christians that as exiles in a foreign country, they "treat that foreign country as their homeland—for the time being, as everything is for the time being." Not confusing that country and its gods with the New Jerusalem, "they accept the opportunity to play their part as citizens, albeit as dual citizens." As such, they take part in the politics of their temporary homeland. At the same time, they experience in the life of the Church a "prolepsis" of the coming kingdom, that "genuinely 'new politics' of the new *polis* that is the City of God." Yet even that is "only a foretaste that whets our appetite for, and sacramentally sustains us on the way toward, that final destination."[189] Hence Neuhaus's "destination ethics," which "reaches toward the good, the hoped-for good, the good that is not yet but may become." That good, the promised reign of God,

---

186. Ibid., 152.
187. Neuhaus, *Naked Public Square*, 119.
188. Neuhaus, *Time Toward Home*, 19.
189. Neuhaus, *American Babylon*, 183–84.

cannot be sought apart from the world, that is, apart from history.[190] But as I have demonstrated, for Neuhaus "history" is Babylon-as-history, over which disordered politics is sovereign. Any public ethic or political theology, subject to future vindication or repudiation, must therefore begin with and operate from within that distorted order. This includes Neuhaus's own, which revolves around defending a supposed American covenant. Thus, Neuhaus's project of authenticating American national identity necessarily contradicts the messianic order the church is to proclaim in liturgy and practice.

Finally, Neuhaus's appropriation of the biblical narrative must be evaluated. Neuhaus often eschews direct appropriations of Israel for America's self-understanding (though he acknowledges their prevalence in historical discourse[191]), preferring to argue for covenant within the more general context. If America has a covenant, it is because America is a part, and a significant part, of creation, which in conjunction with its religious freedom—where the church is "vibrantly free to live and proclaim the Gospel to the world"—means that "America has a peculiar place in God's promises and purposes."[192] Yet Neuhaus makes no direct allusions to the Adamic or Noahic covenants, those usually interpreted as involving all of creation. The only covenant Neuhaus specifically alludes to is Israel's.

For instance, Neuhaus cites the Israelites as a model for America of the complementarity of self-interest and faithfulness to God: "God had inextricably tied his glory to their vindication."[193] And even though he is reticent to tie Israel and America directly together, he suggests that any construction of American public piety is inadequate if it does not consider the covenant imagery of "the other great model in America's historical self-understanding, namely, Israel in the wilderness."[194] At one point, he even goes so far as to state that the covenant at the root of American nationhood is "the narrative of God's dealings with the People of Israel, a narrative borne through time by a society that is incorrigibly, however confusedly, Christian America."[195] He refers ap-

---

190. Neuhaus, *Time Toward Home*, 159–62.
191. Ibid., 30–31.
192. Neuhaus, "Christianity and Democracy."
193. Neuhaus, *Time Toward Home*, 62.
194. Ibid., 201.
195. Neuhaus, "Contract and Covenant."

provingly in the same work to "Lincoln's fine phrase, America is 'an almost chosen people'"; however, three years later, he writes that "we should be uneasy even with Lincoln's sharply modified claim that we are an 'almost chosen' people."[196] There, however, he is not reticent at all to draw allusions between the Christian experience in America and Israel's experience of exile in Babylon, attempting to use Jeremiah's instructions to seek the welfare of the city as normative for the relationship between the church and America.[197] These passages suggest some ambiguity in Neuhaus's understanding of America's relation to Israel, and in the nature of the covenant connection between them. That said, to argue for a public ethic within the context of Babylonian exile necessarily entails a substantive tie to Israel's own covenant narrative. To argue that American democratic freedom prefigures or signals the kingdom of God in a singular manner suggests a continuation of Israel's own singular identity and mission. Like Israel, America is to signal the kingdom of God in its own, intra-communal life. And like Israel's, America's covenant is conditional, which means that "covenant does not confirm us in our righteousness or chosenness but calls us to accountability."[198] As with Israel's, American covenant means America under transcendent judgment.[199]

It is this conception of divine covenant, particularly in relation to Israel, that brings up one of the most significant problems in Neuhaus's political theology and his nationalist account of America. To put it simply, Neuhaus appropriates covenant without election. Granted, particular allusions to Israel notwithstanding, he eschews notions of election ostensibly in order to resist the temptation toward explicit American chosenness, that is, America as the elect nation of God in direct continuity with Israel. However, in so disconnecting covenant from election, the latter of which never enters into his political theology, he detaches covenant from its biblical moorings. Rather than understand-

---

196. Neuhaus, *American Babylon*, 24.

197. Ibid., 26, 55–57. His appropriation here is suspect, in part because he equates "city," which in Jeremiah refers to the immediate communities in which the exiled Israelites might find themselves, with the Babylonian Empire as a whole, including, presumably, its political interests. That "city" and "empire" might not constitute the same set of priorities for Israel—and thus for the church—is a possibility that Neuhaus never entertains.

198. Neuhaus, *Time Toward Home*, 169.

199. Neuhaus, *American Babylon*, 24.

ing covenant as rooted in a particular, divinely ordained identity, it is for Neuhaus a free-floating device for use elsewhere, an abstract and overly malleable concept that can be fitted to contexts arguably foreign to the theopolitics of biblical salvation history. Covenant becomes a product of human initiative—part of the human struggle to which God commits himself[200]—rather than a product of *God's* own initiating act, calling for the *people's* commitment.

A chief manifestation of this problem is Neuhaus's rejection of the past in favor of the future as judgment. The biblical notion of covenant, as explained in chapter 4, is anchored in a historical prologue by which God's acts of deliverance were recounted in order to justify the people's allegiance. Covenant was thus a response to God's *prior* action, an affirmation of a specific calling (election) made within a specific context. As a blueprint for social order, which in Neuhaus's terms means a politics, this covenant (Torah) existed in order to spell out the manner in which election was to be embodied. The prophets appeared to Israel not to suggest that Israel's actions may or may not be vindicated in the future, but rather to indict Israel for failing to live up to its identity previously established in election. Neuhaus effectively reverses this sequence in his political theology, appropriating covenant with no prior calling—that is, no prior warrant or mandate—as the form of America's prominent place in the Christian salvation narrative. Ignoring the biblical narrative of election and covenant as the standard for his move, Neuhaus hopes for future vindication when the kingdom of God comes in its fullness. Advocating the American experience as covenantal is risky, vulnerable to future judgment. Yet this intertwining of narratives is for Neuhaus "the most promising gamble."[201] In the meantime, democratic freedom, as a sign of the future kingdom of God, prophetically safeguards covenant integrity. Those like Yoder, Hauerwas, and their students, who sharply critique defining America in this manner, "have chosen a radically different option, and only the future will reveal if they are right."[202] Yet the biblical text suggests that the criteria needed to resolve that question are already present.

Directly implicated in this problematic reorientation from election to an uncertain eschatological judgment is Neuhaus's realist approach

---

200. Neuhaus, *Time Toward Home*, 61, 164.
201. Ibid., 19.
202. Ibid., 53.

to politics. As I argue in chapter 4, the biblical story of Israel's election and its covenant outworking in Torah prescribed a particular theopolitical orientation over against that of the powers of its day, the power politics of the surrounding kingdoms and empires. The operative political understanding was the reign of Yahweh, which entailed its own sovereignty over the international order and was to be embodied in Israel's communal life. Upon establishing the monarchy in spite of Yahweh's reign, and upon the state centralization inherent in such a move, Israel became something *other* than what its covenant specified. Upon its own (often inept) practice of power politics, Israel was prophetically indicted precisely for that. The significance of this point for Neuhaus cannot be overstated: Israel was not exiled *into* the necessity of "realistic" power politics, as Neuhaus appropriates the Babylon metaphor, but rather for *having already participated* in power politics contrary to its alternative identity and mission as constituted by election and delineated in covenant. Neuhaus, having disassociated covenant from election and then, in abstraction, applied covenant to the American ecclesial context, completely misses this point, one that effectively undermines his political theology. So when he states that "covenant does not confirm us in our righteousness or chosenness," he is correct about righteousness; however, nowhere in the biblical narrative is there national covenant without chosenness. He is quite right to reject a biblical model of election for America, but then this must preclude covenant as well. True to form for nationalist authentication, Neuhaus's intertwining of biblical and American narratives has—even inadvertently—distorted biblical theopolitics to fit his vision of America.

Conclusion

In this final chapter, I have taken up the nationalist discourses of Stephen H. Webb and Richard John Neuhaus, as articulated via their political theologies of providence and historical particularity, respectively. I have explained how, by contrast with the more straightforward historical accounts of Christian Right nationalism, which focuses particularly on recovering lost practices and institutions, both Webb and Neuhaus use political theology to authenticate American national identity via a form of exceptionalism, specifically America's special role in prefiguring the kingdom of God as promised in the Christian Scriptures. I have shown how each must distort the biblical narrative in order to justify their *a priori* nationalist commitments, and how each schema ultimately produces a syncretized narrative or doctrine of salvation history. This is the product of their attempt to authenticate American national identity, which in view of their political theologies, amounts to a problematic theopolitical "holiness" before the Lord Jesus Christ.

I have examined these political theologies, as well as the nationalist narratives in chapter 6, as case studies demonstrating the ways in which nationalism operates as a phenomenon or set of practices apart from state or market direction, emanating not as a force of co-option from outside the church, but as an alteration of theopolitical identity from within. I have further undertaken a theopolitical analysis of them using the theopolitics of the biblical narrative as my primary criterion of evaluation. In doing so, I have attempted to demonstrate that the theopolitical scholarship surveyed in chapters 1 and 3, while operating from a theological orientation I affirm, requires enhancement to properly appreciate and respond to nationalism as a key contemporary challenge to faithful ecclesial identity and practice.

Conclusion

This study began by noting that theopolitical scholarship has accomplished a great deal in terms of identifying and challenging those areas where ecclesial identity and mission are being either co-opted by, or accommodated to, the ways of the powers. I surveyed this literature in chapter 1 because it forms the theological background to the present study; my understanding has been formed in significant ways by their theopolitical work. However, I also noted certain oversights in that work: (1) no robust treatment of nationalism as a substantive phenomenon and/or a challenge distinct from operations of the state, and so far as it challenges ecclesial identity and mission, one emanating largely from within the church; and (2) an inability to adequately respond to the nationalist challenge given the theopolitical literature's inadequate account—and in some cases, neglect altogether—of the theopolitics of the biblical narrative, especially Israel, as normative for the church today.

To supplement the scholarship in these areas, I examined the work of several nationalism scholars who have paid closer attention to this process in terms of the theological roots of nationalism in the West. I noted the links they made between different nationalist movements and various elements of Christian beliefs, liturgies, and practices—including and especially the biblical text and its conceptions of election and covenant—showing how Christian nationalism ultimately amounts to a simulacrum of the Christian salvation narrative. Authentication, that process whereby nationalists determine and propagate the "true self" of the nation, is their pursuit of national holiness; the biblical narrative is selectively interwoven with their version of the national narrative such that the nationalist message becomes a new gospel; and the nation mimics the church, spreading its gospel to exhort the rest of the world to pursue holiness in that nation's own image and thereby to prefigure the kingdom of God. However, I also noted where this same nationalism scholarship does not fully appreciate the theological moves at work in this process, and must therefore attend better to Christian theology to understand precisely what is occurring in nationalist projects.

By way of providing such a theological framework of understanding, I then offered an account of biblical theopolitics. Chapter 4 attended to the theopolitics of biblical Israel, as Israel was delivered from the powers of its day in order to embody Yahweh's alternative way of life in the world, a theopolitics centered around Yahweh's proper worship, and thereby acting as a visible sign of salvation to the nations. I recounted how Israel eventually failed in this regard, adopting rather the political practices of the surrounding kingdoms and thereby altering its own theopolitical identity. I then related how Yahweh, ever loving of his people, then provided a definitive way for covenant to be fulfilled in the form of one person who would incarnate Israel and perform perfect *hesed*. Chapter 5 identified this person as Jesus Christ, in whom both Israel and Yahweh came together, enabling the perfect fulfillment of covenant, the complete embodiment of Israel's election identity. In so doing, Christ, faithful in his suffering, reordered the powers of the world and opened the fulfilled covenant up to all of humanity. He inaugurated the church in order to be the specific embodiment of this fulfilled covenant, the herald and sign of the truly and perfectly established reign of God in Christ, in a world that has not yet fully conformed to that reality. By means of this account, I attempted to address both what I felt was lacking in current theopolitical responses to nationalism, as well as provide a theological criterion of evaluation for Christian nationalist discourse.

Chapters 6 and 7 then took up an empirical analysis of American Christian nationalism. Chapter 6 looked at nationalist discourse by the American Christian Right, which tends toward narratives portraying America as the New Israel, or less directly as the divinely elect nation of the contemporary world chosen to save the world via its politics, economics, and culture, as well as its own innate moral goodness, if only it stays true to its true self. These narratives interweave elements of the biblical narrative with those of American history and myth, resulting in a syncretized nationalist narrative of American chosenness that equates faithfulness to America with faithfulness to Jesus Christ, thus making American national identity a gospel imperative. The discourse examined in chapter 7 accomplishes the same thing somewhat more subtly, filtering this syncretized narrative through political theologies that make America part and parcel of God's redemptive project. Whether through a theory of providence or of historical particularity and transcendence, these theologies locate the heart of Christ's redemptive work in the world today—or at the very least the political outworkings of that work—in the nation of America and in American liberal democracy.

The nationalist discourse surveyed in these two chapters contradicts the theopolitics of the biblical narrative either by de-particularizing Israel as the singular covenant nation in whom God was making his theopolitics real in the world, as fulfilled in Jesus Christ and then embodied by extension in the church; or by missing key lessons in Israel's life by which imitation of the nations and their ways of political life are seen to be directly contrary to the communal existence called for by God in election and covenant; or by ultimately supplanting the church with America as the extension of Israel and the current community called to prefigure the theopolitics of the kingdom of God on earth. In any event, these nationalist narratives—which, in addition to being at odds with the biblical narrative and Christian theology, are shown in both chapters to be marked by internal inconsistencies that in some cases undermine their projects—all demonstrate the distortion of the Christian biblical and theological traditions inherent in their attempts to authenticate a certain vision of the American nation that makes a normative claim on the political identity of Christians. As such, these accounts must be considered inconsistent with Christian identity and practice in view of the theopolitics of both testaments of Scripture.

Nationalism and Theopolitics

If the account I have provided in this study is accurate, then it has implications for the theopolitical scholarship surveyed in chapter 1. Nationalism, as distinct from forces of state and market, is a phenomenon that makes problematic claims on ecclesial identity by syncretizing elements of particular theological traditions with narratives of national history and myth in order to achieve popular acceptance of, and loyalty to, a particular vision of the nation. This demonstrates both the construction and the constraint inherent in the nationalist project, although those factors arguably vary relative to each other in specific instances.

In the case of Christian nationalism, nationalist elites utilize chiefly the biblical narrative, but also other theological beliefs and liturgical practices—elements that act as both external (in terms of available materials and the "wavelength" of the people) and internal constraints (in terms of the elites' own prior formation in those traditions) upon those elites—in order to craft *from within the church itself* an account of the nation as inherent to, and thus indispensible for, God's cosmic project of salvation through Jesus Christ. This often involves the nation in question as engrafted onto biblical Israel, prefiguring in community the inbreaking kingdom of God. The nation thus displaces the church, which according to the biblical narrative is engrafted onto Israel as the embodiment of Christ's fulfillment of covenant and opening of the "new covenant" to the nations. This means that nationalism necessarily distorts Christian theology and ecclesial identity for the sake of imagining the nation; it propagates a theopolitics that necessitates the division of the church along national lines in order to perpetuate its alternative gospel. Ergo, Christian nationalism—as the process of developing national identity in this fashion—cannot be considered orthodox.

The theopolitical scholarship of chapter 1 must take more careful account of this phenomenon. Its preoccupation with the state tends to leave unaddressed how in many cases national loyalty is actually cultivated, not to mention that the loyalties of the people may not coincide with the political apparatuses over them, and may be rooted in other types of community that the state has failed to fully dissolve. This scholarship must pay greater attention to the processes of identity authentication in national politics, the deliberate interweaving and syncretism of narratives that require, not amorphous transhistorical and transcultural notions of "religion," but rather quite particular—and necessarily distorted—faith traditions.

Additionally, this scholarship must take a more robust account of the biblical narrative as the primary source and norm for contemporary Christian theopolitics and ecclesiology. Without adequate attention to the theopolitics of biblical Israel, as fulfilled in Jesus Christ, and as extended into the church, we cannot properly address the claims of nationalism to the ordering of communal life among Christians and beyond, especially where it appropriates that very text to justify its vision. The church must be able to identify and directly challenge those specific points at which nationalist discourse distorts the Bible and Christian theology for its own use, in order to both truly tell the salvation narrative we are called to proclaim (Matt 28:18–20) and to truly embody it before the nations. Thus, while I believe the various proposals for ecclesial renewal put forward by theopolitical scholarship are helpful for the problems they identify, they must be supplemented by more thoroughgoing attention to the matters discussed here if they are to be more complete with regard to faithfulness.

This book is by and large an exercise in critical theology. While it presents a constructive biblical theopolitics, that theopolitics works here to critique American Christian nationalism. Yet, while I emphasize the centrality of the Christ's ecclesia for Christian social and theopolitical identity and mission, at no point do I mean to suggest that there is only one community to which we belong, one narrative alone that forms our imaginations and constitutes who we are. We are members of multiple communities and traditions simultaneously, and severing all ties but one does not seem to be consistent with gospel mission. However, it is just as clear that a simple prioritization of loyalties (God first, then family or country—or in the words of several Christian Right organizations, "faith, family, freedom") is insufficient as well, given that such a move can coexist fairly easily even within nationalism. Rather, we must understand that our relation to Christ and participation in the identity and mission of his ecclesia *redefines* all other relationships. I am still an American citizen, but I cannot be so in the same way as an American who does not call Jesus "Lord." As Paul's identity and citizenship were radically redefined in Christ, rather than eradicated, so must our own.

This prompts a number of questions that the church residing in the United States must ask itself and reflect upon carefully: What does it mean to be American when the very origin of the country is rooted in the act of Christians killing other Christians? What does it mean to be American when the United States constitutes an earthly empire by most measures of the term, that is, military, economic, ideological? What would it mean for the church here to profess and practice the singular identity and mission extended to us in 1 Peter within our own imperial context? How would we need to correct our own telling and embodying of that narrative? How would doing so transform our "Americanness"?

How do we live partly out of American identity when our Christology, ecclesiology, and eschatology all render that identity contingent upon, and in service to, both Jesus Christ and the whole world that is in the process of being redeemed? Can we be American as we live in robust solidarity with non-Americans (or even anti-Americans), especially as Christ has rendered any such divisions or exclusions null and void? These are fairly basic questions of ecclesial mission and identity, of genuine Christian unity, of idolatry and its resulting violence. While they are being answered in multiple contemporary theological discussions, they seem so often to escape congregational reflection. And if nationalism is flourishing, in particular at the congregational level, then perhaps it is time to start asking.

Bibliography

"About AFA." American Family Association. No pages. Online: http://www.afa.net/Detail.aspx?id=31

"About FRC Action: Fighting for the American Family." FRC Action. No pages. Online: http://www.frcaction.org/about-us

"About Liberty." Liberty University. No pages. Online: https://www.liberty.edu/index.cfm?PID=6925

"About Us." Vision America. No pages. Online: http://www.visionamerica.us/about-us/

Anderson, Benedict. "Imagined Communities." In *Nationalism*, edited by John Hutchinson and Anthony Smith, 89-96. Oxford: Oxford University Press, 2001.

Armstrong, John. "Nations before Nationalism." In *Nationalism*, edited by John Hutchinson and Anthony Smith, 140-46. Oxford: Oxford University Press, 2001.

Bader-Saye, Scott. *Church and Israel after Christendom: The Politics of Election.* Boulder, CO: Westview, 1999.

Balthasar, Hans Urs von. *The Glory of the Lord: A Theological Aesthetics.* Vol. 1, *Seeing the Form.* Edinburgh: T & T Clark, 1982.

———. *Mysterium Paschale: The Mystery of Easter.* Edinburgh: T & T Clark, 1990.

Barnes, T. D. *Constantine and Eusebius.* Cambridge: Harvard University Press, 1981.

———. *From Eusebius to Constantine: Selected Papers, 1982-1993.* Aldershot: Variorum, 1994.

Barrington, Lowell W. "Nationalism & Independence." In *After Independence: Making and Protecting the Nation in Postcolonial and Postcommunist States*, edited by Lowell W. Barrington, 3-30. Ann Arbor: University of Michigan Press, 2006.

———. "'Nation' and 'Nationalism': The Misuse of Key Concepts in Political Science." *PS: Political Science and Politics* 30:4 (1997) 712-16.

Barton, David. *America's Godly Heritage.* 2nd ed. Aledo, TX: WallBuilders, 1993.

———. "The Founding Fathers on Jesus, Christianity and the Bible." May 2008. No pages. Online: http://www.wallbuilders.com/LIBissuesArticles.asp?id=8755

———. "God: Missing in Action in America's History." June 2005. No pages. Online: http://www.wallbuilders.com/LIBissuesArticles.asp?id=100

———. *The Myth of Separation.* Aledo, TX: WallBuilders, 1992.

---. "The Separation of Church and State." January 2001. No pages. Online: http://www.wallbuilders.com/LIBissuesArticles.asp?id=123

Baxter, Michael J. "God Is Not American: Or, Why Christians Should Not Pledge Allegiance to 'One Nation under God.'" In *God Is Not . . . Religious, Nice, "One of Us,"* An American, A Capitalist, edited by D. Brent Laytham, 55–76. Grand Rapids: Brazos, 2004.

Beach-Verhey, Tim. Review of *American Providence: A Nation with a Mission*, by Stephen H. Webb. *Political Theology* 10: 2 (2009) 376–78.

Bellah, Robert N. "The Revolution and Civil Religion." In *Religion and the American Revolution*, edited by Jerald Brauer. Philadelphia: Fortress, 1976.

Bellah, Robert N, Richard Madsen, William Sullivan, Ann Swidler, and Steven M. Tipton. *Habits of the Heart: Individualism and Commitment in American Life*. Berkeley: University of California Press, 1985.

"Biblical Support for CWA Core Issues." Concerned Women for America. http://www.cwfa.org/coreissues.asp

Binbaum, Michael. "Historians Speak Out against Proposed Texas Textbook Changes." *The Washington Post*, March 18, 2010. No pages. Online: http://www.washingtonpost.com/wpdyn/content/article/2010/03/17/AR2010031700560.html

Blenkinsopp, Joseph. *Sage, Priest, Prophet: Religious and Intellectual Leadership in Ancient Israel*. Louisville: Westminster John Knox, 1995.

Booth-Thomas, Cathy. "David Barton." *Time Magazine*, February 7, 2005. No pages. Online: http://www.time.com/time/covers/1101050207/photoessay/3.html

Boyd, Gregory A. *The Myth of a Christian Nation: How the Quest for Political Power Is Destroying the Church*. Grand Rapids: Zondervan, 2005.

Boyer, Paul. "Two Centuries of Christianity in America: An Overview." *Church History* 70:3 (2001) 544–56.

Brass, Paul R. *Ethnicity and Nationalism: Theory and Comparison*. New Dehli: Sage Publications, 1991.

Bright, John. *History of Israel*. Philadelphia: Westminster, 1981.

Brubaker, Rogers. *Nationalism Reframed: Nationhood and the National Question in the New Europe*. Cambridge: Cambridge University Press, 1996.

Brueggemann, Walter. "Always in the Shadow of Empire." In *The Church as Counterculture*, edited by Michael L. Budde and Robert W. Brimlow, 39–58. Albany: State University of New York Press, 2000.

---. *The Prophetic Imagination*. Minneapolis: Fortress, 1978.

---. "Scripture: Old Testament." In *The Blackwell Companion to Political Theology*, edited by Peter Scott and William T. Cavanaugh, 7–20. Malden, MA: Blackwell, 2004.

Budde, Michael L. "The Changing Face of American Catholic Nationalism." *Sociological Analysis* 53: 3 (1992) 245–55.

Budde, Michael L., and Robert W. Brimlow, editors. *The Church as Counterculture*. Albany: State University of New York Press, 2000.

Buss, Doris, and Didi Herman. *Globalizing Family Values: The Christian Right in International Politics*. Minneapolis: University of Minnesota Press, 2003.

Caldwell, Deborah. "David Barton & the 'Myth' of Church-State Separation." 2004. No pages. Online: http://www.beliefnet.com/News/Politics/2004/10/David-Barton-The-Myth-Of-Church-State-Separation.aspx
Cameron, Averil, and Stuart G. Hall. "Introduction." In Eusebius, *Life of Constantine*. Translated by Averil Cameron and Stuart G. Hall, 1–53. Oxford: Clarendon, 1999.
Cartwright, Michael G. "Afterword: 'If Abraham Is Our Father . . .' The Problem of Christian Supersessionism *after* Yoder." In John Howard Yoder, *The Jewish-Christian Schism Revisited*, edited by Michael G. Cartwright and Peter Ochs, 205–40. Grand Rapids: Eerdmans, 2003.
Cartwright, Michael G., and Peter Ochs. "Editors' Introduction." In John Howard Yoder, *The Jewish-Christian Schism Revisited*, edited by Michael G. Cartwright and Peter Ochs, 1–29. Grand Rapids: Eerdmans, 2003.
Cavanaugh, William T. "Church." In *The Blackwell Companion to Political Theology*, edited by Peter Scott and William T. Cavanaugh, 393–406. Malden, MA: Blackwell, 2004.
———. "The City: Beyond Secular Parodies." In *Radical Orthodoxy: A New Theology*, edited by John Milbank, Catherine Pickstock, and Graham Ward, 182–200. London: Routledge, 1999.
———. "The Empire of the Empty Shrine: American Imperialism and the Church." *Cultural Encounters* 2:2 (2006) 7–19.
———. "'A Fire Strong Enough to Consume the House': The Wars of Religion and the Rise of the State." *Modern Theology* 11 (1995) 397–420.
———. "God Is Not Religious." In *God Is Not . . . Religious, Nice, "One of Us," An American, A Capitalist*, edited by D. Brent Laytham, 97–116. Grand Rapids: Brazos, 2004.
———. "If You Render Unto God What Is God's, What Is Left for Caesar?" *The Review of Politics* 71 (2009) 607–19.
———. "Killing for the Telephone Company: Why the Nation-State Is Not the Keeper of the Common Good." *Modern Theology* 20:2 (2004) 243–74.
———. "Messianic Nation: A Christian Theological Critique of American Exceptionalism." *University of St. Thomas Law Journal* 3:2 (2005–2006) 261–80.
———. "Reply to Stephen H. Webb." *Cultural Encounters* 2:2 (2006) 26–29.
———. *The Myth of Religious Violence*. Oxford: Oxford University Press, 2009.
———. *Theopolitical Imagination*. London: T & T Clark, 2002.
———. *Torture and Eucharist: Theology, Politics, and the Body of Christ*. Malden, MA: Blackwell, 1998.
Centner, Pat. "TeenPact trains youth for godly government." *AFA Journal*, Nov./Dec. 2002. No pages. Online: http://www.afajournal.org/2002/novdec/christian_activism.asp
Childs, Brevard S. *Old Testament Theology in a Canonical Context*. Philadelphia: Fortress, 1985.
"Christian Worldview Network." Christian Worldview Weekend. No pages. Online: http://www.worldviewweekend.com/christian-worldview-network/
Church-People-State-Nation: A Protestant Contribution on a Difficult Relationship, Report of the Discussions in the South and Southeast Europe Regional Group of the Leuenberg Church Fellowship. Lembeck, 2002.

Clapp, Rodney. *A Peculiar People: The Church as Culture in a Post-Christian Society.* Downers Grove: InterVarsity, 1996.
Connor, Walker. "A Nation Is a Nation, Is a State, Is an Ethnic Group, Is a . . ." In *Nationalism*, edited by John Hutchinson and Anthony Smith, 36–46. Oxford: Oxford University Press, 2001.
Conversi, Daniele. "Mapping the Field: Theories of Nationalism and the Ethnosymbolic Approach." In *Nationalism and Ethnosymbolism: History, Culture and Ethnicity in the Formation of Nations*, edited by Althena S. Leoussi and Steven Grosby, 15–30. Edinburgh: Edinburgh University Press, 2007.
"Culture and Religion." American Values. http://www.ouramericanvalues.org/culture.php
Dawson, Jan. "The Religion of Democracy in Early Twentieth-Century America." *Journal of Church and State* 27:1 (1985):47–64.
Diamond, Sara. "Cultural Projects in Christian Right Mobilization." In *Unraveling the Right: The New Conservatism in American Thought and Politics*, edited by Amy E. Ansell, 41–55. Boulder, CO: Westview, 1998.
———. *Roads to Dominion: Right-Wing Movements and Political Power in the United States.* New York: Guilford, 1995.
Dumbrell, William J. *Covenant and Creation: A Theology of the Old Testament Covenants.* Exeter: Paternoster Press, 2002.
———. *The Faith of Israel: A Theological Survey of the Old Testament.* 2nd ed. Leicester: Apollos, 2002.
Durham, Martin. *The Christian Right, the Far Right and the Boundaries of American Conservatism.* Manchester: Manchester University Press, 2000.
Elshtain, Jean Bethke. Review of *American Providence: A Nation with a Mission*, by Stephen H. Webb. *First Things* 150 (2005) 38–40.
"Ethnicity and Nationalism: A Challenge to the Churches." *The Ecumenical Review* 47 (1995) 225–31.
"Falwell Apologizes to Gays, Feminists, Lesbians." CNN, September 14, 2001. No pages. Online: http://archives.cnn.com/2001/US/09/14/Falwell.apology/
Falwell, Jerry. *Listen, America!* Garden City: Doubleday, 1980.
Fea, John. "Thirty Years of Light and Glory." *Touchstone* 21:6 (2008) 27–30.
Foucault, Michel. "Technologies of the Self." In *Technologies of the Self: A Seminar with Michel Foucault*, edited by Luther H. Martin, Huck Gutman, and Patrick H. Hutton, 16–49. Amherst: University of Massachusetts Press, 1988.
Geertz, Clifford. *The Interpretation of Cultures.* London: Fontana, 1973.
Gellner, Ernest. *Nations and Nationalism.* Ithaca: Cornell University Press, 1983.
Goldberg, Michelle. *Kingdom Coming: The Rise of Christian Nationalism.* New York: Norton, 2006.
Gorski, Philip. "The Mosaic Moment: An Early Modernist Critique of Modernist Theories of Nationalism." *American Journal of Sociology* 105:5 (2000) 1428–68.
Green, Joel B. *1 Peter.* Grand Rapids: Eerdmans, 2007.
Green, John C., James L. Guther, Corwin E. Smidt, and Lyman A. Kellstedt. *Religion and the Culture Wars: Dispatches from the Front.* Lanham, MD: Rowman & Littlefield, 1996.

Green, John C, Mark J. Rozell, and Clyde Wilcox, editors. *The Christian Right in American Politics: Marching to the Millennium*. Washington, DC: Georgetown University Press, 2003.

Greenfield, Liah. *Nationalism: Five Roads to Modernity*. Cambridge: Harvard University Press, 1992.

Grosby, Steven. *Biblical Ideas of Nationality: Ancient and Modern*. Winona Lake, IN: Eisenbrauns, 2002.

Hafemann, Scott J. *Paul, Moses, and the History of Israel: The Letter/Spirit Contrast and the Argument from Scripture in 2 Corinthians 3*. Peabody, MA: Hendrickson, 1996.

Harink, Douglas. *1 & 2 Peter*. Brazos Theological Commentary on the Bible. Grand Rapids: Brazos, 2009.

———. *Paul among the Postliberals: Pauline Theology beyond Christendom and Modernity*. Grand Rapids: Brazos, 2003.

Hastings, Adrian. "The Clash of Nationalism and Universalism within Twentieth-Century Missionary Christianity." In *Missions, Nationalism, and the End of Empire*, edited by Brian Stanley, 15–33. Grand Rapids: Eerdmans, 2003.

———. *The Construction of Nationhood: Ethnicity, Religion and Nationalism*. Cambridge: Cambridge University Press, 1997.

Hauerwas, Stanley. *Against the Nations: War and Survival in a Liberal Society*. Minneapolis: Winston, 1985.

———. "A Christian Critique of Christian America." In *The Hauerwas Reader*, edited by John Berkman and Michael Cartwright, 459–80. Durham: Duke University Press, 2001.

———. *Christian Existence Today: Essays on Church, World, and Living in Between*. Durham: Duke University Press, 1988.

———. "Democratic Time: Lessons Learned from Yoder and Wolin." *Cross Currents* 55 (2006) 534–52.

———. "The Kingdoms of the World." Review of *American Babylon: Notes of a Christian Exile*, by Richard John Neuhaus. *First Things* 192 (2009) 71–74.

———. *The Peaceable Kingdom: A Primer in Christian Ethics*. Notre Dame: University of Notre Dame Press, 1983.

———. *Unleashing the Scripture: Freeing the Bible from Captivity to America*. Nashville: Abingdon, 1993.

———. *With the Grain of the Universe: The Church's Witness and Natural Theology*. Grand Rapids: Brazos, 2001.

Hauerwas, Stanley, and Romand Coles. *Christianity, Democracy, and the Radical Ordinary: Conversations between a Radical Democrat and a Christian*. Eugene, OR: Cascade Books, 2008.

Hauerwas, Stanley, and William H. Willimon. *Resident Aliens: Life in the Christian Colony*. Nashville: Abingdon, 1989.

Heinz, Donald. "Clashing Symbols: The New Christian Right as Countermythology." *Archives de sciences sociales des religions* 59:1 (1985) 153–73.

Hobsbawm, Eric J. "The Nation as Invented Tradition." In *Nationalism*, edited by John Hutchinson and Anthony D. Smith, 76–82. Oxford: Oxford University Press, 2001.

Hobsbawm, Eric J., and Terence Ranger, editors. *The Invention of Tradition.* Cambridge: Cambridge University Press, 1983.

Hollerich, Michael. "Carl Schmitt." In *The Blackwell Companion to Political Theology,* edited by Peter Scott and William T. Cavanaugh, 107–22. Malden, MA: Blackwell, 2004.

Hopson, Ronald E., and Donald R. Smith. "Changing Fortunes: An Analysis of Christian Right Ascendance within American Political Discourse." *Journal for the Scientific Study of Religion* 38:1 (1999) 1–13.

Howse, Brannon. *One Nation under Man? The Worldview War between Christians and the Secular Left.* Nashville: B & H Publishing, 2005.

Huwyler, Beat. "Jeremia und der Volker: Politische Prophetie in der Zeit der babylonischen Bedrohung." *Theologische Zeitschrift* 52 (1996) 193–205.

Ignatieff, Michael. "Nationalism and the Narcissism of Minor Differences." In *Theorizing Nationalism,* edited by Ronald Beiner, 91–102. Albany: State University of New York Press, 1999.

"Israel—God's Covenanted People." In *New Jerome Biblical Commentary.* Edited by Raymond E. Brown, Joseph A. Fitzmyer, and Roland E. Murphy, 1295–1301. Englewood Cliffs, NJ: Prentice-Hall, 1990.

Janzen, Waldemar. "Suffering Servants." In *Suffering,* 20–28. Christian Reflection: A Series in Faith and Ethics. Waco, TX: Center for Christian Ethics at Baylor University, 2005. No pages. Online: http://www.baylor.edu/christianethics/Suffering.pdf

"Jerry Newcombe, D.Min. – Biographical Information." No pages. Online: http://www.jerrynewcombe.com/jerry.html

Johnson, William J. *George Washington the Christian.* New York: Abingdon, 1919. No pages. Online: http://books.google.com/books?id=MzWruWAnHMoC&printsec=frontcover&dq=william+johnson,+george+washington,+the+christian&source=bl&ots=Dz3NyGfrH9&sig=SvedtxZlWrzwooqniwbgY-IBKIbg&hl=en&ei=Aq7ES7_kBoOMNpWrqPYN&sa=X&oi=book_result&ct=result&resnum=3&ved=0CAwQ6AEwAg#v=onepage&q&f=false

Kennedy, D. James. *Character and Destiny: A Nation in Search of Its Soul.* Grand Rapids: Zondervan, 1994.

Kennedy, D. James, and Jerry Newcombe. *What If America Were a Christian Nation Again?* Nashville: Nelson, 2003.

Kerrine, Theodore M., and Richard John Neuhaus. "Mediating Structures: A Paradigm for Democratic Pluralism." *Annals of the American Academy of Political and Social Science* 446 (1979) 10–18.

Kline, Meredith. *The Treaty of the Great King.* Grand Rapids: Eerdmans, 1963.

Kline, Scott. "The Culture War Gone Global: 'Family Values' and the Shape of US Foreign Policy." *International Relations* 18:4 (2004) 453–66.

Kramer, Lloyd. "Historical Narratives and the Meaning of Nationalism." *Journal of the History of Ideas* 58:3 (1997) 525–45.

Kuzio, Taras. "The Myth of the Civic State: A Critical Survey of Hans Kohn's Framework for Understanding Nationalism." *Ethnic and Racial Studies* 26:1 (2002) 20–39.

Kyle, Richard. "The Bedrock Beliefs of the Christian Right." *Direction* 36:1 (2007) 31–42.

Leoussi, Althena S., and Steven Grosby. "Introduction." In *Nationalism and Ethnosymbolism: History, Culture and Ethnicity in the Formation of Nations*, edited by Althena S. Leoussi and Steven Grosby, 1–14. Edinburgh: Edinburgh University Press, 2007.

Levenson, Jon D. *Sinai and Zion: An Entry into the Jewish Bible*. San Francisco: HarperCollins, 1985.

Lienesch, Michael. *Redeeming America: Piety and Politics in the New Christian Right*. Chapel Hill: University of North Carolina Press, 1993.

Lieven, Anatol. "In the Mirror of Europe: The Perils of American Nationalism." *Current History* 103:671 (2004) 99–106.

Lind, Millard C. "Hosea 5:8—6:6." *Interpretation* 38 (1984) 398–403.

Llobera, Josep. *Foundations of National Identity: From Catalonia to Europe*. New York: Berghahn, 2004.

Lohfink, Gerhard. *Does God Need the Church? Toward a Theology of the People of God*. Collegeville: Liturgical Press, 1999.

———. *Jesus and Community: The Social Dimension of Christian Faith*. Translated by John P. Galvin. Philadelphia: Fortress, 1982.

Machinist, Peter. "Hosea and the Ambiguity of Kingship in Ancient Israel." In *Constituting the Community: Studies on the Polity of Ancient Israel in Honor of S. Dean McBride, Jr.*, edited by John T. Strong and Steven S. Tuell, 153–82. Winona Lake, IN: Eisenbrauns, 2005.

Marsden, George M. *Fundamentalism and American Culture: The Shaping of Twentieth-Century Evangelicalism, 1870–1925*. Oxford: Oxford University Press, 1980.

Marshall, Peter, and David Manuel. *The Light and the Glory*. Old Tappan, NJ: Revell, 1977.

Marx, Anthony. *Faith in Nation: Exclusionary Origins of Nationalism*. New York: Oxford University Press, 2003.

McCarthy, Dennis J. *Treaty and Covenant: A Study in Form in the Ancient Oriental Documents and in the Old Testament*. Rome: Pontifical Biblical Institute, 1963.

McKinley, James C, Jr. "Texas Conservatives Seek Deeper Stamp on Texts." *The New York Times*, March 10, 2010. No pages. Online: http://www.nytimes.com/2010/03/11/us/politics/11texas.html

———. "Texas Conservatives Win Curriculum Change." *The New York Times*, March 12, 2010. No pages. Online: http://www.nytimes.com/2010/03/13/education/13texas.html

McNaughton, John. *One Nation Under God*. No pages. Online: http://www.mcnaughtonart.com/artwork/view_zoom/?artpiece_id=353#

Mendenhall, G. E. "Covenant Forms in Israelite Tradition." *Biblical Archaeology Review* 21:2 (1995) 48–57.

Milbank, John. *Theology and Social Theory: Beyond Secular Reason*. 2nd ed. Malden, MA: Blackwell, 2006.

Moaz, Zeev, and Bruce Russett. "Normative and Structural Causes of Democratic Peace, 1946–1986." *The American Political Science Review* 87:3 (1993) 624–38.

Moore, Scott H. *The Limits of Liberal Democracy: Politics and Religion at the End of Modernity*. Downers Grove, IL: IVP Academic, 2009.

Mosse, George. *The Nationalization of the Masses: Political Symbolism and Mass Movements in Germany from the Napoleonic Wars through the Third Reich.* Ithaca: Cornell University Press, 1975.

Murphy, Andrew R. "'One Nation under God,' September 11 and the Chosen Nation: Moral Decline and Divine Punishment in American Public Discourse." *Political Theology* 6:1 (2005) 9–30.

———. *Prodigal Nation: Moral Decline and Divine Punishment from New England to 9/11.* Oxford: Oxford University Press, 2009.

"National Security and International Affairs." American Values. No pages. Online: http://www.ouramericanvalues.org/nationalSecurity.php

Neuhaus, Richard John. "The Ambiguities of 'Christian America.'" *Concordia Journal*, July 1991, 285–95.

———. *American Babylon: Notes of a Christian Exile.* New York: Basic Books, 2009.

———. "Christianity and Democracy: A Statement of the Institute on Religion and Democracy." *Center Journal* 1:3 (1982) 9–25.

———. "Contract and Covenant: In Search of American Identity." 2007 Bradley Symposium (April 16, 2006). No pages. Online: http://www.bradleyproject.org/bradleyprojectessay3.html

———. *The Naked Public Square: Religion and Democracy in America.* Grand Rapids: Eerdmans, 1984.

———. *Time Toward Home: The American Experiment as Revelation.* New York: Seabury, 1975.

———. "The War, the Churches, and Civil Religion." *Annals of the American Academy of Political and Social Science* 387 (1970) 128–40.

Newcombe, Jerry. *The Book that Made America: How the Bible Formed Our Nation.* Ventura, CA: Nordskog, 2009.

Nisbet, Robert. *The Quest for Community.* London: Oxford University Press, 1953.

O'Donovan, Oliver. *The Desire of the Nations: Rediscovering the Roots of Political Theology.* Cambridge: Cambridge University Press, 1996.

Özkirimli, Umut. *Theories of Nationalism: A Critical Introduction.* New York: St. Martin's, 2000.

Pentiuc, Eugene J. *Long-Suffering Love: A Commentary on Hosea with Patristic Annotations.* Brookline, MA: Holy Cross Orthodox Press, 2002.

"Peter Marshall Ministries." No pages. Online: http://www.petermarshallministries.com/index.cfm

Pinches, Charles. "Hauerwas and Political Theology: The Next Generation." *Journal of Religious Ethics* 36:3 (2008) 513–42.

Pixley, Jorge. *Jeremiah.* St. Louis: Chalice, 2004.

Rasmussen, Arne. *The Church as Polis: From Political Theology to Theological Politics as Exemplified by Jürgen Moltmann and Stanley Hauerwas.* Notre Dame: University of Notre Dame Press, 1995.

Redditt, Paul L. "When Faith Demands Treason: Civil Religion and the Prophet Jeremiah." *Review and Expositor* 101 (2004) 227–46.

"Religion and Culture." Family Research Council. http://www.frc.org/religion-culture

Renan, Ernest. "Qu'est-ce qu'une nation?" In *Nationalism*, edited by John Hutchinson and Anthony Smith, 17–18. Oxford: Oxford University Press, 2001.

Robertson, Pat. *America's Dates with Destiny.* Nashville: Nelson, 1986.

Rowe, Paul S. "Render Unto Caesar . . . What? Reflections on the Word of William Cavanaugh." *The Review of Politics* 71 (2009) 583–605.

Schlabach, Gerald. "Continuity and Sacrament, or Not: Hauerwas, Yoder, and Their Deep Difference." *Journal of the Society of Christian Ethics* 27:2 (2007) 171–207.

———. "Deuteronomic or Constantinian: What Is the Most Basic Problem for Christian Social Ethics?" In *The Wisdom of the Cross: Essays in Honor of John Howard Yoder*, edited by Stanley Hauerwas, Chris K. Huebner, Harry J. Huebner, and Mark Thiessen Nation, 449–71. Grand Rapids: Eerdmans, 1999.

Shorto, Russell. "How Christian Were the Founders?" *The New York Times*, February 11, 2010. No pages. Online: http://www.nytimes.com/2010/02/14/magazine/14texbooks-t.html

Siker, Jeffrey S. "Stanley Hauerwas: The Community Story of Israel and Jesus." In *Scripture and Ethics: Twentieth-Century Portraits*, 97–125. New York: Oxford University Press, 1997.

Smith, Anthony D. *Chosen Peoples*. Oxford: Oxford University Press, 2003.

———. *The Cultural Foundations of Nations: Hierarchy, Covenant, and Republic*. Malden, MA: Blackwell, 2008.

———. "Culture, Community and Territory: The Politics of Ethnicity and Nationalism." *International Affairs* 72:3 (1996) 445–58.

———. "The Dark Side of Nationalism: The Revival of Nationalism in Late Twentieth Century Europe." In *The Far Right in Western and Eastern Europe*. 2nd ed. Edited by Luciano Cheles, Ronnie Ferguson, and Michalina Vaughan, 13–19. London: Longman, 1995.

———. "The Formation of National Identity." In *Identity*, edited by Henry Harris, 129–53. Oxford: Clarendon, 1995.

———. *Myths and Memories of the Nation*. Oxford: Oxford University Press, 1999.

———. *Nationalism and Modernism*. London: Routledge, 1998.

———. *The Nation in History: Historiographical Debates about Ethnicity and Nationalism*. Hanover, NH: Brandeis University Press, 2000.

———. "The Origin of Nations." In *Nationalism*, edited by John Hutchinson and Anthony Smith, 147–54. Oxford: Oxford University Press, 2001.

Smith, James K. A. *Desiring the Kingdom: Worship, Worldview, and Cultural Formation*. Grand Rapids: Baker Academic, 2009.

———. *Introducing Radical Orthodoxy: Mapping a Post-Secular Theology*. Grand Rapids: Baker Academic, 2004.

Suny, Ronald Grigor. "Nationalism, Nation Making, and the Postcolonial States of Asia, Africa, and Eurasia." In *After Independence: Making and Protecting the Nation in Postcolonial and Postcommunist States*, edited by Lowell W. Barrington, 279–95. Ann Arbor: University of Michigan Press, 2006.

Tanenhaus, Sam. "In Texas Curriculum Fight, Identity Politics Leans Right." *The New York Times*, March 19, 2010. No pages. Online: http://www.nytimes.com/2010/03/21/weekinreview/21tanenhaus.html

Taylor, Mark Lewis. *Religion, Politics, and the Christian Right: Post 9/11 Powers and American Empire*. Minneapolis: Fortress, 2005.

United States Army. "Army Chaplain Corps." http://www.goarmy.com/chaplain/

Van den Berghe, Pierre. "A Socio-Biological Perspective." In *Nationalism*, edited by John Hutchinson and Anthony Smith, 96–102. Oxford: Oxford University Press, 2001.

Wall, Robert W., and Eugene E. Lemcio. *The New Testament as Canon: A Reader in Canonical Criticism*. Journal for the Study of the New Testament Supplement Series 76. Sheffield: Sheffield Academic Press, 1992.

"WallBuilders Overview." WallBuilders, LLC. http://www.wallbuilders.com/ABTOverview.asp

Walzer, Michael. *Exodus and Revolution*. New York: Basic Books, 1985.

Watson, D. F. "Babylon in the NT." In *The Anchor Bible Dictionary*. 6 vols. Edited by David Noel Freedman. Vol. 1, *A–C*. New York: Doubleday, 1992.

Webb, Stephen H. *American Providence: A Nation with a Mission*. New York: Continuum, 2004.

———. *Blessed Excess: Religion and the Hyperbolic Imagination*. Albany: State University of New York Press, 1993.

———. *The Divine Voice: Christian Proclamation and the Theology of Sound*. Grand Rapids: Brazos, 2004.

———. "Eschatology and Politics." In *The Oxford Handbook of Eschatology*, edited by Jerry L. Walls, 500–17. Oxford: Oxford University Press, 2008.

———. *Good Eating: The Bible, Diet, and the Proper Love of Animals*. Grand Rapids: Brazos, 2001.

———. "On the True Globalism and the False, or Why Christians Should Not Worry So Much about American Imperialism." In *Anxious about Empire: Theological Essays on the New Global Realities*, edited by Wes Avram, 119–28. Grand Rapids: Brazos, 2004.

———. "Response to William T. Cavanaugh." *Cultural Encounters* 2:2 (2006) 21–25.

———. *Taking Religion to School: Christian Theology and Secular Education*. Grand Rapids: Brazos, 2000.

———. "The Very American Stanley Hauerwas." *First Things* 124 (2002) 14–17.

Wells, Jo Bailey. *God's Holy People: A Theme in Biblical Theology*. Journal for the Study of the Old Testament Supplement Series 305. Sheffield: Sheffield Academic Press, 2000.

Weinfeld, Moshe. ברית. In *Theological Dictionary of the Old Testament*, edited by G. Johannes Botterweck and Helmer Ringgren, 2:253–79. 12 vols. Grand Rapids: Eerdmans, 1977.

"Who Is AFA?" American Family Association. http://www.afa.net/Detail.aspx?id=31

Wilcox, Clyde, and Carin Larson. *Onward Christian Soldiers? The Religious Right in American Politics*. Boulder, CO: Westview, 2006.

Wildmon, Don. "The building called America." *AFA Journal*, Jan. 2003. No pages. Online: http://www.afajournal.org/2003/january/don.asp

Wolff, Hans Walter. *A Commentary on the Book of the Prophet Hosea*. Translated by Gary Stansell. Edited by Paul D. Hanson. Philadelphia: Fortress, 1974.

World Council of Churches Commission on Faith and Order. "Ethnic Identity, National Identity, and the Search for Unity." No pages. Online: http://www.wcc-coe.org/wcc/what/faith/kuala-docs13-makarios.pdf

Worldview Weekend. http://www.worldviewweekend.com

Yack, Bernard. "The Myth of the Civic Nation." In *Theorizing Nationalism*, edited by Ronald Beiner, 103–18. Albany: State University of New York Press, 1999.

Yoder, John Howard. *Body Politics: Five Practices of the Christian Community before the Watching World*. Scottdale, PA: Herald, 1992, 2001.

———. *The Jewish-Christian Schism Revisited*. Edited by Michael G. Cartwright and Peter Ochs. Grand Rapids: Eerdmans, 2003.

———. *The Original Revolution: Essays on Christian Pacifism*. Scottdale, PA: Herald, 1971.

———. *The Politics of Jesus*. Grand Rapids: Eerdmans, 1972.

———. *The Priestly Kingdom: Social Ethics as Gospel*. Notre Dame: University of Notre Dame Press, 1984.

Index

allegiance, monolithic conceptions of, 24
alternative theopolitical communities, 240
America. *See also* United States
   applying the biblical covenant model to, 187
   as battleground between God and Satan, 168–69
   as chosen community, 204
   covenant of, 243, 244
   decline of, 158, 175–81, 209–13, 231–32
   failures of, defined as extraordinary, 188
   fundamental principles of, 199
   as global sovereign, 213–20
   history of, filtered through a covenant lens, 187–88
   importance to, of the early settlers, 169
   mediating democracy, capitalism, and Christianity to the world, 201
   military strength of, 193
   miraculous power of, 208
   narrative of, interwoven with Christian themes, 159
   narrative of its providence, providentially formulated, 208
   national identity of, meaning of, 185
   as new Israel, 42–43
   as primary bearer of democratic ideal, 228
   providence as key to national identity of, 204
   public purpose of, 225–26
   relation of, to Israel, 178–79, 244
   renewal of, 181–84
   as sacred land, 168–69
   saga of, as salvation history, 194
American Babylon (Neuhaus), 239
American Center for Law and Justice, 166n60
American Civil Liberties Union, 178
American civil religion, Christian themes and symbols in, 28–29
American covenant, less certainty regarding, 226
American exceptionalism, 29, 74–75, 156–57, 207, 230
   Neuhaus sliding in and out of, 228
   as providence, 217
American Family Association, 156, 158
American jeremiad, 150, 152–54, 162
American Providence: A Nation with a Mission (Webb), 201
American Revolution, 172–74, 189
American Values, 156, 158
Anabaptists, 47n23
Anderson, Benedict, 20, 21, 22, 24, 42n6
Ashcroft, John, 163n40
Augustine, 14

Index

authentication, 6, 26–28, 33–34, 51–52, 55, 151, 153, 186, 200, 225, 235, 243
authority, political, 214, 215

Babylon, 239
  America as, 231
  politics for, 242
Babylon-as-history, 243
Bader-Saye, Scott, 64, 76–80, 88, 89, 93, 97
Bancroft, George, 191–92
baptism, 66–67, 72, 74, 79
Barrington, Lowell, 31, 32
Barth, Karl, 222
Barton, David, 155, 191n170
Bauer, Gary, 156
Baxter, Michael, 221n86
Beach-Verhey, Tim, 207, 217
Bible
  centrality of, in cultivating European nationalism, 24
  formal vs. popular understanding of, 47–48
  indigenization of, 45
  narrative of, interwoven with America's story, xii
biblical exceptionalism, 29
biblical narrative
  Neuhaus's distortion of, 221
  as primary source and norm for contemporary Christian theopolitics and ecclesiology, 252
biblical religion, 234
Blackwell Companion to Political Theology, The (Cavanaugh, ed.), xiv–xv n6
Blenkinsopp, Joseph, 102
Book of Martyrs (Foxe), 42n8
Bradford, William, 164
Brass, Paul, 24, 25, 151
Bright, Bill, 163n40
Bright, John, 116, 117–18
Brownback, Sam, 163n40
Brueggemann, Walter, 74, 86
Bush, George H.W., 182

Calvin, John, 209
capitalism, 24
Cartwright, Michael, 67–70
Catholicism, varying inspirations for, 45
Cavanaugh, William T., 2, 11, 12–20, 23–24, 26, 28–29, 73–76, 193, 199, 212–13, 217, 238
CBN, 166n60
Center for Reclaiming America for Christ, 165n48
Character and Destiny (Kennedy), 176n103
chosen community, 150, 204
chosenness, transferred from an ethnic community to the universal church, 52
chosen people, presenting a new social reality, 92
Christ. *See also* Jesus; Jesus Christ
  inaugurating the messianic age, 128
  incomplete victory of, 240
  proclaiming a social order that transcends Torah, 128
  sovereignty of, 139
Christian Coalition, 166n60
Christian ethics, 4
Christianity
  as alternative social body, 61
  Christian nationalism in the United States as gravest national threat to, 46
  embracing, as prelude to entering world markets, 206
  empirical and true, distinguishing between, 30n76
  encouraging literature, 43–44
  functionalist approach to, 192–93
  political models of, 45
  political nature of, 72
  as religion of translation, 44
  role of, in globalism's success, 219–20
Christian nation, biblical model of, in Old Testament Israel, 44
Christian nationalism, 1–2, 224–25, 252

misappropriating the biblical narrative, 63
replacing some theological understanding, 26
Christian Right (U.S.)
  aligned with American neoconservatism, 160
  authors' misappropriation of Scripture, 188–89, 195
  characterized by overlapping agendas, 160–61
  combining national identity with broader conservative theology, 156–58
  interweaving a vision of America with elements of Christian theology, 186
  as nationalist movement, 159–62
  nostalgia as element of, 184–85
  ongoing influence of, in shaping the American national identity, 156
  presenting a particular narrative of American national identity, 162–63
  seeing itself as God's preferred people, 46
  seeking to project a countermythology for America, 161
  supplanting the church and Jesus Christ as Lord, 194–95
  using the past to set parameters for national life, 162
  viewing itself as defensive, 161
Christians
  altering their identity in the church of Jesus Christ, 99–100
  asked to get in the game of history, 202
  losing skills to discern their level of compromise, 9
  patriotism of, 4
  sharing power, without being part of the powerful, 7
Christian Worldview Network, 157–58
church
  acting as exemplar for the world, 67
  alignment of, with the powers, 3
  catholicity of, suffering because of nationalism, 4
  constituted by God's own choosing, 140
  criticizing the American experiment, 235
  depoliticization, of, 76
  as distinct society, 236
  domestication of, 12, 16
  embodying an alternative politics, 74
  embodying an exilic identity, 67
  fit of, with America's global sovereignty, 218–19, 220
  foremost task of, 65–66
  forfeiting its ability to serve as alternative to state politics, 5
  grafted onto Israel's identity and mission, 82–83, 126, 127, 194, 203
  identity of, informed by biblical theopolitics, 145–48
  identity and mission of, rooted in Israel's election, 76
  losing ability to be critical, 4
  merging in, of the political and theological, 145
  in the messianic age, 140–42
  mission and identity of, stemming from God's being, 147
  moral practices of, narrow focus on, 10
  nationalist discourse emanating from, 1
  as New Israel, 48
  not requiring conventional politics for faith, 140
  as pilgrim community, 144
  playing the role of globalism's other, 219–20
  political nature of, 66
  practicing its vocation and mission, 145–46
  praising God through its formation, 78
  realizing when it's not being church, 89
  relegated to chaplaincy, 4

church (*continued*)
    as resident advisor to the state, 219
    separateness of, 140–41
    sharing in divine power, 141
    as signal community, 229, 234
    as social body, 66
    subjected to state power, 219
    task of, in relation to Israel, 134
    tentative nature of, 64
    theological unity of, with Israel, 143–45
    transnational, as threat to state unity, 16
    undermining its own ethic in seeking for power, 3–4
    uniqueness of its identity and mission, 146–47
church militant, retrieving the model of, 234
civil community, 5
civil religion, 4, 6, 8–10, 225
clergy, lower
    consolidating national identities, 43–44
    as educators of the populace, 48
coercive power, renunciation of, 5
Columbus, Christopher, 168, 169–70
community, 50, 163. *See also* civil community; chosen community; covenant community; imagined communities; signal community; theopolitical communities
    cohered through ritualistic practices, 49
    formed by story, 70
    role of, in producing habits of virtue, 72–73
Concerned Women for America, 158
Connor, Walker, 31
Constantine, 2, 3
Constantinianism, 2–7
conversion, 181
Coral Ridge Ministries, 165n48
counter-politics, 9, 18
covenant
    affecting church's role in shaping America, 235
    conditions linked to, 88, 89
    in context of biblical narrative and American history, 226
    without election, 244–45
    elements of, 94
    essential core of, unchanging from Old to New Testaments, 139–40
    established after Israel's salvation, 56
    first major institutional departure from, 100–102
    as form of Israel's fulfillment of election, 93
    growing out of election, 83
    with Israel, unconditionality of, 79
    as lens for filtering American history, 187–88
    militating against nationalism, 188
    new, distinguished from old, 129
    as product of human initiative, 245
    as response to God's prior action, 245
    self-appropriation of, 50, 51
    theopolitical nature of, 83
    tied to social contract, 226–27
    transcendent, 232
covenant community, 93–99, 119, 136
covenant-contract dialectic, 229–30
covenant-style Christian nationalisms, 52
Creasy, Edward Shepherd, 191–92
creation continua, 202
cult of authenticity, 51–52, 53, 55, 58, 59
cultural renewal, 151
culture, as force of history, 222
culture war, 177, 184

Davidic covenant, 101n49
    distorted view of, 119
    establishment of, 113–15
Davidic throne, legitimacy of, 104–6
Decalogue
    at the heart of the Torah, 97, 98–99
    role of, in Jewish and Christian theology, 74–75
Declaration of Independence, as religious act, 172

Declaration of Marlborough
    (Massachusetts), 173
deities, nation-specific, 85
democracy
    as appropriate social form for
        Christian society, 9
    commitment to, as a type of
        idolatry, 227
    presented as amenable to
        Christianity, 205
    providing form for evangelization,
        29–30
    radical, 8n17
    reflecting Neuhaus's theology, of
        historical particularity and
        contingency, 227
    theological importance of, 227
democratic freedom, 199, 227
depoliticization, 16
destination ethics, 242–43
destiny, 183. *See also* glorious destiny
    for a nation, 44–45
    related to national identity, 54–55
Diamond, Sara, 160n31
diaspora, 141
disciples, 133, 134
dominion theology, 181–82n136
Dukakis, Michael, 182
Dumbrell, W. J., 84–85, 90, 92, 95,
    102, 103, 105–6, 108–10, 131,
    144–45

ecclesial identity, 10–11
*Ecclesiastical History of the English
    People* (Bede), 42n8
ecclesiology, theopolitical, xiii
education, universalization of,
    definitive for rise of national
    identity, 21–22
Edwards, Jonathan, 171
election
    exodus and, 84–92
    giving Israel its mission in the
        world, 83
    personal, as corollary of communal
        election, 76
    response to, 56
    self-appropriation of, 50

theopolitical nature of, 83
elites, 161, 232–33, 252
    exploiting religious belief, 39–40
    formed by prior identity and
        culture, 40
Ellul, Jacques, 232n144
Elshtain, Jean Bethke, 213
empire, 45, 216–17, 230–31
emulation of the holy, 57
England, merging in, of nation and
    national identity, 42
Enlightenment exceptionalism, 29
eschatology, 237–40
ethics of responsibility, 242
ethnic election, 50–51, 56
ethnohistory, 53
ethnosymbolism, 26
Eucharist, 18, 72–73, 74, 79, 236. *See
    also* Lord's Supper
Europe, national identities in,
    solidification of, 46
Eusebius, 3n1
evangelism, 181
exceptionalism, 29–30. *See also*
    American exceptionalism;
    biblical exceptionalism;
    Enlightenment exceptionalism
exceptions, to democratic political
    order, 214–15
exodus, election and, 84–92

Falwell, Jerry, 160, 163, 166, 171, 179–
    80, 183, 185, 192–94, 194, 195
family of God, community of, 135
Family Research Council, 156, 158
Fea, John, 163
First Peter, 140–44
founding fathers, 166, 178
FRC Action, 156
free church theology, 69n19
freedom. *See* democratic freedom
    ideal of, 29
    resulting from training in Torah
        practices, 77
free enterprise, 179–80
free speech, theology of, 205
Friedman, Milton, 179, 193–94

friend-enemy distinction, in political
    theology, 214

Gellner, Ernest, 21–22, 27, 32
general providence, 202
George III, 173
globalism
    Christianity's role in the success of,
        219–20
    church playing the role of other,
        219–20
    economic and religious, 206–7
globalization, capitalist, central
    importance of, 205–6
global salvation, 51, 57
glorious destiny, 150
glorious past. See golden age
God
    as Absolute Future, 223, 225, 226
    character of, 139
    governing history, 3–4
    history realized in, 223
    personally concerned about our
        historical experience, 223–24
    rule over Israel, developed in three
        aspects of the Torah, 98
    transforming the world and
        protecting freedom, 91
gods, nation-specific, 85
golden age, 53–54, 150, 151, 162, 163,
    169–70
gospel, proclamation of, as powerful
    speech act, 205
Great Awakening, 171–72
Great Commission, 137
Green, Joel, 143
Greenfield, Liah, 51n30

habit of thought, 10
Hafemann, Scott, 129
Harink, Douglas, 69, 101n50, 138–42,
    144, 146, 240, 212
Hastings, Adrian, 24, 41–48, 61, 194
Hauerwas, Stanley, xiii, 2, 7–11, 70–73,
    76, 199, 207n26, 210–12,
    232n144, 245
Heinz, Donald, 161, 185
Herbert of Cherbury, Lord, 15–16

Heritage Foundation, 154, 160
hesed, abandonment of, 102
history
    as God's project, 222
    as history of redemption, 224
    naturalization of, 53
Hobbes, Thomas, 16
Hobsbawm, Eric, 20–21, 22, 25
holiness, 51, 142
Holy Spirit, directly affecting Marshall
    and Manuel's work, 190
homeland, 52–53
Hosea, book of, 100, 102–12
Howse, Brannon, 157, 158

identity
    as continuous phenomenon, 112
    story as central to, 82
idolatry, Israel guilty of, 110
imagined communities, 20, 22
inherited traditions, 22, 25
invented traditions, 20, 25
Israel, biblical
    abandoning its theopolitical
        identity, 99
    achieving form and purpose
        through election, 91–92
    allegiance of, to Yahweh, 93–94
    alternate politicization of, 138
    called to be visible sign of God's
        salvation to the world, 64
    called to war against the Canaanite
        tribes, 96–97
    calling of, 84, 146
    church engrafted into, 82–83, 126,
        127, 194, 203
    church's theological unity with,
        143–45
    civil religion of, 121
    competing views of, as political
        community, 47
    as counter-model to the
        surrounding kingdoms, 95, 96
    covenant of, giving way to state,
        100–102
    as covenant community, 93–99
    covenant failure, linked to state
        centralization, 104

demanding a human king, 100–101
depoliticization of, 137–38
election of, 69–70, 88, 89
election and covenant in, 83–99,
   126
embodying the drama of sin and
   salvation, 74
finding its identity in the Creator
   God, 98–99
foreign alliances of, 109–10
identity of, 72, 91, 112
identity and mission of, as means
   toward global salvation, 57
Jesus' attention directed at, 132–36
mediating Yahweh's grace to the
   world, 95
military weakness of, 193
misappropriated for use in
   American context, 190
as model of nationhood, 41, 42
national identity of, related to
   conserving the law, 107
nationalist model derived from, 56
nationalist narratives rooted in,
   falsity of, 126
as new form of political
   community, 93
new identity of, 87–88
not entirely accepting Jesus'
   mission, 134
particular mission of, in the world,
   82
political and religious practices of,
   linked, 108–12
power politics in, 246
as quintessential formulation of
   divine action and covenant, 52
realization of its election, 88
realpolitik of, theological
   implications, 108
reason for election of, 90–91
relationship of mutuality with
   Yahweh, 77
secularization in, 117
separateness of, from the rest of the
   world, 90–91
statehood of, 75

as template for God's future use of
   nation-states, 203
theopolitical identity of, 99
theopolitics in, 63, 75–76
as tribal league without centralized
   covenant, 95
uniqueness of, 203
United States portrayed as modern
   extension of, 164–65, 168
withdrawn from Yahweh, 102
as Yahweh's treasured possession,
   88
Israel-Jesus story, continuity of, 71–72

Janzen, Waldemar, 124
Jefferson, Thomas, 175, 192
Jefferson Bible, 175
jeremiads, 151–53, 184, 198–99
   progressive, 220
   traditionalist vs. progressive,
      153–54
Jeremiah, 113, 115, 242
   arising as prophet, 117–19
   book of, 100
   encountering another prophet,
      122–23
   subverting one national identity in
      favor of another, 120
Jeremianic model, for spreading the
   gospel, 141
Jeremianic turn, 67–68
Jesus. *See also* Christ; Jesus Christ
   attention of, directed at Israel,
      132–36
   ethical teachings of, read in light
      of the gospel about God's
      kingdom, 135
   exaltation of, 137
   fulfilling the covenant, 68, 130–31
   fulfilling the law of Sinai, 135
   as both Israel and Yahweh, 132
   as messiah, 130
   messianic age of, 138, 141–42
   noncoercive ethic of, 10
   perfectly embodying Torah, 129
   resurrection of, 132

274 Index

Jesus Christ. *See also* Christ; Jesus
   divine intervention of, reordering the world, 65–66, 68
   fulfilling Israel's election and covenant, 126
   reign of, present now, 139
   sovereignty of God in, 136–39
   sovereign over the world, 137
Johnson, Paul, 191–92n170
Judah, elected and blessed by Yahweh, 123

Kennedy, D. James, 160n32, 163, 165–66, 170–71, 172, 175, 176–78, 181–82, 183, 185, 190–92, 194, 195
Kennedy, Robert F., 200n2
King, Martin Luther, Jr., 200n2
kingdom of God, 131–32, 135, 202, 237–38, 240
kingship, 102–3, 104, 106, 108–9, 172–73

LaHaye, Tim, 160n32
land, sacredness of, 167–68
language, creating basis for national identity, 20
Lemcio, Eugene, 143
Letter to Diognetus, 242
Levenson, Jon, 85, 94, 95, 111
liberal democratic state, 7
liberalism
   as agent of modern Constantinianism, 7
   associated with a limited state, 7–8
liberal Protestants, acquiescing to the elites, 233
liberal state, insoluble paradox of, 8–9
liberation theology, 212–13
Liberty University, 166n56
Light and the Glory, The (Marshall and Manuel), 155, 163–65, 186–90
Lind, Millard C., 107, 109
Listen America! (Falwell), 193
literature, Christianity encouraging, 43–44
liturgy, 72–73, 74, 235–39
Llobera, Josep, 23

Locke, John, 16
Lohfink, Gerhard, 90, 91, 95, 97, 98, 105–6, 120, 123, 129–30, 131, 132–36, 146
Lord's Supper, 66. *See also* Eucharist
loyalty, to God and nation, syncretization of, 30

Machinist, Peter, 103–4, 108
Manuel, David, 163–65, 168, 170, 172–74, 176, 181, 184–85, 210, 186–90, 194, 209
Marshall, Peter, 155–56, 163–65, 168, 170, 172–74, 176, 181, 184–85, 210, 186–90, 194, 195, 209
martyrdom, 139, 142
Marx, Anthony, 25, 32, 37–41, 46, 61
Mather, Cotton, 171
McLeroy, Don, 154
McNaughton, John, xi–xiii
Melville, Herman, 28–29
membership, in a nation, 33
memory, territorialization of, 53
messianic time, 141–42
Milbank, John, 207n26
mobilization, through religious communities, 24
modernist school, nationalism and, 19–28
modernity
   assuming separation of politics and theology, 12
   creation myth for, 17
   as greatest challenge to orthodox ecclesial identity, 12
   proposing a political sphere outside the covenant, 77
   theopolitics of, 18
monarchy
   corruption in, 121
   perspectives on, 104–7
   success of, as a central element of Israel's national identity, 121
monasticism, 47n23
Moral Majority, 154, 160n32
Moyers, Bill, 200n2
Murphy, Andrew R., 150–54, 162, 169, 184, 198–99, 220

Index   275

mythologization, purpose of, 43
Myth of Religious Violence, The
    (Cavanaugh), 13

naked public square, 231–32
Naked Public Square, The (Neuhaus),
    223n95
narratives, interweaving of, 2
nation
    boundaries of, 33
    as Christian development, 43
    claiming divine election for, 44–45
    definitions of, 31
    distinguished from state, 10, 32
    etymological roots of, 42
    merging with religious identity, 43
    as messiah, 29
    as object of secular mythology and
        religion, 49
    purification of, 34
    as recognizing shared attributes of
        others, 21
    sacred foundations of, 49
    shared sense of purpose among its
        people, 31–32
    structured according to God's will,
        10
national communion, 54–55, 60
national holiness, pursuit of, 151
national identity, 4–5
    alternate notion of, to the monarchy
        and ruling elite, 121
    American, covenant and contract as
        part of, 226–27
    authenticated vision of, 30
    built on four sacred foundations, 50
    Christian Right authors merging
        their personal identities with,
        185
    determining, 25
    as form of political holiness, 200
    maintenance and reinterpretation
        of, 49–50
    position of, relative to other
        identities, 224
    required for redemption, 203
nationalism
    in academic theologies, 199

    as alternate religious system, 60–61
    always contested, 24
    anti-state, 23
    authentication and, 33–34
    as challenge to the church, xiii, 33,
        251–54
    as Christian development, 43
    created away from the state, 23
    defined, xiii
    definitions of, 32
    discussed little in theopolitical
        scholarship, 1–2
    emanating from within the church,
        12
    fusing narrative elements from
        distinct peoples, 61
    fusing the political and theological,
        xiii
    importance of, for theopolitics, xiv
    as link in state's reordering and
        unification of society, 60
    modernist scholarship on, 19–20
    modernist school's approach to,
        19–28
    as movement, 32–33
    narrow conception of, 18–19
    as new form of social organization,
        21–22
    parodying the symbols and
        practices of the church, 60
    as political identity formation, 24
    political by definition, 24–25
    as a political religion, 81
    power of, xiv
    problem of, as practiced in the
        church, 148
    processes involved in, 32–34
    as project of the modern state, 19
    reconstructing earlier nationalist
        elements, 59
    relation of, with traditional
        religions, 58–59
    as religion of the people, 49, 56
    religion's role in, 55
    as reparticularization, 28–30
    repoliticizing the faith community,
        61
    rise of, in early modern Europe, 38

nationalism (*continued*)
  sacred foundations of, 49
  scholarship on, suffering from lack of attention to theology, 81
  secular, 14
  syncretizing the nation with specific features of faith tradition, 28
  as theological virtue, 159
  twofold project of, 148
  undergirding or resisting states, 32
nationalists
  distorting the Christian gospel, 147
  formulating a vision of a "true nation," 55
  limited options of, in crafting their message, 26
  preformed, according to cultural and religious traditions, 25–26
  redefining Christian identity, 37
  reinterpreting existing cultural resources, 27
national renewal, 151
National Rifle Association, 154
national salvation drama, 54–55
nationhood, biblical Israel as model of, 42
Nations and Nationalism (Gellner), 21–22
nation-state, 32n82, 45
  centrality of, in Webb's theology of providence, 202–3
  God moving through, 212
  peripheral role of, in divine plan, 203
  political nature of, 213–14
nature, historicization of, 53
Nehemias Americanus, 171
Neuhaus, Richard John, 7–8, 199–200, 220–46
Newcombe, Jerry, 191n170
New Israel, church as, 48
New Testament
  emphasizing the people of God, 130
  Hauerwas's almost exclusive focus on, 71–72
  viewed as apolitical, 47
Niebuhr, H.R., 234
Niebuhr, Reinhold, 216

1950s, nostalgia for, 184
1960s, noted as beginning of America's decline, 175–76, 184–85, 210, 231
North, Gary, 182n
nostalgia, in Christian Right jeremiads, 184–85
Novak, David, 52n35
novus ordo seclorum, 229–30

O'Donovan, Oliver, 92, 94, 98, 104–7, 121–22n102, 137, 138–39, 146n62, 147n63, 203
Old Testament
  covenants of, Falwell's misunderstanding of, 193
  discussing individual responsibility, 130
  priority in, of the communal and the political, 77
  structural role of, in 1 Peter, 143–44
One Nation Under God (McNaughton), xi–xiii

pacifism, 211
particular-universal relationship, 228–29
patriotic piety, 225
peacemaking, 5
Pentecostalism, 205, 206
Pentiuc, Eugene J., 111
people, as object of nationalism-as-religion, 49
people of God
  called into political community, 74
  emphasized in the New Testament, 130
  establishing the unique identity of, 144
  identity-forming practices for, 73
  as the Israel that knows itself to be chosen, 133–34
  Old and New Testament visions of, 46–47
  theopolitical understanding of, 83
personal God, belief in, 202
Peter Marshall Ministries, 155

Pharaoh
    oppressiveness of, 86
    Yahweh setting himself against, 86–87
Pixley, Jorge, 119, 120
political conflict, converging with religious strife, 38–39
political theology, 214
    America's place in, 201
    realistic, 241
political theory, salvation narrative of, 13
politics, xiii
    coercive, 4
    as function of salvation history, xiii–xiv
    presenting itself as alternate soteriology to Christianity, 73
    religion providing a moral rationale for, 222–23
    as response to God's activity in the world, 12
    sovereignty of, in making of history, 222
    unrealistic, 211
politics-faith dichotomy, falseness of, 60–61
politics of small accomplishments, 8n17
populist theology, 210
poverty, as teaching tool, not ideology, 206
power politics, 246
    idolatry of, 110
    problem of, as practiced in the church, 148
powers
    Christ's reordering of, 65–66, 68
    rebelling against their divine mandate, 84
priestly kingdom, 90
print-capitalism, 20
progressive jeremiad, 199, 200n2, 220
prophetic critique, 99–100
prophets, envisioning a future with hope, 123–24

Protestantism
    functioning like the US Constitution, 205
    liberal, 233
    political situations of, applying Old Testament precedents to, 45
providence, 199
    general and special, 202
    as key to American national identity, 204
    linked with political authority, 215
    political theology of, 201
    rejection of, 210
    role of, xii n3
    theologies of, 209
providential rhetoric, decline in, 210
providential theology, recovery of, 201
public ethic, 241–42
public narrative production, control of, 185–86
public piety, 225, 229, 231, 234, 235
publishing, 20, 24
Puritans, 28, 170–71, 208–9
purpose, shared sense of, 31–32

radical democracy, 8n17
Rasmussen, Arne, 8
Rauschenbusch, Walter, 7
Rawls, John, 16
Reagan, Ronald, 154, 182
realized eschatology, 237–38
realpolitik, 94, 100, 101, 102, 113, 118, 120, 130, 132
Redditt, Paul L., 121, 122
redemption
    requiring national identity, 203
    of the world, 84–85
Reformation, 15
religare, 222–23
religio, 14–15
religion
    contestability of term, 14
    doctrinal departicularization of, 15–16
    driving politics and history, 235
    as intellectual exercise, 15–16
    invention of, 15
    as normative concept, 16–17

religion (*continued*)
  providing moral rationale for politics, 222–23
  as transhistorical and transcultural phenomenon, 13
religious, distinguished from secular, 13–14
religious homogeneity, 41
religious identity, merging with nation, 43
religious institutions, as mediating structures, 234–35
religious nationalism, Marx neglecting the theological content of, 41
religious violence, 13–14
  myth of, 17
  scholarship on, three groups of, 14
reparticularization, 28–30
responsibility, ethics of, 242
Robertson, Pat, 163, 166–67, 171, 172, 174, 178–79, 182, 183–84, 192, 194, 195
Rousseau, Jean Jacques, 16, 49
Rushdoony, Rousas John, 182n

sacraments, 66–67, 72–73, 74, 79, 236
sacred destiny, 163
sacred foundations, 150, 163, 198
sacred languages, 44n15
sacrifice, 54–55, 183–84
saeculum, 238
salvation
  achieved by emulating the holy, 57
  concerned with creating community, 12
  global, 51
  involving exaltation of the American national identity, 195–96
  viewed in distinctly national terms, 195
salvation drama, 59–60
salvation history, 237
  alternative, 12
  Babylon as current form of, 239–40
  as story of Christ's suffering, 65
salvation narratives, 64
  as character of the jeremiad, 152

  politics, of, xiii–xiv
Satan, involved in sinking the Pinta, 168
Schmitt, Carl, 213–16, 218
scripture, rendered apolitical, 211–12
secular, distinguished from religious, 13–14
secular nationalism, 14
security, as Israel's ultimate reality, 120–21
selective domestic exclusion, 38
self-perception, as part of defining a nation, 31–32
separation of church and state, 175, 192
September 11, 2001, 177n, 180–81
700 Club, The, 166n60, 180
shared sacrifice, 150, 163
Sheen, Fulton, 46n21
Shklar, Judith, 16
signal, significance of, in Neuhaus's thought, 229
signal community, 229, 234
Siker, Jeffrey, 70–71
sin
  redemption of, restoring primal unity, 73–74
  theopolitical, 102
Siniatic covenant. *See also* covenant
  consecrating Israel's national life, 94
  establishing a political community, 93
Smith, Anthony D., 25, 26–27, 31, 32, 33–34, 48–59, 61, 150, 163, 169, 198
social contract, covenant tied to, 226–27
social forms, as parables of the coming of God's kingdom, 202
soteriology, of the state, 17–18
sovereign, authority of, 215
special providence, 202, 218
Stanley, Charles, 160n32
state
  as agent of nationalism, 21–22
  body of, compared to the Eucharist, 18
  bringing violence instead of peace, 17

concentrating on order
  maintenance, 21
concern with, linked to another
  identity, 23
confused with the covenant
  community, 119
creating a direct tie to the
  individual, 11
creating an identity for its citizens,
  20
identified with its own form of
  culture and communication, 22
nation distinguished from, 10, 32
salvation narrative of, 13
saving humanity from religious
  division, 17–18
seeking passionate loyalty by using
  religion, 39
seeking to surpass its limits, 7
state centralization, linked to Israel's
  covenant failure, 104
state cults, 102
state nationalism, 21–23
status elites, 161, 210
story, central to identity, 82
Stout, Jeffrey, 16
Suffering Servant, 124–25, 128, 130,
  141
Suny, Ronald, 31
supersessionism, 69
suzerain-vassal covenant model, 93–94
symbol competition, 151
symbol selection, involving competition
  among elites, 24–25
syncretism, 99–100, 151

temple, building of, 114–15
Ten Commandments. *See* Decalogue
territory, 33, 52–53, 150, 163, 167–69
Texas Board of Education, 154–56
theological education, 48
theology
  American, ecclesiological deficit in,
    236–37
  anti-American, 216
  political, 214
  populist, 210

theopolitical communities, alternative,
  240
theopolitical scholarship, xiii–xiv, 1, 63
theopolitical sin, 102
theopolitics, misappropriation of, 10
Thomas, Cal, 163n40
Thomas Aquinas, 15
Time Toward Home (Neuhaus), 223n95,
  236n166
Torah
  centrality of, to covenant, 77
  people obeying, under the new
    covenant, 129
  social order established through, 68
  social project of, 97
traditionalist jeremiad, 153–54, 198,
  199, 200n2
transcendence, judgment of, 235
transcendent covenant, 232
transnational church, as threat to state
  unity, 16

United States. *See also* America
  as Christian nation, 10–11, 165–66
  Christian nationalism in, as
    gravest nationalist threat to
    Christianity, 46
  as empire, 230–31
  as the new Israel, 10–11, 28
  portrayed as modern extension of
    Israel, 164–65, 168
  presented as a chosen nation,
    161–62
  secularization of, 158
US Army Chaplain Corps, 4n4
US Constitution
  divine connection of, 167
  signers of, 175

vernacular languages, 20
vernacular literature, 42, 43–44
Viguerie, Richard, 160
violence, 5
  nationalist, 23
  religion as source of, 13
virtue deficit
Vision America, 158

voluntarism, 57
von Balthasar, Hans Urs, 130, 136, 139

Wall, Robert, 143
WallBuilders, 155
war, 18
Wars of Religion, 16–17
Washington, George, 164, 174
Watson, D. F., 239
Watts, Isaac, 42n8
Webb, Stephen H., 29–30, 199–200, 201–20, 232n144
Weber, Max, 21
Weigel, George, 218–19
Wells, Jo Bailey, 87, 88, 143–44
Weyrich, Paul, 160
What If America? (Kennedy), 176–77n103
Whitefield, George, 171
Winthrop, John, 164, 170, 171

Wolff, Hans Walter, 103, 108, 110

Yahweh
  acting outside covenant for Israel's sake, 125
  concerned with Israel's destiny and identity, 87–88
  delivering Israel into a new theopolitical order, 85–86
  exclusive worship of, 98
  intent for Israel, contradicted with emphasis on state interests, 120–21
  power of initiation, 91–92
  reasserting divine kingship, 138
  setting himself against Pharaoh, 86–87
  usurped as king, 109
Yoder, John Howard, xiii, 2–7, 47, 64–70, 130, 132, 232n144, 245

www.ingramcontent.com/pod-product-compliance
Lightning Source LLC
Chambersburg PA
CBHW021653230426
43668CB00008B/610